Social Policy, Social Welfare and Scandal

Social Policy, Social Welfare and Scandal

How British Public Policy is Made

Ian Butler and Mark Drakeford

First published 2003 by
PALGRAVE MACMILLAN
Houndmills, Basingstoke, Hampshire RG21 6XS and
175 Fifth Avenue, New York, N.Y. 10010
Companies and representatives throughout the world

PALGRAVE MACMILLAN is the global academic imprint of the Palgrave
Macmillan division of St. Martin's Press, LLC and of Palgrave Macmillan Ltd.
Macmillan® is a registered trademark in the United States, United Kingdom
and other countries. Palgrave is a registered trademark in the European
Union and other countries.

ISBN 0–333–74762–3 hardback

This book is printed on paper suitable for recycling and made from fully
managed and sustained forest sources.

A catalogue record for this book is available from the British Library.

A catalogue record for this book is available from the Library of Congress.

10   9   8   7   6   5   4   3   2   1
12 11 10 09 08 07 06 05 04 03

Printed and bound in Great Britain by
Antony Rowe Ltd, Chippenham and Eastbourne

Dan, Emma, Jonathon, Mark, Matthew and Tony

Contents

Notes on the Authors

Ian Butler is a qualified social worker with considerable practice and managerial experience. He has worked in residential and field settings, mainly with children and their families, in the statutory, voluntary and independent sectors. He also worked as a parliamentary research assistant for members of the Labour Party before taking up post as a Lecturer in Social Work at Cardiff University. He was Director of Social Work Studies at Cardiff before moving to Keele University, where he is now Professor of Social Work. Together with Mark Drakeford, he is currently editor of the *British Journal of Social Work*.

Mark Drakeford is a Senior Lecturer in Social Policy and Applied Social Sciences at the University of Wales, Cardiff. For fifteen years he worked as a probation officer and community development worker. Together with Ian Butler, he is the current editor of the *British Journal of Social Work*.

Since 2000 he has been seconded to work as the Cabinet's health and social policy adviser, and special adviser to the First Minister, at the Welsh Assembly Government.

Acknowledgements

Jo Campling has been an invaluable supporter of this project, since we first discussed it with her some three years ago. We are grateful, as always, both for her support and for the confidence which comes with knowing that she is involved in the publication.

We are grateful also to Professor Olive Stevenson for her invaluable insights on the conduct of the Maria Colwell Inquiry which are reflected in chapter 5 of this book. We are grateful to the staff of the Public Records Office at Kew for their help in gaining access to papers relating to the Ely Hospital Inquiry (chapter 3) and to the staff of *The Sentinel* for access to their cuttings, files. We would also like to acknowledge Sue Hayes of Cardiff University's School of Social Sciences for her help with the preparation of the manuscript and Pat Smail and Clare Drakeford for their help with proof reading.

We would especially like to say thanks to all of the students at Cardiff and Keele universities who have sat patiently and listened, even occasionally expressed enthusiasm, as we worked out the details of this book in the lecture courses on which it is based. You taught us a lot! Thanks are due also to various colleagues at Keele and Cardiff who have helped with the teaching, especially to Jenny Swindle for her help when the course became just too big!

IAN BUTLER
MARK DRAKEFORD

1
Scandal

> It is public scandal that constitutes offence, and to sin in secret is not to sin at all.
>
> Molière (1622–1673)

Introduction

While scandals are relatively rare, sin is common enough. As this book will demonstrate, neither the chronic administrative failings, small carelessnesses and institutional brutality of the long-stay hospital, nor even the abuse of children or the violent deaths of innocent bystanders, are sufficient cause for scandal. This book is about the process whereby such everyday tragedies are transformed into something extraordinary; the process whereby events which are local and personal become national and public; the process whereby the specific comes to stand for the general and where meanings and historical significance become attached to acts and events which at other times might have passed almost unobserved.

Whilst the means whereby scandal is constructed and sustained is a central concern of the book, our particular interest is in how scandals illumine the process whereby public policy is produced and, specifically, welfare policy. The obvious connection between a scandal and the production of welfare policy is the Committee of Inquiry and the workings of such inquiries are also a key object of our interest. But scandals do not appear in a policy vacuum; rather they develop in very particular contexts at very particular times and it is the complex, reciprocal relationship between scandal, the Public Inquiry and the development of policy with which this book is concerned.

1

Scandal

It is central to the argument of this book that a scandal is not coterminous with the underlying events from which it springs. Often the events will have been in train for many years before they are construed as scandalous, as in the case of Ely Hospital, the subject of chapter 3. The underlying events may not even be perceived as 'sinful' by those directly involved. On the contrary, they may be the subject of official approval, as in the case of the Staffordshire Child Care Inquiry described in chapter 9. Even where the underlying event quite clearly represents a fundamental violation of shared moral norms – as in cases of murder – it cannot be assumed that scandal will follow. Some murders assume greater significance than others, as the contrasting cases of Isabel Schwartz and Stephen Zito, described in chapter 7 demonstrate. A few years or a few miles in between ostensibly similar sets of circumstances seem to make a great difference.

Two questions immediately arise from these observations: 'Why do some, highly selected events become scandals and others not?' and 'How is the transformation achieved?' We seek to answer both of these questions in this book. We have chosen to focus on two broad areas of welfare policy: services for children and services for adults with mental health problems or learning difficulties. (It is an unfortunate side effect of historical research that we are forced to use terms which, although faithful to their period, jar with a modern audience. Often, we find ourselves talking in terms of services for adults who are mentally ill or mentally handicapped.) For each broad area of welfare practice, we take what we consider to be the most important scandal of the postwar period and explore its life course in some detail. Because the processes of scandal formation are different and because the dynamics of the underlying events are also different, for each area of welfare practice, we consider one 'institutional' scandal (Ely Hospital; Pindown) and one 'community' scandal (Maria Colwell; Zito/Clunis). In each of these scandals, we explore how their emblematic status was achieved.

We will show that far from just happening, scandals are assiduously prosecuted (and resisted) by key individuals or groups whom we identify as primary claims-makers. The variety of claims-makers which people the various scandals we consider is surprisingly wide. Not all are powerful individuals with 'specialist' or 'insider' knowledge. Many occupy relatively powerless positions, at least initially. We will examine how serendipity as well as coincidence of interests with other groups can hinder or facilitate the development of a momentum to escape the gravitational pull of the status quo, vested interests or the indifference of a wider public. At several points, we examine the role of the press in the process of 'discovery', a necessary first stage in the progress towards scandal.

This is not to relegate in importance the structure and pattern of the underlying events of scandal themselves. We will suggest that they share certain vital characteristics. For example, the events usually stand in stark contradiction to the locations in which they occur: cruelty in a place of healing; brutality in the home at the hands of those who are supposed to care. Similarly, the iconic status achieved by the underlying events of scandal is often enhanced by their genuine dramatic content. Observing the process through the record of events provided by a Committee of Inquiry does not necessarily lessen the sense of 'what if?' in many of the scandals we report, any more than the second reading of a favourite novel might.

Perhaps the most important question that we seek to answer in terms of understanding scandal, however, is not so much 'why' or 'how' but 'why *now*?' Each of the landmark scandals that we consider is prefaced by a chapter spelling out the policy context in which the scandal occurred as it is our view that scandals occur *only* at certain stages in the development of public policy. At some points and in some policy contexts, scandals simply do not and can not happen. Where there is consensus, for example (even a consensus of disinterest), while there can be tragedy and injustice, there cannot be scandal. The condition of young offenders currently is a case in point (Butler and Drakeford, 2001a). Given the strong political consensus around youth justice policy, the abusive and brutal conditions in which youngsters are imprisoned hardly merits a second glance.

The appetite for particular scandals can wane as well as wax and what was scandalous once can just as easily disappear beneath the waves of interest which for a time buoyed it up. It is our primary purpose to provide an analysis of both the particular policy contexts in which key scandals came into being and to describe more generally the kind of policy environments in which scandals can and do play a decisive role.

The Committee of Inquiry

The Committee of Inquiry is the most obvious point of connection between the scandal and the operations and interests of the State. We are concerned, through an examination of the minutiae of their operation, to demonstrate that much of the historical significance of a scandal is constructed in the formal inquiry which follows. The way in which the 'facts' are pursued, re-assembled and re-told by the men and women (they are not gods) who sit as part of Committees of Inquiry can contribute powerfully to the 'meaning' of each scandal. Personal courage and enmity on the part of members of such committees; professional habits of thought and ways of 'seeing the world'; even styles of writing – each of these factors can add a particular layer to the final 'truth' that scandals tell.

We will suggest that Committees of Inquiry are important sites where a variety of professional, ideological and personal positions compete for dominance. They are sites which come to be occupied by interests entirely outside the experience or control of those sitting in the room in which the inquiry takes place. Deeper social and political undercurrents can well up and almost completely obscure the immediate topics of concern. These can emerge in the cross-examination of witnesses, as in the case of Maria Colwell; the authorial tone of the published report, as in the case of Pindown; or in the actions of individual chairs of committees, as in the case of Geoffrey Howe in the Ely Hospital Inquiry. In so far as Committees of Inquiry are the creation of particular social and political forces, so too are they active participants in the making of history. They can also be made to be the foundations on which history can be rewritten, and we will show that they have proved fertile grounds for a variety of moral and intellectual entrepreneurs seeking authority or precedent for their own particular analyses of the present.

For all their claims to rest on the 'facts', reports of Committees of Inquiry are interesting artefacts in their own right, as we have suggested. Some are written with all of the pace and style of a good 'airport novel'. Almost all contain stock heroes and villains and many descend (or are elevated, depending on your point of view) to little more than morality plays. Some are rather cool in tone and written with all the clipped politeness of a high-ranking civil servant. Others are almost messianic in the zeal with which they go about recording their findings. Some find receptive audiences, others fall into the wrong hands entirely. Almost all come to stand for the whole inquiry itself. In fact, the report is only one record of events. Newspaper accounts, official papers now in the Public Records Office, and later recollections by those present are equally articulate commentaries on any particular scandal and we try to make use of all of these sources in our account.

Public policy

We have suggested already that there is a symbiotic relationship between scandal, the Committee of Inquiry and public policy. We have hinted that there are times when scandals are more likely to occur than others. It follows therefore that there are times when public policy is more susceptible to change and to have that change traced to or associated with the appearance of scandal. This is the ultimate 'chicken and egg' question that we seek to explore in this book. Which came first: the scandal or the shift in policy/practice?

Across the broad sweep of history, it is possible to pick out critical moments or turning points that seem to represent some qualitative shift both in thinking about welfare and in welfare practices. Often these do occur in close proximity to a welfare scandal, but this is not invariably the case. This is not surprising given that it is rarely possible to isolate historical variables precisely or to identify the exact point at which evolution turns into revolution. Accordingly, our answers to the various questions we pose in this book cannot be final ones. However, it is possible to discern a clear pattern.

We have likened this pattern to the occurrence of earthquakes. These happen along particular faultlines where the old landmasses of the past disappear beneath the emergent foundations of the future. Tensions can occur as the old and the new slide past each other. Sometimes an accommodation is made without too much difficulty. At other times, there is resistance. The pressure builds until there is some cataclysmic event which can overwhelm all of those unfortunate enough to be caught in the wrong place at the wrong time. Scandals are the policy equivalent of the earthquake; they are a powerful signal that change is occurring, or that the pressure for change has reached unsustainable levels. After an earthquake, we have to reconstruct the world we inhabit, metaphorically as much as literally, in order to take account of our experiences. In the wake of a scandal, we re-design the architecture of our professional or intellectual worlds just as much as we adapt our buildings in the aftermath of a physical earthquake. With the passage of years, however, it is easy to forget that the world around us once shook. Like the real seismologists, our analysis of scandals remains a better explanatory than a predictive science, but we believe that we are beginning to understand the fundamental tectonics of policy development.

It is central to our argument that scandal is constructed out of a very particular set of events and processes, inhabited by real people and built on unique experiences. Yet, simultaneously, we are suggesting that scandals also constitute a class of social phenomena that has discernible commonalities and enduring attributes and an important relationship to the development of public policy. In this way, it is the aim of this book to both particularise and generalise, much in the manner of scandals themselves.

2
'Gothic Nightmare'
Madness and Public Policy from the Eighteenth Century

Introduction

This chapter aims to provide the essential background against which the scandals which took place in mental health institutions during the 1960s and 1970s can be understood and assessed. As chapter 1 suggested, scandals are the product of culturally and historically specific reactions to particular events. Such events are themselves shaped by the social policy context within which services are provided in any era. This chapter will end by identifying the key currents running in the social welfare world which produced the first major institutional scandal of modern times – that at Ely Hospital in Cardiff. In order to understand these events, however, the roots of mental health policy over a longer period need to be identified and discussed.

More, perhaps, than in any other branch of social welfare, a social constructionist understanding is capable of yielding rich insights when applied to changing understanding of madness. Jones (1996: 126–7) suggests that for nearly three hundred years after the closure of the monasteries in the English Reformation, attitudes towards mad people were characterised by harshness:

> The mad were increasingly seen as different and dangerous: sub-human, irrational and the bestial. Through giving into their madness they had forfeited their claims to be human and to be treated as such. Their madness was seen as their own fault, the result of self-indulgence, and excess of passion and egoism … Madness became redefined as the result of the deluded ideas and an unrestrained and violent imagination.

Foucault, in particular, has been highly influential in suggesting that, throughout Europe, the eighteenth and nineteenth centuries were characterised by a great confinement in which mad people were rounded up into asylums or prisons. The evidence for such a development in eighteenth-century Britain has been contested but it does seem clear that, even during an era of undiluted laissez-fairism, growth took place in the provision of private madhouses, catering for the better off in society. Confinement of poor people who were mad was still likely to be within pauper workhouses. The reputation, and the operation of private madhouses was highly variable but even at the more humane institutions treatment was predicated on what Jones (1996: 127) describes as 'the assumption that the mad were sub human and punishable'.

During the eighteenth century, therefore, only the first stirrings are detectable of a more interventionist, state-sponsored approach to provision for the mentally ill. For the most part these were driven along by one of the great enduring themes of British mental health policy, and one which was highly productive of scandal – the fear of unlawful confinement in a mental institution. In 1763 a House of Commons Select Committee was appointed to investigate claims of cruelty and illegal confinement in madhouses. A Bill followed which reached the statute book in 1774 as the Madhouse Act. According to Hervey (1985: 98–9), 'the main aim of this legislation was to prevent illegal reception of the sane, and for this reason it concerned itself little with the mechanics of inspection, or indeed with the real plight of madhouse inmates.' The system of certification set up by the 1774 Act did not apply to pauper patients, nor did it set up an inspectorate genuinely independent of asylum proprietors.

These inadequacies led to further attempts to reform the inspection and provision of institutional care of mentally ill people at the start of the nineteenth century. Discovery of ill-treatment of patients at York and at the London Bethlem Asylum in 1814 drew together a coalition of interested groups – philanthropists, evangelicals, asylum governors and magistrates – who, as Hervey (1985) suggests, lay behind the appointment of a House of Commons Select Committee in the following year and the drafting of Bills in 1814, 1816, 1817 and 1819. In the terms suggested in chapter 1 of this book, these groups represented primary claims-makers, utilising the raw material of revelation to campaign for reform. At this stage, however, only minor legislation followed. The 1828 Madhouse Act repealed the 1774 Act, and the County Asylums Act of the same year required asylums to make returns of admissions and discharges to the Home Office. Beyond these rather technical changes, more powerful policy principles, opposed to the extension of state control over private enterprise, prevailed.

Cumulatively, as Scull (1996: 8) argues, the evidence of abuse within the system added energy and urgency to the efforts of the reformers. A continuing series of parliamentary inquiries – the Public Inquiries of their day – appeared, writes Scull (1996: 9),

> to provide lurid confirmation of the public's worst Gothic nightmares about what transpired behind the high walls and barred windows of the madhouse. The reports of the select committees … contained a compelling amalgam of sex, madness, maltreatment, and murder, mixed together in a fashion guaranteed at once to titillate and repel: patients bled and drugged into insensibility; their public display, 'like animals in a menagerie'; unregarded deaths from botched forced-feeding and the brutality of uncaring attendants, the corrupt confinement of the sane, amidst the shrieks and raving of the mad.

Scandal depends upon the mobilisation of some of the most fundamental archetypes of human emotion and reaction. The reform movement of early Victorian Britain, culminating in the 1845 Lunatics Act and the establishment of the Lunacy Commission, was adept at harnessing such ingredients in pursuit of its aims.

Beyond such individuals, however, there were wider social forces which lay behind the particular reforms in the field of mental health. Mental health asylums undoubtedly form part of that broader picture in which, together with workhouses and prisons, the deviant, disruptive and economically burdensome populations of early Victorian Britain were segregated and controlled. The precise weight to be attached to different elements underpinning such developments is contested but it does seem clear, as Busfield (1986: 136) suggests, that 'public asylums were developed as a solution to the problems of social and economic order created by economic, social and personal dependency and had a clear motive of collective social control.' In a later text she concludes (1993: 137) that, in turning their energies and reforming zeal to the facilities for those suffering from mental illness, the Victorians found that 'professional advantage, humanitarian concerns and the economic and political interests of the state combined'.

The key component of the 1845 Lunatics Act, however, was that all counties were required to provide adequate asylum accommodation for 'pauper lunatics', defined as those persons whose maintenance came wholly or in part from public funds. These new institutions were to be small in scale and run according to the principles of 'moral treatment', an approach which had emanated from the Quaker reforms of the York Asylum. These, in turn, had roots in an older tradition, which Borsay

(1998: 646) traces from more than a hundred years earlier, in which economic rationality and morality were combined in the aim of returning 'hospital patients to the community as physically fit and morally healthy workers'. 'Moral treatment' in the field of mental illness depended upon a humanitarian approach which emphasised the minimal use of physical restraint and the maximum effect of a tranquil environment, upon patients whose behaviour would be shaped by the role-modelling example of those employed to attend to them. Quite certainly, however, the optimism which moral treatment provided included an economic as well as a therapeutic element. By restoring the mad to health the economic burden of caring for them would also be relieved as the effect of the moral regime educated its charges 'in ways of orderly living' (Borsay, 1998: 657). An additional wider social purpose could be identified in the new treatment regimes. Andrew Scull, amongst others, has emphasised the thoroughgoing means of control which such a system placed in the hands of the custodians, as well as the hidden threat of punishment and restraint upon which the system still depended.

Overseeing the new pattern of mental health provision was the Lunacy Commission, set up under the leadership of Lord Shaftesbury and provided with powers of visitation over County asylums, workhouses, and hospitals. Their powers were considerably greater than those provided under the 1774 Act and included particular powers to inspect and alter the regimes of private asylums where patients were kept for profit. The Commission is of particular relevance to the subject matter of this book because it acted, in many ways, as an early equivalent of the modern Committee of Inquiry. Scandal was soon a feature of its practical operation when, as Hervey (1985: 123) points out, in the year following its establishment, 'scandal erupted at Haydock Lodge ... a grossly overcrowded private asylum in Lancashire [where] paupers were underfed and ill treated.' The responses which the Commission were able to make to such eruptions were, of course, shaped by the wider views of madness and the treatments available for it which prevailed at the time. Hervey (1985: 104–5), for example, notes the ambivalent influence which Lord Shaftesbury provided in this regard: 'Shaftesbury often gave the lead to his colleagues, making crude generalisations about mental illness. In 1859 he informed the Select Committee on Lunatics that the main cause of insanity was intemperance ... He ascribed it at other times to commercial speculation and railway travel.'[1]

---

1. Such social constructionism was not unchallenged by alternative interpretations. According to Hervey (1985: 122) 'Florence Nightingale is recorded as having remarked of Lord Shaftesbury that, had he not devoted himself to reforming lunatic asylums, he would have been in one himself.'

Within the particular framework of contemporary understanding, however, the Commission proved itself capable of taking decisive action where it felt moved to do so. In 1851 it gained access to the Bethlem Hospital in London, recording its findings in the Annual Report which followed. Bethlem had long been the focus of agitation amongst those seeking reform in the mental health field. The Commission now proceeded to act in the role of secondary claims-maker. According to Hervey (1985: 110), 'the commissioners entered Bethlem with a preconceived notion of what to expect, and made extensive use of leading questions in their inquiry to elicit faults they intended to find.' The ostensible role of independent inspectorates, be they commissions or public inquiries, is to provide objective and impartial insight into events and actions. Below this surface, however, a far more active construction is taking place, in which particular interpretations of events are shaped into those 'master-narratives' which inquiries produce. In the Bethlem case, Hervey suggests, the Commissioners made 'ruthless use' of their Annual Report, emphasising the evidence which contributed to their case for reform while minimising the impact of any contradictory testimony.

The Commission's work continued throughout the Victorian era and beyond, punctuated regularly by scandal and shaped by the wider changes in attitude and understanding towards mental illness of the period. During the nineteenth century, the social understanding of madness and the policy responses to that understanding were successively reconstructed so that, as Scull (1981: 6) describes it, 'the Victorian age saw the transformation of the madhouse into the asylum into the mental hospital; of the mad doctor into the alienist into the psychiatrist; and of the madman (and mad woman) into the mental patient.' A number of these developments are especially important for an understanding of the policy context of modern mental health scandals and need to be considered here in some detail.

The growth of the asylum

The single most important factor which came to dominate the provision of institutional care for the mentally ill, and which produced a direct impact upon the scandals of the modern era more than a century later, is to be found in the massive growth in the number of individuals admitted to them almost as soon as the new buildings which followed the 1845 Act had been completed. According to Rogers and Pilgrim (1996: 46), 'The increase in lunatics was massive and far outweighed the growth in the population. In the half a century following the introduction of the compulsory asylums system the population grew by 80% whilst the numbers of lunatics quadrupled.' As Parry-Jones (1981: 207) makes clear, the demand for asylum places appeared to be insatiable. No matter how quickly new buildings were added to the old, 'the asylums were literally besieged by previously unheard of applicants for admissions'. Jones (1996: 130), taking the example of the West Riding Asylum, shows how its population grew from 150 in 1818 to 1,469 in 1900. By her estimates, 'whereas in England in 1800 there were around 1000 asylum inmates, by 1900 there were 100,000'. Gittins (1998: 13) suggests that two years after the 1845 Act there were 5,247 pauper patients in 21 county and borough asylums in the publicly placed sector in England and Wales. By 1914, the number had grown to 138,000.

This rapid rise in public asylum population did not reflect a cross-section of society as a whole. The numbers were overwhelmingly drawn from 'pauper lunatics' who, as Showalter (1981: 316) demonstrates, 'quadrupled between 1844 and 1890, formed the overwhelming majority of the total inmate population, and by 1890 were indeed 91% of all mental patients.' Despite their therapeutic intent, these figures suggest that asylums were overtaken by the institutional bias which was so characteristic of the New Poor Law. In the absence of outdoor relief a 'demand' for asylum care was created. As Busfield (1996: 138) puts it, asylums rapidly became 'like other Poor Law institutions: places of last resort where those for whom little could be hoped in the way of improvement were to be found.'

More broadly still, as Scull (1981: 16) has suggested, 'there is evidence that the public viewed any slackening of the rigid segregation of the mad with more than passing trepidation'. The reluctance to accept mentally ill people in the community – as expressed by George Eliot in the opening pages of *Middlemarch* (1872), for example, where the novelist assures us that, 'Sane people did what their neighbours did, so that if any lunatics were at large, one might know and avoid them' – acted to ratchet up even further the numbers admitted to asylums.

As numbers in the asylums grew, so the 'moral treatment' regimes under which they had been established deteriorated. Neither money nor numbers of staff were available to provide adequate regimes for the rapidly growing numbers. The result, according to Walton (1981: 169), was to 'push the new institutions towards a custodial holding operation ... and ensured a drift towards impersonality, regimentation, and the institutionalisation of routine.' The same author (1981: 169) concludes that the nature of patient admitted to the new institutions was also changing:

> the local Poor Law administrators generally sent the patients who were most troublesome and expensive to maintain in the workhouse or in the community, rather than those who seemed most likely to be curable. Instead of the recent cases for whom they held out the highest hopes, the asylum authorities found their institutions swamped by older and chronic patients.

The legacy of such a development, and the implications for regimes within institutions, will be a theme to which chapter 3 will return in some detail. Within the Victorian institutions themselves the effect was to bring about a rapid decline in the proportion of patients considered curable. According to Parry-Jones (1981: 207), for example, in the period '1844 to 1870 the proportion of curable patients fell from 15% to 7%'. Walton (1985: 138) quotes the superintendents of the county and other asylums and registered hospitals of England and Wales in 1867 as regarding 2,491 patients as 'probably curable', and 22,257 as 'probably incurable'. As he concludes:

> the asylum superintendents had given up hope for about 90% of their patients; and the ratio in the workhouses must have been much worse. An expensive system had promised cures, and failed to deliver; ... most of the successes were alcoholics who had dried out, exhausted, half-starved, over-worked women who recovered after a few weeks of limited exertion and reasonable diet, and cases of post-natal depression.

Summarised simply, the small-scale, curative enterprises of 1845 had become, in less than twenty years, large-scale custodial warehouses in which an ever-growing population of chronic, long-stay patients had overwhelmed any optimism that most of those admitted could be returned to health and to the community.

Madness and the family

As well as being drawn very heavily from the ranks of the poor, the inmates of the Victorian asylums were the product of family life. As Prior (1996: 87) puts it:

> the inevitable conflicts which arose between parents and their children could always be readily reinterpreted as expressions of their

madness ... In any event given that most of the people who entered the asylum were committed there on the say-so of their relatives, it seems fair to suggest that the appeal to madness as an underlying explanation for family conflicts and tensions was far from being rare or unusual.

Given the heavily skewed power relationships within Victorian families, also, it is hardly surprising to find that women were particularly highly represented within asylum populations. In some cases, confinement appeared to be the product of simple coercion, as when Walton (1985: 138) identifies a case reported, in 1879, in the language of scandal in which 'the commissioners found two women in the Blackburn work-house, confined as lunatics without proper certification and paid for by relatives'. In one case a husband paid ten shillings per week to keep his wife on pauper fare; and 'the second case was that of a girl who had been dissipated and disobedient to her parents, who sent her to the workhouse as a lunatic, and paid for her maintenance.' This latter case is resonant of a second, and wider, pattern of asylum confinement, in which morality rather than madness appears to have been the cause of admission. Showalter (1981: 324), who convincingly shows the way in which life within the asylum obliged women to live according to the narrowest of Victorian sex stereotypes – recording, for example, that 'five times as many women as men patients in the Colney Hall Asylum were punished by seclusion in padded cells in the period 1865 to 1874' – also suggests that disobedience or rebelliousness (and especially sexual rebelliousness) were easy grounds upon which fathers, brothers, and husbands could find doctors willing to certify women as lunatics. As late as 1895, she records the case of Edith Lanchester, a socialist convert living in Battersea with her lover, a mechanic, who was kidnapped by her father and brother and committed to an asylum on the authority of Dr G. Fielding Blandford, who judged her insane 'because he believed her opposition to conventional matrimony made her unfit to take care of herself.'

More broadly than the treatment of women, McCandless (1981: 351) and others have suggested that 'the greater adherence to respectable behaviour demanded [by the new Victorian] moral code paved the way for a broadened definition of insanity ... The person who seriously overstepped the bounds of acceptable conduct – through drunkenness, licence, gluttony, or extravagance – courted an accusation of madness.' In the case of men as well as women, the Victorian obsession with masturbation provided fertile ground for mixing matters of sexual morality and madness. As McCandless (1981: 355) notes, 'Doctors pointed to the asylum as a place where the moral patient could be cured of his vices, or at least prevented from indulging them and so bringing shame on himself and his family.'

Fear of improper confinement

The ease with which it appeared possible to arrange for the confinement of a family member in a mental asylum set off a countervailing reaction against the powers of doctors compulsorily to admit individuals against their will. Scull (1981: 25) links the periodic outbursts against 'mad-doctors' and the confinement laws to the sort of diagnoses set out above. In his view, 'it was not that doctors and relatives conspired to incarcerate the sane ... Rather the very bases of physicians' judgements were often heavily value-laden, so that in their eyes insanity and immorality at times became all but indistinguishable.' In other cases, judgements were less value-laden than straightforwardly spurious. When the eminent Dr George Burrows declared that maniacs emitted a particular smell – 'a symptom so unerring, that if detected in any person, I should not hesitate to pronounce him insane, even though I had no other proof of it' – such claims were the cause of disrepute, even amongst contemporaries. When these fears were layered upon the distrust of the asylums which campaigns against their abuses inevitably engendered, it is not surprising that so much Victorian energy was consumed in the investigation of alleged cases of wrongful confinement and in the framing of laws to prevent it.

McCandless (1981: 342) provides an instructive insight into the ways in which scandals concerning wrongful confinement appeared to develop a cyclical pattern in Victorian Britain. At regular intervals, 'some real or imagined injustice aroused public opinion to a high pitch of excitement. During these lunacy panics, newspapers and magazines often printed articles demanding inquiries and suggesting reforms.' One such case involved the case of Edward Davies, a tea dealer who was confined in an asylum at the instigation of his mother. Amongst the reasons given for supporting confinement were that Davies was incapable of managing his business affairs, even though the doctor providing this rationale later admitted that he had never inquired into the way in which these affairs had been actually conducted. According to the account provided by McCandless (1981: 350):

> When the jury heard this evidence they stopped the case without hearing Davies' witnesses and returned a unanimous verdict in his favour. The spectators greeted the decision with loud and general applause.

In Davies' home town of Newtown, Montgomeryshire, the citizens held a public demonstration to celebrate this triumph over cruelty and oppression. Sheep were roasted in the marketplace for the benefit of the poor; the respectable held a supper at the Castle Inn; and the evening was brought to a close with the burning of Davies' mother in effigy.

Yet such attention seldom lasted for long. Interest would be lost and attention shifted elsewhere. The production of scandal relies upon a combination of factors – the event itself, its being brought to the notice of individuals or groups with an interest in connecting the particular happening to a more general cause, and the successful dissemination of such a portrayal to a wider audience. There can be little doubt but that the raw material for scandal – in the shape of wrongful detention – did exist in Victorian Britain, even if the scale of such detentions is disputed. As McCandless' account (1981: 342) also makes clear, there existed a well-organised if small group of dedicated primary claims-makers – mostly former mental patients or relatives of patients – who 'wrote books and pamphlets, investigated alleged abuses, and, campaigned for changes in the law'. Drawn almost exclusively from the middle classes – for it seemed inconceivable that anyone would wish to commit a pauper offering no prospect of monetary gain to an institution – such individuals were responsible for the strikingly-named Alleged Lunatic's Friend Society (founded in 1845) and its successor, the Lunacy Law Reform Association (founded in 1873). A receptive audience was regularly available for the stories which such groups produced. Scull (1981: 18) suggests that the public remained 'always fascinated by tales of the dark underside which asylum might have and perpetually fearful of improper confinement in these institutions'. The periodic waves of alarm which followed produced a pattern which was to become familiar in our own times. Agitation by primary campaigners led to two major parliamentary inquiries on the issue in 1858–59 and again in 1876–77. Paradoxically, as in the modern media treatment of paedophilia, fears appeared to increase as successive attempts were made to allay them.

At the root of the scandals which surrounded improper confinement lay a double ambivalence. On the one hand, contemporary public attitudes were capable both of powerful support for the compulsory detention of the lunatic and of powerful hostility towards the prospect of the unlawful detention of the sane. At the same time, the successful colonisation of mental illness as the province of medicine – in which the legal framework of certification provided an important guarantee of respectability – was undercut by the enduring sense of stigma which clung to the whole lunacy business. Nor was such a sense confined to those suffering from mental illness itself. As Scull (1981: 11) puts it, 'somehow, close and unremitting contact with the stigmatised and powerless carries with it its own peculiar reward – a share of their stigma and the marginality.' In the scandals which form the main focus of this text, the sense of stigma which appears to be inherent in social welfare undoubtedly played an important part. The way in which such a feeling was connected to workers in the lunacy field during the nineteenth century provides some instructive parallels, as the following two sections illustrate.

The medicalisation of madness

For many historians of the Victorian period, the capturing of mental health as the province of medicine represents a major triumph of professional imperialism. Rogers and Pilgrim (1996: 46), for example, quote the 1858 editorial of the *Journal of Mental Science* in its pronouncement that 'Insanity is purely a disease of the brain. The physician is now the responsible guardian of the lunatic and must ever remain so.' 'These two sentences', Rogers and Pilgrim suggest, 'capture a political project of organised medicine which was to last for over a hundred years: madness was a biological disorder and only doctors could oversee its management.'

Despite this, the combination of continuing public ambivalence and the remaining subjectivity of psychiatric diagnosis meant, as Scull (1981: 11) suggests, that at the end of the nineteenth century, real dangers remained that 'the newly consolidating psychiatric profession could look forward to no more than a dubious status as a barely legitimate branch of medicine.' Gittins (1998: 3) concludes that, well into the twentieth century, mental health physicians were regarded:

> more as custodians than doctors and were seen by the rest of the medical profession as poor cousins, Cinderellas of medicine. The track record of cure in psychiatry was very poor indeed; some treatments, such as bromides, paraldehyde, continuous baths and physical restraint by straitjackets, helped to alleviate, sedate and control, but at this point there were no more real 'cures' in evidence than there had been a hundred years previously or, indeed, a thousand years previously.

Staffing questions

Of more significance in the small change of institutional scandal was the persistent complaint – amongst the Lunacy Commissioners, family members and amongst some asylum workers themselves – that the quality of staff in asylums was consistently low. Hervey (1985: 112) provides detailed information from one Kent asylum in which the average working life for attendants dropped from three years in the 1840s, to only one year in the late 1850s. Between 1876 and 1878 the words most frequently used to describe attendants in official records were 'brutish', 'dirty', 'ugly', and 'rude' and the author concludes that, 'it is clear from the servants' book that size and strength were the important criteria in staff selection.'

The long hours of difficult work, combined with the personal restrictions which asylum employment entailed, made the recruitment and retention of suitable staff persistently difficult throughout the nineteenth century. In striking pre-echoes of the scandals dealt with in the next chapter of this book, the employment conditions of staff prescribed dismissal for any attendant who was caught striking a patient, or appearing on duty in a state of drunkenness. Attendants were also forbidden to receive items from patients or to carry out any business on their behalf. At times of economic prosperity, especially, asylum work appeared unattractive, an impression which grew as the numbers entering institutions mushroomed and regimes retreated towards the custodial. In some parts of the country, too, wage rates within asylums remained very low. Davies (1996: 372) calculates that, in West Wales, the daily rate paid to attendants was consistently lower that the amount spent per day on each inmate. In some places, he suggests, even more senior staff 'were themselves virtually paupers'. Scandals involving unsuitable staff were the result. Walton (1985: 187) reports a case involving the prosecution of two attendants who, in March 1870, 'were found guilty of manslaughter for beating and kicking a patient to death'. A number of features of the case are worth noting. Firstly, the criminal trial which followed was marked by what the prosecuting counsel characterised as a 'malign esprit de corps' amongst the 'warders', in which other attendants had contributed financially towards the defence of their colleagues. Secondly, it became clear that, at ward level, the asylum was in the hands of staff left alone with the patients with the minimum of supervision. An internal subcommittee of inquiry into the causes of the scandal recommended closer supervision of the wards by the chief attendant and his assistant medical officers. As Walton (1981: 141) suggests, 'its most important paragraph showed a revealing awareness of the root of the trouble: "We would therefore strongly urge upon the superior officers frequent and irregular visits to the wards."' Thirdly, scandals involving ward-level staff illustrated the extent to which institutional inertia had come to militate against the primary purpose of asylums – the cure of inmates. Within the institution many patients provided the labour upon which the efficient and economic operation of the asylum depended. As Walton (1985: 142) writes, it became easier to get 'inmates to contribute to the smooth running of the asylum than to decant them into the outside world'. Moreover, as the same writer suggests, 'Poor Law penny pinching and concerned custodial control combined to make a gentle assimilation into the outside world almost impossible. Patients had to be released suddenly and without resources, into a harsh and unfriendly world.' With this echo of the community care scandals which appear in later chapters of this book, we now turn to a final, and relatively hidden aspect of nineteenth-century provision for the mentally ill – the arrangements for the care of individuals outside the asylum.

Community care

Three essential ways existed through which mental health patients in Victorian Britain might be cared for outside their own families but not within the confines of the asylum. The first does not qualify for any form of 'community care' attribution but consists of the large number of mentally ill people who found themselves retained within the workhouse or who languished in prison. The complaints of the Lunacy Commission in 1866 and 1867, that excited or uncontrollable workhouse lunatics were being disciplined by spells in prison instead of being referred to the care of the asylum (Walton, 1985: 138) will become familiar in later chapters when we turn to consider arrangements for the community care of mentally ill people in our own day. In the following year, the Commission complained again that the retention of mentally ill people in workhouses (often on the grounds of economy) only acted to deny them the necessary treatment as well as 'the comforts and indulgences their malady or their helplessness so urgently needs' (quoted in Davies, 1996: 369).

The second means of care outside the institution represented an extension of the asylum into the community, rather than any real alternative to it. 'Single lodgings' had long existed where, in theory at least, single patients were looked after within private houses. In some parts of the country, these remained the dominant form of provision well after the 1845 Act. In Wales, for example, the Lunacy Commissioners found that, in 1860, 988 patients out of 1,754 remained in single lodgings (Davies, 1996: 367). Despite particular powers provided to the Commission, such lodgings proved especially difficult to locate and supervise. With the growth in the asylum population, patients were moved from asylums into private lodgings where they were supervised by attendants. These were commercial arrangements, brought about, as Hervey (1985: 116) suggests, by the fact that 'private lodgings were the ideal form of care for wealthy families, as they avoided a stigma of asylum admission'. In a further business arrangement, asylum practitioners would endorse particular lodgings, supplying them with patients. Single lodgings were used in the same way and Hervey concludes that 'patients were rarely registered, they had no safeguards to their liberty at all, and with the increasing difficulty of confining these borderline cases in asylums, due to better certification procedures, it is tempting to speculate that the number of patients in single lodgings rose'.

On a grander scale of moving the asylum into the community, Parry-Jones (1981: 207) describes an experiment conducted by the superintendent of the Devon County Asylum which provides an instructive commentary upon the contemporary concerns explored further in later chapters dealing with contemporary mental health policy. Overcrowding at the main Exeter Asylum was relieved by the opening of a temporary branch asylum at Exmouth and by housing patients in local cottages in the neighbourhood. This development caused great alarm amongst local residents, who petitioned the Secretary of State against the move. As Parry-Jones suggests, 'subsequent events would be familiar to anyone who has been involved in new developments within the community involving the mentally ill'. The objections raised by the local inhabitants were the following:

> That the existence of the pauper lunatic asylum at Exmouth would prevent invalids and tourists visiting the town as a marine watering place; that the hotels and houses let as lodgings would be unoccupied; that the value of house property would be greatly deteriorated; that the residents would be distressed and terrified by painful scenes, and that in taking their usual walks upon the beach and the sands, they would be in danger from the violence of the patients whom they would meet.

The third form of non-asylum care was more consciously developed as an alternative to the institution. Scull (1981: 14), quoting John Buckrill from 1880 reminds us that, despite the powerful rise of the asylum in Victorian Britain, 'in some quarters the heretical thought was voiced that "the curative influences of the asylum have been vastly over rated and those of isolated treatment in domestic care have been greatly under valued" (Buckrill, 1880).' Examples exist of extended experiments of this sort, such as that reported by Parry-Jones (1981: 207) in relation to the Lunatic Colony at Geel which he describes as an 'indisputable... prototype for an alternative approach in the care of the chronic insane to that offered traditionally within the asylum system'. Dispersing chronically ill lunatics was claimed to be both more humane and – in anticipation of contemporary debates – cheaper than institutional care.

Nor was this form of dispersed treatment immune from scandal. A colony on the Scottish island of Arran was disbanded because of brutal treatment. Parry-Jones (1981: 211) summarises the objections which were regularly made against such a system: 'poor selection of patients; inadequate supervision; the impossibility of obtaining consistent and reliable custodians and the difficulties inherent in any training; the insufficiency of proper official inspection; the liability of improper treatment and the misuse of patients; and the fears of moral injury to the custodian's family, especially its younger members'. By contrast, those who were not fit to live outside the asylum, would be better provided for within an institution where they would be happier, freer, and would have a higher standard of care.

Despite these reservations, the scale of 'community care' of pauper lunatics in Victorian Britain was not insubstantial. Parry-Jones (1981: 212) estimates that in England and Wales, in 1870, 62 per cent of pauper lunatics were in asylums, 23.5 per cent in workhouses, and 15 per cent boarded-out. Certainly the scale was large enough to merit that essential Victorian vehicle, the society dedicated to its interests, with the founding of the Mental After Care Association in 1879 under the patronage of the ubiquitous Lord Shaftesbury.

Reforms to mental health services and the legislative framework surrounding them continued throughout the Victorian period. The last major Act of Parliament in this field was the 1890 Lunacy Act, described by Rogers and Pilgrim (1996: 52) as 'the culmination of custodialism in the latter part of the 19th-century, which continued into the first decades of the twentieth.' The Act was infused with what Busfield (1986: 134) terms the 'therapeutic nihilism of the latter part of the 19th century', in which the optimism of the asylum movement had been thoroughly dissipated. Asylums had been transformed into understaffed, overcrowded establishments, housed in buildings whose very size and appearance, as Parry-Jones (1981: 207) suggests, 'spoke of authority and repression'. The 1890 Act responded to these changed conditions by concentrating almost entirely on a legalistic approach, prioritising once again the need to prevent wrongful certification and detention of the sane, rather than improving the conditions or civil liberties of the patient. Within the walls of the institution, the asylum population came to be dominated more and more by the chronic and the aging. They had, according to Scull (1996: 7),

> degenerated into more or less well attended cemeteries for the still living ... it was this spectre of chronicity, this horde of the hopeless, which was to haunt the popular imagination, to constitute the public identity of the asylums, and to dominate the Victorian and Edwardian psychiatric theorising and practice.

It is against this background that, during the early years of the twentieth century, medical attention in relation to mental health issues turned in a new direction, heavily influenced by more general preoccupations with social decay and deterioration. Of particular interest to this book is the impact of such thinking upon services for what came to be known as the mentally handicapped. A distinction between mental illness and mental handicap was largely absent from Victorian activity in the lunacy field. The rudimentary provisions of the Idiots Act of 1886 were short-lived and overtaken by the 1890 Lunacy Act, in which any distinction between the two categories had disappeared. During the Edwardian era, however, *mental deficiency* came far more to the fore, with a supposed link between mental deficiency and social problems – criminality, promiscuity – leading to calls for the sterilisation and the segregation of people with mental deficiency. In response, the Government set up a Royal Commission on the Care and Control of the Feeble Minded (1904–08). Although heavily influenced by the Eugenics Society, the Commission rejected a policy of sterilisation. It nevertheless favoured what Porter (1996: 395) describes as 'removal of defectives from the community ... in the interests of national efficiency – so as to prevent criminality, idleness, and the multiplication of low-grade types'. A pamphlet issued in support of the Parliamentary Bill which followed, and sponsored amongst others by the Archbishops of Canterbury and York argued that action was necessary: 'BECAUSE they are frequently producing children, many of whom inherit their mental defect, and nearly all of whom become the paupers, criminals and unemployables of the next generation' (quoted in Porter, 1996: 394).

Thus were laid the foundations of the 1913 Mental Deficiency Act, which recommended that each local authority establish a 'colony' as a basis for specialist care. This would provide a completely self-contained and segregated environment where mentally deficient people of all ages could live, train, work and relax, with villas for residences, schools, workshops, churches, recreational facilities and a farm. It required each local authority to set up a Mental Deficiency Committee to provide an administrative system for such non-institutional provision. While this was by no means 'care in the community', it was the first stirrings of an organised, supervised, non-institutional care of mentally handicapped people.

The implementation of the 1913 Act was delayed by the onset of the 1914–18 War and by the challenge which the mental health conse-quences of that conflict produced for psychiatry. Given the scale of men-tal distress which participation in the war created, and the indiscriminate way in which 'shell-shock' afflicted men from all social classes, eugenic theories of genetic decline or faulty breeding became difficult to main-tain. The aftermath of the fighting left some 100,000 additional mental health patients from this source alone. Consideration of the issues involved were summarised in a War Office Report (War Office, 1922). It contributed to a recognition of the environmental causes of mental health problems. According to Rogers and Pilgrim (1996: 59), the chang-ing emphasis further undermined the legitimacy of those asylum doctors whose theories had rested upon eugenic explanations. The extent of dis-illusionment is noted by Freeman (1998: 226) who suggests that, in the setting up of the 1924 Royal Commission on Lunacy and Mental Disorder, 'the inferior status of psychiatrists is illustrated by the fact that it had only two medical members, neither of whom was a psychiatrist.' Once again, according to Busfield (1986), the major impetus for the Commission came from renewed concerns about unlawful detention, brought about by a scandal exposed at the Prestwich Asylum in 1921. The Mental Treatment Act of 1930 which followed, however, did contain some softening of the purely legalistic approach of the 1890 Lunacy Act, replacing it with a greater emphasis upon the treatment needs of mental health sufferers. It renamed asylums as 'mental hospitals' and introduced three types of admission: voluntary, temporary and certified. The balance of power was shifted gently away from the law and towards the medical profession, now responsible, according to Rogers and Pilgrim (1996: 61), for the oversight of 'a nationwide network of grand and extensive build-ings near every major population point. England and Wales had 98 asy-lums which contained 120,000 patients.' With this Act, suggests Freeman (1998: 226), 'the modern era of mental health policy in Britain may be said to have opened.'

On the mental handicap front, the Report of the 1929 Wood Committee supported some of the main thrusts of the 1913 Act, but placed a greater emphasis on the classification of the mentally deficient. It identified those capable of living a normal sociable life in the community under some form of supervision, as well as those needing institutional care because of their antisocial or dangerous behaviour. It thus reinforced the emphasis on care outside institutions for some categories of the mentally deficient. Nevertheless, the interwar years saw a rapid expansion of specialised institutions for the mentally handicapped. Starting with 2,040 individuals in such establishments in 1914, the figure rose to 46,054 in 1939.

Reaction against institutions

Rogers and Pilgrim (1996: 61) describe the interwar years as a period of 'business as usual' in British mental health policy and practice. Institutional provision dominated the field, dwarfing a weak outpatient sector. The hospitals themselves were 'really little different from the Victorian asylums. They were merely the same buildings but with a new treatment rhetoric.' In legal terms, too, little had altered. In the mid-1930s, some 90 per cent of patients were still compulsorily detained.

Real change, then, did not take place until the second half of the twentieth century. The state of mental health services at the point of National Health Service foundation in 1948 vividly illustrates the tension between the weight of demand within the system and the scarcity and inexpert nature of resources devoted to that demand. Freeman (1998: 229) estimates that in the year in which the NHS became responsible for mental health services, 44 per cent of all hospital beds nationally were in mental illness or in mental deficiency hospitals. Yet in the decade which was to follow, the Medical Research Council devoted fully 1 per cent of its £8 million budget to research into mental illness and mental deficiency. Admission rates to mental hospitals in the postwar period were also rising sharply. The number of beds in institutions caring for mentally ill people was yet to reach its peak of around 149,000 in 1955. While Freeman suggests that this was 'then regarded as a laudable process, indicating that more people were willing to accept treatment at an earlier stage of illness', the numbers added to the problems of overcrowding and staff shortages with the effect that, in many mental hospitals, beds were placed in corridors or crammed into wards. In mental handicap the position was worse, with waiting lists for the country standing at 9,000, of whom nearly half were children (Jones, 1972: 290). Yet, when, in 1948, a duty was placed upon local health authorities to provide officers who could undertake compulsory admissions to mental hospitals, the state of staff training and expertise was such that there was no requirement for these people to have any knowledge of mental illness.

It was against this background that changing professional and public attitudes began to produce a movement in political perceptions. Yet it was, once more, the whiff of scandal which produced one of the earliest direct assaults on mental health institutions. This came about with the 1951 publication of the National Council for Civil Liberties pamphlet *50,000 Outside the Law* which argued that mentally subnormal people, as they were then called, lacked some of the legal safeguards available to the mentally ill against wrongful detention, and that the methods of testing young people for mental deficiency failed to distinguish temporary backwardness from permanent deficit. Conditions in mental deficiency institutions created a 'vested interest' in retaining people rather than releasing them. Patients often did work which would otherwise require additional paid staff, and hospitals took on commercial work without adequately paying patients.

At this point a series of factors came together in a way which was to produce a quantum shift in mental health policy. Some forty years later, the House of Commons Health Committee (1994) was to summarise the different elements as: the public concern about deteriorating conditions and neglect in the mental hospitals and the disabling and stigmatising effects of long-term hospitalisation; the availability of drugs enabling the management of many mental disorders outside hospital and the development of other flexible forms of treatment; and research showing the benefits of treating and supporting people in their own homes and other community-based settings.

To this must be added the upsurge in interest from social scientists in mental hospitals, especially in America. As summarised by Korman and Glennerster (1990: 13–14) they found, unsurprisingly, an organisational structure that encouraged custodial care rather than cure or rehabilitation. Hospitals were characterised by an acute shortage of professional staff of all types, with ward-level treatment and the management of patients determined by the ward attendants, the least well-trained of all staff. These individuals spent most of their time supervising able patients to do work which they themselves were officially paid to undertake, such as washing and cleaning the wards, and washing and feeding other patients. The prime needs of ward staff were for order and control, and these tended to override the needs of patients. Relationships between medical and nursing staff were characterised by suspicion, avoidance and hostility and the presence of doctors in substantial parts of hospitals was minimal. The most extreme shortage of staff was among trained social workers, exaggerating rather than mitigating the fractured links between patients and their families, so that patients who might have benefited from being discharged were less likely to be so.

This analysis was carried further in the seminal work of Goffman (1961: 17) and his influential concept of the 'total institution' – a place where all aspects of life for inmates took place within institutional boundaries and under institutional control; where the daily round of activities was unvarying and rigidly pursued according to institutional needs; where the individual was subjugated to the collective and where the actual and ostensible practices of the organisation were very far apart.

While the attack on institutions was less strident in Britain than in America, the notion that the old asylums were part of the problem of mental health services, rather than being the solution, preventing rather than providing treatment, gathered ground on both sides of the Atlantic. It provided a context in which the shift from institutional to community care was driven not so much out of knowledge of the positive advantages of domiciliary care as by an increasing awareness of the disadvantages of treatment within institutions, and the damage which could be caused by them.

More positively, change was also informed by new methods of treatment, many of them based upon the new generation of tranquillisers which contributed to the capacity of mental hospitals to abandon many of their security practices and to introduce new 'open-door' policies. Porter (1996: 401) suggests that, 'the new drugs did not so much inaugurate as expedite' the era of care in the community. It all added up to a fresh onrush of therapeutic optimism which is perhaps best illustrated in Jones' (1972: 340) quotation of the views of the Conservative Minister, Sir Keith Joseph, that 'psychiatry is to join the rest of medicine. The treatment of psychosis, neurosis and schizophrenia have been entirely changed by the drug revolution. People go into hospital with mental disorders and they are cured.'

Against this background, the first signs of political interest came when Kenneth Robinson, later to be a Labour Minister of Health, initiated a debate on mental health matters in the House of Commons in February 1954. It was, reported Freeman (1998: 229), the first time since 1930 that the subject had been discussed in Parliament. The establishment of a Royal Commission on Mental Illness and Mental Deficiency followed. According to Kathleen Jones (1972: 289), 'there had been no major revision and consolidation of the law relating to mental illness and mental deficiency for 64 years. The Lunacy Act of 1890, although to some extent by-passed by the 1930 Mental Treatment Act and Mental Deficiency Acts of 1913 and 1927, was still in force.'

The Royal Commission marked a fundamental shift in policy-making. In place of the century-old obsession with compulsory detention and certification, it proposed the principle of voluntary admission. In place of the emphasis on treatment within institutions, it proposed a transfer of resources and patients to care in the community. According to Freeman (1998: 230):

> there is considerable uncertainty as to how the community care policy began, but the first reference in an official document to the unsuitability of mental hospitals for modern treatments seems to be in the Ministry of Health's *Annual Report* for 1955 ... In the following year, the Chief Medical Officer's report made the first reference to a 'comprehensive' service and identified three main foci for development: developing community services, expansion of general hospital facilities and upgrading mental hospitals.

When the Royal Commission proposals were embodied in a Parliamentary Bill, the Minister of Health, Derek Walker-Smith, introduced the debate by declaring that, 'One of the main principles we are seeking to pursue is the re-orientation of the mental health services away from institutional care towards care in the community.'

Such a reorientation clearly had considerable potential consequences for existing forms of provision. By 1961 it was officially predicted that within 16 years the number of beds in mental institutions would fall from over 160,000 to about 80,000. Both the sense of mission which had come to surround the policy shift, and the sense of struggle which was to be involved in translating the policy into practice, is captured in the words of the then Health Minister, Enoch Powell (1961), who expressed it thus:

> these bold words ... imply nothing less than the elimination of by far the greater part of this country's mental hospitals as they stand today. This is a colossal undertaking, not so much in the physical provision which it involves as in the sheer inertia of mind and matter which it requires to be overcome. There they stand, isolated, majestic, imperious, brooded over by the gigantic water-tower and chimney combined, rising unmistakably and daunting out of the countryside – the asylums which our forefathers built with such solidity. Do not for a moment underestimate their power of resistance to our assault.

Set against the determination to close the old asylums there were thus a series of doubts about the community care arrangements with which they were to be replaced. There is in social policy, as well as in other fields of human history, a temptation to tell the story as though dominant trends were unambiguous. Community care was undoubtedly a 'winning' trend from the late 1950s onwards. Yet, from the start there were questions raised which were to become more important by the late 1980s and 1990s. These included an emphasis on the fact that, for certain mental illnesses and handicaps, no amount of deinstitutionalisation, normalisation or reverse labelling, could deny the existence of severe handicaps and the need for special services. Writers who emphasised these points noted that, contrary to the thrust of Goffman-like thinking, institutions did not simply create disabilities: the disabilities really did exist and needed attention.

Even amongst those who accepted the case for community care in principle, voices existed to question the readiness of replacement facilities. As Sedgwick (1982: 192) suggests:

> in Britain, as in the USA, the reduction in the register of patients resident in mental hospitals (from a peak of 154,000 in 1954 to around two-thirds of this total in recent years) has been achieved through the creation of a rhetoric of 'community care facilities', whose influence over policy on hospital admissions and discharge has been particularly remarkable when one considers that they do not, in the actual world, exist.

Earlier voices had already signalled the importance of this argument. Titmuss (1963: 223) had put it powerfully when he suggested that 'to scatter the mentally ill in the community before we have made provision for them is not a solution'. In the figures he provided, the 1950s – the decade of the onset of community care – had witnessed a decrease in local authority expenditure on mental health services per head of the population, rather than the 'ratcheting up' of services which would be needed if hospitals were to close. While the same decade might truthfully enough be described by Goodwin (1989: 27) as the period which brought about, 'a transformation in policy regarding the treatment of mentally ill people in England and Wales', it is not surprising to find Kathleen Jones (1972: 325) describing the launch of community care as one characterised more by 'a chorus of discussion' than by one of congratulation.

In the event, the predicted reduction in beds was only partially realised. Yet, throughout the period the staff of mental hospitals felt that they faced an uncertain future. The plan did not generate confidence; rather the reverse. Unsurprisingly, the first to be resettled were generally those patients who were the more acute, younger and more hopeful; those who stayed were older and more severely mentally infirm. Morale, therefore, was almost inevitably going to be damaged and the nursing task made more difficult and probably less rewarding.

There were doubts, too, about the physical future of hospital buildings. Many were badly antiquated and in need of major repair. In 1950 the Minister who had founded the National Health Service, Aneurin Bevan, wrote a memorandum to the Cabinet in which he declared that, 'Most of the hospitals fall far short of any proper standard ... indeed some of the mental hospitals *are very near to a public scandal* and we are lucky that they have not so far attracted more limelight and publicity' (quoted in Klein, 1995: 80, emphasis added). Yet, if they were to be closed, what was the point of spending great sums on them?

At a local level, it seems that hospitals for the mentally ill concentrated such resources as were available on admission wards and short-stay facilities, working on the reasonable principle that the first priority was to stop new patients becoming chronic and, if possible, to keep them out of hospital altogether. Thus the converse of the bright coin of the therapeutic revolution was a comparative neglect of its darker side, the long-stay 'back wards' inhabited by patients for whom there seemed little hope, and nursed by staff with equally low expectations. Full employment in the labour market, furthermore, meant that staff recruitment was difficult, and nursing administrators could be faced with a choice between recruiting doubtful candidates or doing without staff altogether. Sometimes older staff found it difficult or impossible to adapt to new methods, thus exacerbating the potential for conflict between the newly trained and their less qualified, but experienced seniors.

During the nineteenth century, the development of policy had been regularly punctuated and prompted by the eruption of scandal, as earlier parts of this chapter demonstrated. As provision for the mentally ill and the learning disabled shifted in favour of institutional settings, as optimism rose and then gave way to pessimism, as medicine and the law jostled for supremacy in the governance of mental health services and patients, so sufficient policy fluidity existed for scandal to be an effective tool in the hands of particular policy proponents. In the first half of the twentieth century, that sense of struggle had subsided. Those few paths of policy progress which were attempted were quickly submerged in wider upheavals or foundered in rapid disillusionment. Without the possibility of change, scandal lacked an essential lever for its own mobilisation. Thus, despite the reservations which Bevan and others expressed, the quality of institutional services for long-term patients did not appear to attract such early attention. It was this ground which was about to shift dramatically, beginning with the publication of a letter to the Editor of *The Times* newspaper, dated 10 November 1965:

Sir,

We the undersigned, have been shocked by the treatment of geriatric patients in certain mental hospitals, one of the evils being the practice of stripping them of their personal possessions. We have now sufficient evidence to suggest that this is widespread.

The attitude of the Ministry of Health to complaints has merely reinforced our anxieties. In consequence, we have decided to collect evidence of ill-treatment of geriatric patients throughout the country, to demonstrate the need for a national investigation. We hope this will lead to the securing of effective and humane control over these hospitals by the Ministry, which seems at present to be lacking.

We shall be grateful if those who have encountered malpractice in this sphere will supply us with detailed information, which would of course be treated as confidential.

Yours faithfully,
Strabolgi, Beaumont, Heytesbury, Brian Abel-Smith, Edward Ardizzone, Audrey Harvey, John Hewetson, Barbara Robb, Bill Sargent, Daniel Woolgar, O.P.
10, Hampstead Grove, NW3

3
'The Corruption of Care'
The Ely Hospital Inquiry 1969

Introduction

> There is no doubt that the occasional scandal does an enormous
> amount for a social service.
> > (Sir Keith Joseph, House of Commons 12 July 1971)

The newspaper story which broke with the *Times* letter quoted at the end
of chapter 2 contained many of the ingredients from which scandals are
constructed. One of the signatories, Barbara Robb, was a claims-maker of
the first rank. Founder of AEGIS (Aid for Elderly in Government
Institutions), Mrs Robb was the mobilising spirit behind the attention
which was now drawn to conditions in some of Britain's oldest and least-
well-resourced institutions. Life within the hospitals in which geriatric
medicine was practised continued to reflect their Poor Law heritage. The
daily routine relied upon a series of practices which Goffman identified
as characteristic of 'total' institutions. The enclosed nature of the world
which emerged in the wake of the *Times* letter can be gauged from this
extract, taken from one of the early Inquiry Reports which was to follow
the AEGIS agitation which was now set in train. A psychiatric social
worker had complained about the reception afforded to her father,
referred to as Mr Tasburg, on admission to Friern Hospital. In response,
the Report (25) records the account of the Charge Nurse responsible:

> it was his practice as a Charge Nurse to request relatives to take home
> articles that the hospital would supply: and he had naturally been
> reluctant to allow Mr Tasburg to keep a razor as he might still have
> suicidal tendencies ... the patient's money (except loose change) had
> been handed in to the Admissions Office together with other articles,

as was the prescribed procedure with which the Committee find no fault; and that Mr Tasburg had wrapped the loose change in a handkerchief and put it under his pillow. Such an action was to be deprecated because of the risk of petty theft, but it was difficult to prevent; and the Committee think that on balance it was (and is) better to placate disturbed patients by allowing them to retain small sums or minor valuables rather than to upset them by requiring nightly or *total surrender.* (emphasis added)

The group of signatories who had been assembled for the *Times* letter, including members of the House of Lords and senior academics, ensured that its contents could not go unnoticed, while the status of the newspaper itself added weight to the charges which were made. A group of people determined to bring a scandal to public notice had found a vehicle through which the wider public might be contacted. The result was immediate and highly successful. Several hundred letters were received in response to the invitation to be supplied with detailed information of ill-treatment and malpractice in health service hospitals caring for older people.

Sans Everything

In June 1967, these responses were gathered together and published in a book edited by Barbara Robb entitled *Sans Everything: a Case to Answer.* As Korman and Glennerster (1990: 15) suggest, 'the book suggested that callous indifference to patients, exploitation, rough handling, removal of glasses, hearing aids, dentures and other indignities, were portrayed as customary procedures'. While the territory set out in *Sans Everything* was to become heavily disputed, the immediate impact was considerable. By now, Kenneth Robinson had been appointed Minster of Health in the Labour government. He responded by asking the Hospital Boards responsible for six hospitals identified by the authors of *Sans Everything*, to set up independent Committees of Inquiry. Jones and Fowles (1984: 108), who provide a generally unsympathetic account of the book, conclude that 'the whole affair was a very skilful exercise in public relations; and despite the flamboyance, the distortions and the inaccuracies, it worked'.

The results were published together in the following year. A general introduction set the scene for the assembled reports. The views contained in *Sans Everything* had given 'rise to much public concern, and were of a nature which clearly called for investigation'. The terms of reference provided to the Inquiries were 'to investigate the allegations made ... and also to enquire into the present state of affairs at these hospitals'.

In establishing the different Inquiries, a number of key patterns of institutional response to scandals in mental health institutions were laid down. As the Report makes clear:

> the Chairmen of these Committees were Queen's Counsel whose names had been suggested by the Lord Chancellor at the request of the Minister of Health; the other members of each Committee were a doctor, a nurse and one or more persons not professionally qualified in medicine or nursing but experienced in the administration of hospitals or other public concerns.

This structure – an independent lawyer as chair, a medical and/or nursing representative and an administrator – was to become the usual mode of inquiry in such cases. It combined insider-knowledge with independence from the particular circumstances under consideration. Importantly, in working through the Lord Chancellor's Department, it established a quasi-judicial framework for Inquiries which was to be highly influential.

The legacy of the court-room proved significant in a number of different ways. It had an impact upon the formality with which Inquiries went about their business. In some, for example, Inquiry members would process in and out at the start and conclusion of each day's hearing, just as in a Court of law, as illustrated in the case of the Colwell Inquiry in chapter 5. The conduct of Inquiries, too, rapidly drew upon this heritage, calling witnesses, appointing barristers and so on, as later chapters of this book will demonstrate. From the outset, such origins influenced the atmosphere of Inquiry hearings. Even where more informal approaches were attempted, the impact upon potential contributors was that of appearing in a forum where their conduct was under examination and their veracity under question. Finally, it produced a profound impact upon the task which Inquiries regarded themselves as embarked upon. From the conflicting and competing accounts provided by witnesses, sometimes of events which had taken place a considerable time beforehand, the Inquiry's task was to establish the 'truth' and to reach judgements upon individuals and organisations. The construction of that account appeared, at least to those who embarked upon the earliest mental health Inquiries, a relatively straightforward affair. The 'truth' really did exist. The task of the Inquiry was to establish it.

In all this, the decision to provide the Lord Chancellor's Department with the right of nominating Inquiry chairs retained a very powerful tool in the hands of the government in general and the legal establishment, in particular. The choice of such individuals, as the seminal Inquiries of Ely and Colwell demonstrate, was to have considerable impact.

For the most part, this book is concerned with the attempt to fashion an understanding of those conditions in which scandal takes a grip of the public imagination and impacts upon the policy-making process. In moving towards such an appreciation, it is important to explore, also, those conditions in which scandal fails to take root, or where its potential effect is diffused and fended away by those upon whom it might have been influential. The detailed discussion of this aspect of scandal is to be found in chapter 6 of this text. Here, it is important to note that the basic decisions made at the outset of the *Sans Everything* Inquiries had already sown the seeds of the stunted growth and limited immediate effect which was to follow their publication.

Thus it was that the individual *Sans Everything* Reports varied enormously in length, from the relatively extended treatments in the case of Friern and Bodmin, to the page and a half which deals with the allegations at Springfield Hospital in Manchester and the three pages in which allegations at two further hospitals in Leeds and Kirkburton were set out, evaluated and assessed as to their future significance. Those responsible for *Sans Everything* had agreed to identify the actual institutions which appear disguised in the book, but had declined to release the names of individuals, leaving it to Inquiry team members to make their own assessments. The main difference between the very short and longer reports lies in the success, or otherwise, which Committees were able to achieve in dealing with this position and hearing from relevant witnesses. A single thread, however, links the different Reports together, making their communality more significant than the differences between them. Unanimously, the Reports concluded that the complaints raised in *Sans Everything* should be dismissed, most often in a cloud of congratulations to the 'vital, healthy and progressive atmosphere' (p. 54) at the institutions under investigation.

Martin (1984: 4) notes that the diaries of Richard Crossman, later to be Secretary of State at the Department of Health and Social Security, suggest that Kenneth Robinson had set up Committees of Inquiry to investigate six hospitals in 'retaliation' against the allegations made. Even if this represents some post hoc rationalisation it does seem clear that, in some cases at least, Inquiry teams were quickly on the offensive, positively attacking the accusations which had led to their establishment. In the case of Bodmin, for example, the Committee heard from 'Nurse Craythorne' who had made the original *Sans Everything* criticisms. Having taken the reader, paragraph by paragraph, through her complaints, and dismissed each one, the Report concludes with a Summary of Findings:

> As the result of exhaustive examination of the allegations we have no hesitation in saying that in our unanimous opinion there is no substance whatever in the allegations of cruelty by staff to patients as alleged in the article. We found no evidence to support any such allegations. To adapt the words of the sub-title of the book we find 'there is no case to answer'.

It is not possible, given the space available here, to provide a full account of each of the *Sans Everything* Reports. For our purposes, we must concentrate upon events at Friern Hospital, the subject of the longest Report in the collection and notable because the *Sans Everything* chapters setting out allegations about that institution had been written by Barbara Robb herself. The Report spares no effort in attempting to discredit her. Its first main paragraph suggests that some sinister purpose had motivated the decision not to identify institutions by name in the original allegations: 'Mrs Barbara Robb *has admitted* to the Minister that the allegations starting on these pages in the book relate to Friern' (21; emphasis added). Dealing with the decision not to identify individuals, the Report was equally judgemental: 'Fortunately the Committee were able in the course of their enquiry to dispel some of the aura of anonymity with which Mrs Robb sought to cloak her charges' (27).

The bulk – but by no means all – of the allegations at Friern related to an elderly individual whom Mrs Robb had befriended. The Report sets the context for these allegations by casting doubt upon her motivation in doing so: 'The Committee accept that for some obscure reason, Mrs Robb had a genuine desire to assist the anonymous patient who was virtually a stranger to her and that she is possessed of an almost fanatical zeal to further the interests of geriatric patients in mental hospitals' (27).

The effect of this 'fanatical zeal' had been to lead the complainant into a series of misjudgements. Complaints that patients were under-stimulated were the product of unrealistic expectations: 'many of these older patients desire nothing more than just to sit or loaf around owing to their mental condition. They may appear bored and dejected: in fact they are often incapable of animation.' Complaints that patients were left without basic equipment, such as spectacles or hearing aids, were both denied and dismissed: 'Neither spectacles nor hearing aids, if totally absent as Mrs Robb implies but the Committee do not accept, would have been of much use to most of them' (30).

Underpinning all the *Sans Everything* complaints, the Report suggests, was a basic failure, 'to appreciate the mental condition of many senile patients, whether at Friern or elsewhere, who are frequently schizophrenic, deluded or what doctors would not inaptly describe as "vegetables" '(37).

As a result, the Committee concluded their investigation of Mrs Robb's complaint by turning the charge of scandal back on those who had originally made it (41):

> In conclusions the Committee would say that in the light of the evidence available and their own investigations and inquiries they are satisfied that none of the allegations of cruelty towards or ill-treatment ... in particular or ... in general is justified; that the charges of laziness and dishonesty ... are false and scandalous.

A series of common themes run through these Reports, in their universal conclusion that all was well in Britain's mental institutions. The social construction of scandal does not depend simply upon those who wish to bring matters to public attention in a way which attributes wider significance to particular events. Rather, a set of counter-claims is often mounted by those whose actions come under scrutiny, or from those responsible for examination of that conduct. In the case of the *Sans Everything* Inquiries a series of such counter-claims were deployed in order to diminish or demolish the charges of scandal which the original claims-makers had advanced. These may be summarised as follows.

Attacking individual complainants

A standard tactic, in attempting to discredit allegations of scandal, is to cast doubt upon the credentials of those making them. The Friern Inquiry's assault upon the good faith of Barbara Robb was not their only effort in this direction. In dealing with the complaints concerning the Mr Tasburg with whom this chapter began, the Inquiry concluded: 'the allegations by Miss Tasburg are based on a gross distortion of many of the facts, a suppression of other facts, and a remarkable inability in a psychiatric worker to perceive or accept the truth. They dismiss her complaints' (26).

Even when Committees were less inclined to attribute culpability, it was possible to dismiss individual complaints by casting doubts on competence or insight. At Cowley Road in Oxford, complainants who criticised standards of professional practice might have been well-meaning but, the Committee concluded, such witnesses were 'not accustomed to use vulgar language [while] for some of the auxiliary staff it may have been normal speech' (16). The Bodmin Inquiry summarised its assessment of the central witness in that case, in this way:

> Nurse Craythorne proved a most unreliable witness, whose judgement was manifestly unsound... [she] is a rather solitary person with a *somewhat simple mind*... Her sentimental approach no doubt conflicted with the objective attitudes which perforce have to be adopted by doctors and nurses who deal with very grave matters of life and death. (78; emphasis added)

'Doctor knows best'

The first, and most obvious, rejection of complaints rests – as in the case of those brought by Nurse Craythorne – upon the basis that, while others might lack the knowledge to understand the reasons why, decisions made by medical personnel were ipso facto the correct ones. Mrs Robb's questioning of electro-convulsive therapy applied to her elderly friend was dismissed in the same way: 'the doctors and nurses were the best judges of the appropriate treatment' (34). The circularity of such arguments represents, as well as anything else, the triumph of medicalisation as traced in the previous chapter.

Problematic quality of staff

Even doctors cannot be everywhere, and a number of Reports – echoing the complaints of their Victorian predecessors – make reference to the difficulties which medical staff faced in the quality of individuals employed at ward level. At Cowley Road Hospital in Oxford, where doctors had a record of considerable achievement in new and successful treatments, the Report concluded that such offences as might have been committed were the product of 'unsuitable people who have necessarily been employed in order to meet the demands for staff' and, as the Clinical Director commented, 'if you are employing people of low intellect, of lower ability to adjust to stress and strain, they are more likely to be exasperated' (16).

In other places, the same complaints were accompanied with a specific race dimension. The Banstead Report, for example, suggested that, in relation to nursing staff, 'The only criticisms appeared to stem from shortage of staff and difficulties arising from the employment in the wards of foreigners who could scarcely speak English' (3).

'Bad apples'

In only one of the *Sans Everything* Reports are allegations and incidents of ill-treatment found to be authentic and these are dealt with in the shortest of all the documents, that relating to the Springfield Hospital in Manchester. Even here, however, the Committee concluded that the cause for disquiet was largely at an end. A slightly off-colour apple, in the shape of 'a Chief Male Nurse who was in poor health and clearly found it difficult to exercise the supervision and discipline which is necessary in a hospital of this kind' had been removed by retirement. As a result, the Report concluded, 'the danger of such incidents has considerably lessened (and) ... there remains little need for anxiety so far as the future treatment of patients in this hospital is concerned' (83). This tendency, to portray specific instances of neglect and abuse as 'aberrations rather than the tip of the iceberg' (Hopton and Glenister, 1996: 112), was to remain an explanatory thread in many of the mental health scandals which were to follow over the next 15 years.

'The patient's to blame'

A further contender in this catalogue of ways in which allegations of apparently scandalous treatment might be countered and rejected is the notion that patients brought ill-treatment on themselves, through their own behaviour. Staff might be a little rough and ready, but they needed to be ready for the roughness of the tasks in which they were engaged. For example, the South Okendon Report of 1974 records the views of the consultant in charge of one of the wards as: 'about a dozen (patients) were regularly violent and the incidence of violence seemed to me to be really extreme, it occurred every day. Very often it was against staff' (para. 62). At St Augustine's Hospital in Kent, the Inquiry of 1976 reported that, 'Quite often the ward charge nurse would make derogatory comments about patients either during the changeover or to their face, e.g. "you dumbo, I'm sure you're being deliberately awkward".' Whether under the provocation of deliberate awkwardness or extreme violence, the argument emerged that staff reaction – or retaliation – was explicable or even (as in the case of Farleigh Hospital discussed in chapter 6 below), acceptable.

Policy context

As well as pointing the finger at individuals, a number of reports explore the general policy context within which work was undertaken at particular hospitals. Some concentrate upon the Poor Law legacy of buildings and resources. The Cowley Road Report makes a point of reminding readers that it had been opened in 1865 as 'a workhouse of a size sufficient to hold 330 persons, men, women and children, properly classified' (11). At the time of NHS investment on 5 July 1948, less than twenty years before the complaints had been made, 'we have been told that at that time the buildings and the hospital services were in a deplorable condition' (11). Since then, considerable investment had improved the position, but the effect of the legacy lingered on in some parts of the building and the attitudes and approaches which went with it. The Report at Banstead was more resigned: 'We have examined the situation in the wards today and found that they are being managed and the patients are being treated as well as the conditions set by Banstead's heritage will allow' (5).

The same Report contained an early suggestion of the impact of the policy of running down hospitals in favour of community care, one Banstead doctor telling the Inquiry that 'there was then very little stimulus or constructive planning for the future and [he] felt that an impression that the policy was to "run down" the hospital with a view to closure in about ten years was necessarily detrimental to the interests and welfare of staff and patients alike' (3–4).

Standards of judgement

There is an inevitable danger of anachronism in applying contemporary standards to the judgements reached at previous times which would not have been recognised by those concerned, as the last chapter of this book suggested. It is perhaps sufficient, therefore, to suggest that the conclusions reached by most of the *Sans Everything* Reports, at least when dealing with those complained against, rather than complaining, tended towards the charitable. Cowley Road may stand as an example of this more general trait when it concluded that, if incidents had taken place, then these must have been 'rare occasions when an auxiliary nurse, and sometimes a pupil nurse or male orderly, has spoken crossly, rudely or improperly to a recalcitrant or annoying patient'. That these rare events had not been addressed was itself a tribute to the finer feelings of senior staff. Acknowledging that the complaints of one witness which had been recorded in *Sans Everything* had not been acted upon, the Report concluded that Matron, to whom they had been put, 'took no action upon the complaints put forward ... principally because she did not believe them and also because, being a kindly and gentle person, she did not wish needlessly to upset her staff by seeming to entertain unjust reflections upon their professional competence' (16). Happily for those concerned, the Cowley Road Inquiry concluded that 'we found no evidence of anything which called for disciplinary action against anyone', a sentiment shared by each of the six other Committees.

In a text which traces the disputed ground over which charges of scandal are traded there can be little doubt but that the *Sans Everything* Inquiry Reports were a bitter source of disappointment to those who had made them. Certainly, the reports allowed ministers and other politicians to treat the complainants as misguided at best and as wilful trouble-makers at worst. The Minster of Health, Kenneth Robinson, described the original complaints as 'totally unfounded or grossly exaggerated', while Dr Shirley Summerskill asked if he would take steps to 'prevent the publication of another similar book or the publication of exaggerated stories of this kind…giving a distorted impression to the public of conditions in hospitals?' (House of Commons Debates, 9 July 1968, cols 214–16).

Almost as these words were spoken, however, and just as it seemed that counter-claims-makers had won the day, the hearings were already underway in relation to a new and major Inquiry, which was to generate a very different response. It is to Ely Hospital in the Welsh capital city Cardiff, a place where, as the eventual Report was to suggest, 'officials are doing everything to prevent a scandal' (para. 172), that this chapter now turns.

Ely

Ely Hospital, at the time of the Inquiry in 1968–69, housed more than 660 patients in buildings largely left over from the Victorian era. Medical care of these vulnerable individuals was the responsibility of one part-time and two full-time doctors. Founded in 1862 as a Poor Law Industrial School for Orphaned Children, it was adopted as a workhouse in 1903, before being incorporated within the National Health Service on vesting day, July 1948. The state of the buildings presented a challenge from the outset. In February 1966, three years before the Inquiry took place, Ely's bid for priority within a remedial capital works programme was assessed by the Principal Assistant Medical Officer of the Welsh Hospital Board in this way, 'Although Ely is bad, North Wales, Denbigh and Neath could all be stated to be worse' (BD 18/2588).

Even at this distance in time, it remains moving and shocking to read the records of patients such as John Sisch, admitted as a 19-year-old before the outbreak of the First World War, when Franz Joseph was Emperor of Austro Hungary, before the assassination of Archduke Franz Ferdinand, before Lloyd George was Prime Minister, and still at Ely more than half a century later. Or Bertha Battiscombe, born when

Gladstone was Prime Minister and Queen Victoria was on the throne. She was also still a patient at Ely when Harold Wilson's government conducted its Inquiry. John Sisch, his record said, was admitted as a diagnosed 'imbecile', while Bertha Battiscombe was an 'idiot'. It might be tempting, at first glance, to discount such attributions as the product of an entirely bygone age, the period of the 1888 Idiots Act and the 1904 Inquiry into the Care of the Feeble Minded. Such comfortable conclusions are exploded, however, when the records reveal exactly the same diagnoses recorded for individuals admitted to Ely in the 1960s.

Generating scandal

Events at Ely Hospital came to public attention in the summer of 1967 when a Nursing Assistant at the hospital made a series of specific allegations concerning the treatment of patients in the hospital and the pilfering of property by staff members. The man, known in the Report as XY, passed information to the Ministry of Health in July. Not only patients spring out of the Public Record Office papers, but also those most closely associated with the Inquiry do too. We know from the papers that XY was a Mr Pantelides, upon whose account the Inquiry were, somewhat reluctantly at first, to place great weight. Within a month of his complaints being published in the newspapers, he had resigned his employment, as from 24 September 1967. When no action followed the complaint made by Mr Pantelides to the Ministry, he forwarded a copy of his dossier to the *News of the World*, a newspaper specialising in sensation, but one which also had a long-standing interest in covering certain social problems. It had already, for example, been the source of one set of allegations covered in the *Sans Everything* Inquiries. It published Mr Pantelides' allegations on 20 August 1967, although without disclosing the identity of the hospital or the staff concerned. Doig (1988: 328) concludes that 'scandals are not welcomed by politicians ... Only rarely do scandals happen under their control or with their connivance. Their political routine and their authority is undermined, and the temptation is to ensure the quickest possible resolution of the scandal.' Certainly, in the case of Ely, the scandal which the *News of the World* publication produced led directly and swiftly to the establishment of a Committee of Inquiry.

In terms of this book's concern to explore the genesis of scandal, these earliest elements in the Ely story are significant. When the Inquiry Report was presented to the Ministry, nearly three years later, it emerged that members of its Nursing Division had visited Ely three or four years earlier and had reported 'scandalous conditions, bad nursing, the basis

of the *News of the World* revelations' (Crossman, 1977: 593). The difference was that this report, and others like it, had simply been filed at
Whitehall. It is one of the particular features of the institutional episodes
considered in this book, that the *conditions* of scandal had almost always
been present over a long period. It is the *revelation* of those conditions
which distinguishes those events which transformed the potential for
scandal into its reality. Discovery may be the first prerequisite of scandal
but, as Ely demonstrates, the necessity of drawing attention to that discovery follows closely behind. Conditions at Ely had already been discovered by far more powerful individuals than Mr Pantelides, exercising
prerogatives of inspection which were quite outside his own remit.
What he possessed, as much as they lacked, was the determination to
bring these discoveries to the attention of others. In the terms adopted
in chapter 1, he was clearly a first-rank claims-maker, upon whom the
earliest steps in the construction of scandal depended.

Once the Ely allegations became a matter of public concern, the
Minister responsible, following the pattern of the *Sans Everything*
reports, instructed the relevant Hospital Board to set up an inquiry. The
membership also closely followed the earlier approach, although including representatives of both nursing and medical professions. In addition
to its chairman, it was made up of a retired Nursing Officer, a member of
another Regional Hospital Board and a psychiatrist who was at the time
Professor of Mental Health at the University of Bristol. It was, however,
in its chairman, Geoffrey Howe, QC, that the Ely Inquiry departed most
radically from the earlier examples. The minister responsible for setting
the Inquiry in motion, Richard Crossman – the Secretary of State at the
combined Ministry of Health and Social Security – described the choice
in his famous *Diaries* (1977: 426) in this way:

> (Howe) was not a young Tory seeking to make party capital but inter-
> ested in the Committee and what the inquiry would do, good or bad,
> to his career. He told me he had taken a great risk because undoubtedly
> he would make himself unpopular in legal circles which determine
> what kind of inquiries and jobs of this kind Q.C.s get.

The risk which Howe was to take lay in his determination to broaden the
base of the Inquiry beyond the events at the hospital itself. According to
Crossman (1977: 426):

> the Lord Chancellor's office had more than once emphasized how
> important it was for Q.C.s to keep this kind of inquiry narrow, but he

[Howe] had felt strongly about this episode and so had two members of his Committee. They had all believed that they really ought to widen their responsibilities and carry the inquiry outside Ely up to the Hospital Management Committee, up to the Regional Hospital Board, really up to the Ministry, so that the report was not only a Report on Ely but one which illustrated a defect in the structure of the Health Service.

Thus, from the outset, the forces were ranged both in favour of making claims that the particular events at Ely represented a scandal and also, crucially, of identifying the specifics that had taken place at this hospital as emblematic of more general scandals within the whole system. There are, as chapter 1 suggested, some factors in the generation of scandal which are a matter of chance and accidental circumstance. The decision of Mr Pantelides to send his allegations to the *News of the World* set a tone of public revelation which may have been intentional. Less deliberate, however, was the timing of the allegations which, arriving in the month of August, found themselves without competition for the front-pages. Once within the public domain in this way, the momentum of events created its own claims. The creation of scandal is, most often, a dynamic process in which time as well as place and person plays a critical part in convincing an audience that events have been discovered which demand a particular response. Once the fuse of the Ely had been lit, the momentum of revelation and response led very rapidly to the establishment of an Inquiry.

Public Record Office papers

In addition to the text of the Report, and the academic literature which it has since generated, it is now possible to provide some additional insights into the Ely Hospital Inquiry, through the placing in the public domain of the papers held about it at the Public Record Office at Kew. Under the Thirty-Years Rule, the bulk – but not quite all – of the information held in the relation to the Inquiry is now available for public inspection.

An investigation of these documents assists the purposes of this book in a number of important ways. In the first place, it allows us to decode some of the more hidden details of the Ely events or, as Schlesinger et al. (1991: 398) put it, the papers allow us to see into 'the conflictual processess that lie behind the moment of definition'. The published Report itself was particularly secretive. To an extent which none of its successors were to follow, it disguised the names of individuals and, to a lesser extent, the nature of events which it described. While much of this information would have been available locally, and some might still be obtainable by a determined inquirer from other sources, the Public Record Office papers add to our knowledge about events at Ely in a fuller and more coordinated way than before. Secondly, it provides us with new insights into the practical actions of public bodies and policy-makers. Scandals are always interesting to social policy students and historians because they provide a moment at which the curtain is lifted upon the apparently smooth and uncontentious round of social welfare policy-making and implementation. Behind the scenes, the engine room of policy production emerges as rather dirtier and less tranquil than might have been anticipated. Now Ely has already provided something of a case study in this respect, because the Secretary of State at the time, Richard Crossman, published his diary account of these and other events. What the Public Record Office papers provide is a further set of instances and insights into the way in which social welfare organisations respond to this sudden eruption into the public view of their hitherto private concerns and the invasion of that private territory by a powerful set of inquiring outsiders.

The allegations

The allegations made by Mr Pantelides were summarised on the first page of the Ely Hospital Report:

(a) Cruel treatment of four particular patients by six named members of staff;
(b) generally inhumane and threatening behaviour towards patients by one of the staff members already referred to;
(c) pilfering of food, clothing and other items belonging to the hospital or the patients;
(d) indifference on the part of the Chief Male Nurse to complaints that were made to him;
(e) lack of care by the Physician Superintendent and one other member of the medical staff.

As well as investigating past events, the terms of reference provided to the Inquiry included 'to examine the situation in the wards of the hospital at the present time'. According to Martin (1984: 6), the main differences between Ely and the *Sans Everything* Inquiries in this regard was that 'the allegations were wide-ranging but specific and the principal informant had worked in the hospital for about nine months before bringing the allegations to the notice of the press'. The complaints to be investigated also moved beyond accusations of individual cruelty to include direct allegations of managerial complicity. In pursuit of its objectives, the Committee spent 15 days hearing evidence. It made extensive visits to the hospital, advertising itself in local papers and on radio and receiving a considerable public response. It invited parents and others who had written to give evidence. It attempted to persuade – not always successfully – staff and former staff to do the same. The final transcript of evidence ran to more than a thousand pages.

The ingredients of scandal: heroes, victims and villains

A number of key ingredients are to be found in those social welfare scandals which succeed in becoming lodged in the public and professional memory as the embodiment of a particular moment in policy and practice. Essentially, these ingredients revolve around the extent to which the raw material provided in any instance allows both the banalities and the complexities of social welfare activity to become dramatised and simplified into a struggle between elemental forces such as good and evil. Ely provides a series of such essentials which now need to be disentangled in order to cast some light upon the impact which the Inquiry Report was eventually to produce.

In the first instance, the setting of the scandal is itself significant. Ely was a *hospital*, a place dedicated to the care and betterment of vulnerable individuals. As Knapp has suggested, societies have sacred places which transform the nature of public reaction to events which happen within them. The relatively minor acts of cruelty and dishonesty which were alleged at Ely were transformed by their setting: harm in a place of healing, corruption amongst those whose calling spoke of incorruptibility. It was the stage, as much as the events which took place upon it, which set the scandalised tone of the *News of the World* reporting. Nor is this dramatic metaphor accidental. As in so much drama, audience involvement depends not just upon the intrinsic attractions of the plot but upon the lessons for their own lives which can be drawn from the unfolding events. Hospital scandals draw their saliency from the notion which lurks in the minds of onlookers that *this could be them*. The portrayal of older, mentally frail individuals, left at the mercy of indifferent or callous keepers, struck just such a chord. Many families have older members being cared for in state institutions. We all grow old ourselves.

Such social welfare scandals draw their force from this connection with these deep-rooted fears within our own lives.

Secondly, and continuing the dramatic metaphor, scandals which penetrate the public consciousness depend upon the characteristics of particular actors within the events reported by them. Put simply, scandals depend upon heroes and villains. Ely's hero came in what appears, at first sight, to be the unlikely shape of Mr Pantelides, the Nursing Assistant whose complaints led to the *News of the World* story. He, we are told, was born in Cyprus in either 1915 (he said) or 1918 (his passport said) and educated at the American Academy at Larnaca until 1933. He worked in a variety of responsible occupations and locations between then and arriving in Cardiff in October 1965. He was able to obtain employment as a Nursing Assistant in Ely in September 1966. The way in which the Committee formulated its conclusions were bound by the conventions and ways of thinking which prevailed at the time – over thirty years away from today's experience. Yet, as in the case of the *Sans Everything* reports, the attitude of the Committee towards XY had that faint whiff of racism about it. Thus, the Committee thought it necessary to note that, 'he is obviously not British-born – although his command of English is very good, surpassing that of many less well-educated Britons' (24). He possessed, however, that well-known native dislike for hard work – 'he did not seem to have a natural enthusiasm for hard physical work' (24). In an uncanny echo of the complaints brought against staff at the Kent asylum discussed in chapter 2, the Committee rejected his complaint that Charge Nurse 'A' had deliberately forced him and a group of patients to remain in an outdoor 'Airing Court' on a February day on the grounds that XY was 'comparatively unaccustomed to the Welsh climate' (119). And although clearly of the view that the post of Nursing Assistant was not commensurate with the individual's abilities, the Report could not suppress a side-swipe at XY's contention that 'he came to the United Kingdom because, as he put it, he wanted to practise his "profession" as a Health Inspector' (23).

Despite these prejudices, and no doubt to its credit, the Committee came to form a favourable view of this witness. In the words of the Report, 'What then of his credibility? Initially sceptical about this, we were more and more impressed by the number of points on which other, independent evidence finally came to confirm what XY had told us ... he seldom, if ever, identified smoke without fire. He struck us as substantially accurate in his direct evidence about what he had actually seen' (26–8). XY's 'heroic' standing was thus created out of his 'outsider' status. The unlikelihood, in the minds of the Committee, of his providing promising material, rebounded to his advantage as a claims-maker when his essential allegations proved to be correct. And in being so, XY stands at the head of a long line of outsiders upon whom the discovery of institutional scandals depend. Despite the carefully-worked-out complaints procedures which hospitals possessed, the scandals which were to become endemic in the mental health sector were uniformly to be brought to public attention by individuals who were, in one way or another, marginal and outside the mainstream of the organisations against which they complained.

XY, however, did not only possess credibility. He also possessed the essential heroic ingredient of integrity. As the Report makes clear, he had received no money from the *News of the World* and harm rather than any advantage to his personal prospects seemed to be the likely outcome of his actions.

If scandals require heroes, then villains are also an essential part of any presentation of events which secure a place in public consciousness. Ely's villains were real, even if the Report shared the charity towards them which had been established in the *Sans Everything* Inquiries. Nothing in the main text of the Report captures quite the strength of Mr Pantelides' accusations against Assistant Chief Male Nurse, John Edwards. As these appear in the Public Record Office papers these read (D9):

> In Ward 23 there is a charge nurse named John Edwards who everyone considers to be a sadist. He has an assistant named Kay who falls into the same category. A young patient named Kevin is constantly going into the kitchen which is out of bounds. He is regularly beaten by the two nurses. On one occasion Edwards took him to his office and beat him. I heard the screams.
>
> Edwards takes a thick stick on his rounds and threatens patients with it if they are not quick enough. About four weeks ago he had a number of patients in the yard and told them he was going to give them a bath. He ordered them to strip and started hosing them down with cold water. One patient was screaming.
>
> Edwards caught sight of another nurse watching him from a balcony and he handed the hose to Angus. Angus is a mentally retarded but powerful man. He is allowed to beat other patients on the slightest excuse and without any remonstration from the staff. When they sit in a line waiting for a shave, Angus will walk along the line, slapping them.

The Report's interpretation of these events was generous. Commenting on the treatment of Kevin (or 'Masefield' as he appears in the text) the Inquiry team concluded: 'We regard this conduct as symptomatic not of malice towards the patient but rather of old fashioned and unsophisticated nursing techniques' (113). When nursing staff, having unsuccessfully worked their way through a bowlful of ill-assorted false teeth, completed their search for a pair to fit the patient 'Dryden' by removing a set from the mouth of a sleeping patient and rinsing them under a tap, while comforting his wife with the consoling explanation that 'most of the dentures in the communal bowl "belonged to dead patients" ' (53), the Committee concluded that the incident had demonstrated 'some lack of sympathy and insensitivity towards the family of the patient Dryden' (57). Confronted with evidence that Angus (or 'Jonson' as the Report calls him) shared the same 'old fashioned and unsophisticated' approach to keeping order displayed by some of the nursing staff, the Physician Superintendent told the Inquiry that this came to him as 'a big surprise' (116).

Counterpoised against the treatment of patients, the Inquiry Report sets out the difficulties which had been experienced by the authorities in recruiting staff – the Deputy Medical Officer whose training had been obtained at the French University of Beirut, via a spell in the Polish Airforce Medical Corps and who had failed to obtain the certificate in psychiatric medicine, 'despite a number of attempts to do so'; the Junior Hospital Medical Officer, for example, had come into mental illness and subnormality medicine following a career spent largely at the nearby Caerphilly District Miners' Hospital. As the Report noted, 'He makes no claim to specialist knowledge or experience of mental illness or mental subnormality, has attended no specialist conferences or other comparable hospitals, training centres or institutions and reads no specialist literature' (373); the nurse recruited from the Airforce on the strength of a telephone reference which failed to include any questions relating to health and who turned out to have a pronounced propensity to return to the wards late in the afternoon, worse for drink, keen to borrow money from patients and who was himself admitted to another Cardiff psychiatric hospital on three separate occasions during the period of his employment at Ely.

The Public Record Office papers provide fresh insights into these staffing difficulties. The press release put out by the Hospital Management Committee to coincide with the publication of the Report itself pointed out that attempts to appoint a Senior Occupational Therapist had failed because not a single application could be obtained for the post, and this despite 'continual efforts having been made to recruit additional staff – not merely by traditional advertising methods but also by direct contact with members of organisations such as St John's Ambulance Brigade and Civil Defence Corps' (BD 18/2558). In what appears to be an unbroken line from the earliest days of lunatic asylums, the problem of staff recruitment clearly lay behind many of Ely's difficulties.

In tracing its account of daily life at Ely, and parading its cast of characters before the Report's audience, of course, the Committee were welding together the 'master-narrative' which Bogen and Lynch (1989) identify as the core task of any official Inquiry. It saw it as its business to make judgements upon individuals, both those making allegations, and those denying them, and to dispose of particular incidents according to its assessment of witness 'credibility' and the standards of care which it identified as acceptable. In doing so it concentrated, as Crossman had suggested, upon the defects which it identified at managerial and systemic levels.

Management failures included complicity with theft of food and clothing, as well as an almost total neglect of the training needs of hospital staff. The Hospital Management Committee was responsible for 'an ineffective system of administration; the effective isolation of Ely from the mainstream of progress and the absence of any well-informed stimulation towards an improvement of standards'. The Regional Hospital Board, whose meetings were taken up with a disproportionate devotion to gardening issues, was criticised for failing to take 'any responsibility for the inspection or supervision of standards at Ely'.

From these management failures, a series of difficulties had resulted which amounted, in Martin's (1984: 87) phrase, to a 'corruption of care'. The hospital emerged as an institution cut off from the mainstream. No doctor had specialist qualifications. No doctor and only a single senior nurse had ever visited another hospital dealing in the same area of specialism. No single training event had been attended since the 1950s when a different Charge Nurse had taken part in a course on the role of nursing in the event of an atomic war!

Within the hospital, life had already begun to be influenced by the onset of community care. The more able patients were being prepared for discharge and the more forward-looking and progressive staff were often to be found in those hospital wards where the new plans were being put into practice. In the 'back wards', where the oldest and least able patients were gathered together, medical staff appeared almost never to venture. Instead, regimes in these areas had become individual fiefdoms of particular members of the nursing staff where, in the privacy of their own enclosed worlds, different standards of conduct became the norm, powerfully resistant to criticism, suppressing it where it emerged and victimising those who made complaints. Amongst senior staff a culture of 'cover-up' protected those involved. The highly perceptive Mr Pantelides described the situation to the Inquiry in this way (272):

> The senior staff were very closely knitted together. One was saving the other from anything that might arise against one of them, and nobody had a chance of complaining...There is not leadership in this hospital. I would not say that the top does not care, but I think that through the years they have committed themselves in one way or another to something irresponsible...and therefore they do not dare impose their ideas or use their authority for the better management of the hospital.

Responding to the Report

One of the subterranean currents of policy-making which the Ely papers allow us to consider emerges in relation to the advance access which some organisations, and some individuals, were allowed to gain to the contents of the Report. The Welsh Hospital Board were in possession of a draft at least six months before publication. By 4 November 1968, the chairman, vice-chairman and group secretary of the Hospital Management Committee were also provided with full copies, while all other members were allowed access to the Conclusions and Recommendations section. An ad hoc committee of the Board decided, at an early November meeting, to contact Geoffrey Howe 'for further elaboration' and for 'rewording' of those sections to which it took exception.

Rehearsing intensively for the media questioning which was bound to follow, officers of the Welsh Hospital Board prepared a set of probable questions, and model answers, for their members. These emphasised both the problems which the Board had faced, and the actions it had taken. A round of meetings struggled to find the right form of words to deal with one of the most difficult issues – the retention on night duty, right through the Inquiry process, of a charge nurse against whom the Report strongly urged that disciplinary action should be taken. In the end, the prepared line suggested that the Board's actions be defended on the grounds that to have moved the individual concerned in advance of the publication of the Report would have been 'unjust' and 'would have led to questions which, before the publication of the Report, could not have been answered', while conceding that 'probably, with hindsight, we would have taken some different course of action'.

It is clear from this extended period of negotiation that the organisations criticised in the Report did not, as it sometimes seems from the outside, simply acquiesce in its conclusions. Nor were their objections confined to 'behind-the-scenes' bargaining. On publication of the Report, the Hospital Management Committee, for example, both rejected a number of criticisms and challenged the Inquiry's methods. 'We question', it said, 'the fairness of quoting snippets from the transcript to make a point on an unrelated matter'. Nor did it 'accept the recommendation that their present organisation and administration needs to be critically reviewed and overhauled'. When the day for publication came, the HMC were able to use its privileged access to an advance copy, to be able to employ one of the standard tactics of counter-claims-makers. The criticisms levelled by the Inquiry were, it said, already out of date: 'The Report makes 50 specific recommendations and we have already implemented 26 of them and 20 others are currently being pursued' (IIBD 18/25581).

Protection for some ...

In comparison with Inquiries which were to follow, the Ely Report was noticeably benevolent in its treatment of those figures against whom it laid any blame. Yet, in the aftermath, the consequences were rather differently negotiated. In relation to nursing staff, an ad hoc Committee of the Welsh Hospital Board met on 4 December 1968, 'to consider and if thought fit to take action upon the Report of the Committee of Inquiry upon allegations made by Mr Pantelides'. It decided that five nurses were to be told that 'their continued employment at the hospital be conditional upon their pursuing a course of study at some suitable hospital to be nominated by the HMC'. Disciplinary proceedings were to be instituted against a sixth. In the case of the Physician Superintendent, by contrast, discussions were to be opened, 'to review and redefine his functions'.

It was not until a meeting of 21 March 1969 that this gentleman-like approach was amended. An unsigned note in file 18/2561 suggests that:

> the chairman, Mr Hewell and I met the Minister and his colleagues at the Welsh Board of Health. During the course of the meeting ... the future of medical staffing at Ely was made quite clear by the Minister. He stresses that Dr Jenkins [Dr Cyril Wynn Jenkins, the Physician Superintendent] would have to leave Ely. It was made clear that

Dr Jenkins would have to agree to this pending any disciplinary proceedings and that such action would not take place prior to the publication of the report.

The central message of this note should not be overlooked. It was *ministers* rather than officials who insisted that the Physician Superintendent
could not survive publication of the Report. Those inside the system
clearly took a different view, right up until the moment of publication.
Protracted negotiations followed, complicated by the fact that
Dr Jenkins was not amongst those privileged to have sight of an advance
copy. With only days to go before publication, a meeting took place
between the Superintendent and the writer of the note, at which
Dr Jenkins agreed to take two weeks' annual leave and 'I suggested to
him that at the termination of his annual leave he have himself med-
ically examined in view of his past history: this he agreed to do'. So it
was that, in the run-up to publication, Dr Jenkins came to be on leave.
On the eve of the publication of the report he was admitted to a different Cardiff hospital, diagnosed as suffering from the recurrence of an
earlier coronary ailment. There he remained during the next two weeks,
unavailable for any public contact or comment. On 31 July, the *Liverpool
Daily Post* recorded that the former Physician Superintendent had been
allowed to retire on medical grounds.

... negligence for others

For Mr Pantelides, the position was far worse. The Public Record Office
papers contain a series of exchanges in which the issue of future employment for him was discussed. He is recorded as having left Ely Hospital,
'having apparently found the atmosphere uncomfortable' (MH 159
314). It seems clear, today, that he left as a result of an assault by other
staff members, in which he was thrown down a flight of stairs and
injured.[1] He then turned to the Welsh Hospital Board for assistance in
finding another job. Little help was forthcoming, despite regular pressure from the Ministry in London, during which the Secretary of the
Board was reminded that, 'unlike the authors of the allegations in *Sans
Everything*, Mr Pantelides readily agreed to cooperate in the investigation'. The nub of their concern was summed up in an internal memorandum which made it clear that 'we have urged staff at the hospitals

---

1. Personal communication from Charles Webster, historian of the NHS, Bangor,
   March 2000.

who see things are wrong to make complaints without sheltering behind anonymity: Mr Pantelides did so. He deserves well of the hospital service.' Instead, quite the opposite appeared to be taking place. The danger was directly identified: 'it is likely to become a public scandal if the apparent outcome of his complaint is long unemployment'.

Despite these warnings, nothing was done. Mr Pantelides exhausted his entitlement to National Insurance benefits and disappears from the records as someone who, in the assessment of the Department for Employment and Productivity, 'has not proved a very easy person to place'.

The aftermath of Ely

The local struggles over the content of the Ely Report were mirrored in a parallel struggle over its publication which was waged in London. The Committee had submitted its report to the Ministry in September 1968. Officials were determined that only a summary of its findings should be made public, and engaged in a correspondence of increasing acrimony with the Inquiry Chair over his equal determination that the fullest possible text should be publicly released. An issue of timing resulted in the actual date of publication becoming, itself, surrounded by a sense of crisis. On 1 April 1969 responsibility for health services in Wales was to be transferred to the Secretary of State for Wales. As this became apparent, so the pressure to publish the Ely Report became acute. The *Crossman Diaries* record the Minister's reaction on Monday 10 March, when being:

> suddenly told that I had to agree [to publication of a shortened version of the Report] before March 31st, the date on which I hand over the control of Health in Wales to the Secretary of State for Wales. I was furious because it was outrageous to bring it to my notice on Monday night, giving me two days to agree with it when I could have seen it any time in the last three months.

On the following day, Crossman summoned the Chief Medical Officer and the Under-Secretary at the Department, to inform them that he was not prepared to come to a decision without reading the whole Report. He did so in bed on the following evening, summoning officials to a round table meeting on the Wednesday morning. The *Diaries* describe a 'long, long argument about which version should be published'. The official record shows only the Secretary of State informing others that 'He favoured the full report as did the Prime Minister when he outlined the position to him.' As the *Diaries* concede, this last point 'produced real movement', and the decision was made. Crossman (1977: 408) summed up the position in this way:

> The report had been 83,000 words long and straight away the Ministry had said that there must be a confidential report in full for the Department and a shortened version for publication. 'Not on your life', Geoffrey Howe had said, 'I must get out the essential facts'. For three months the Department and Howe had fought about the character of the report ... in my view of the situation there was no alternative to publishing the full, unabridged, 83,000 words. If I published any less Geoffrey Howe would be entitled to go on television and talk about suppression.

Yet the sense of drama, and of scandal, which surrounded Ely was still not over. The importance of claims-makers in this field was re-emphasized when Crossman took time, over the weekend of 22–23 March, to telephone the editor of the *News of the World*, briefing him about developments and offering 'to give him an exclusive article'. Then, at the Cabinet Social Services Committee on Monday 24 March, he agreed that 'I would announce this and take upon myself the responsibility of the scandal', sparing the embarrassment of George Thomas, the Secretary of State for Wales, in whose constituency the hospital was situated and who was about to take responsibility for the health service in Wales. He, Crossman noted, 'has been tricky and jumpy but I have managed to carry him along'. From the Cabinet Committee, discussion moved to the Cabinet itself on the following day. Here, Crossman says, members 'were pretty aghast. They thought, "My God, another bloody scandal".' The Prime Minister's mind was preoccupied with a rather different scandal – the scandal, as he saw it, that the Report's findings were to be announced on a Thursday when three by-elections were due to take place, a fact which had been overlooked both by Crossman and by the Leader of the Commons.

Crossman concluded (1977: 409):

> the whole thing had to be published. The report completely substantiated the *News of the World* story and I might as well make the best of it by outright publication. But I was also clear in my own mind that I could only publish and survive politically if in the course of my Statement I announced necessary changes on policy including the adoption by the Ministry and the RHBs of a system of inspectors,

central and regional, such as there are in almost every other Ministry, and such as the Health Service has never yet permitted itself.

The policy impact of scandal

One of the key concerns of this text is to assess the impact which Public Inquiries in social welfare scandals might produce upon future policy formation. The landmark nature of the Ely Report can be established at a number of different levels.

Locally, its publication was accompanied by what staff at the hospital felt was grossly unfair treatment in the tabloid press. The faults of the few were laid at the doorstep of the many. For a while staff were actually ostracised in public places. In order to mark the Welsh Office's assumption of health service responsibility, George Thomas, in whose Cardiff West constituency the hospital stood, visited Ely. The visit was described in a contemporary official report as 'of great significance because the morale of staff was very low, particularly as they were the subject of largely unjustified hostility from the public' (FBD I 8/2558). A newspaper report of the visit shows Mr Thomas being accosted by Ward Sister Gwen Martin, of whom the Inquiry had said that 11 years in charge of a children's ward had 'got on top of her'. Sister Martin objected to the criticism and asked Mr Thomas to reopen the Inquiry. More than three months later, the local branch of NALGO was still being reported in the *Medical News* as claiming, 'The staff at Ely Hospital were denied British Justice. The inquiry was based on a procedure which was most unfortunately wholly unjust.' Tumber (1993: 51) suggests that in the aftermath of institutional scandal 'the problems (of image) may haunt for some time and this effect is particularly acute for those in direct contact with the public.' This was quite certainly so in the case of Ely. Personal communication during the writing of this book shows that, for those who were directly involved at the time, such feelings, when recalled, remain potent, more than thirty years later. At the time, however, other changes were also in place by the time the Report itself was published. The Hospital Management Committee was replaced and reorganised. There was an increase in nursing staff and in revenue funding. Medical staff were moved. The reinstatement of victimised nurses was referred to the Hospital Board.

Regionally, a rapid report for the Welsh Hospital Board showed that the conditions and conventions prevailing at Ely were far more widespread than might have been suggested. The effect was to produce a twin set of changes which were symbolic of wider alterations which were to follow Ely on a national scale. On the one hand, revised priorities led to a substantial increase in funds to the long-stay sector while, on the other, as Martin (1984: 68) suggests, 'It also led the Board to formulate new policies for the mentally handicapped, and the publication in 1971 of *Charter for the Mentally Handicapped Patient*, emphasising the concept of normalisation, and making it the aim of policy.'

Taken together, the effect was to provide a further impetus upon the road to community care. Outside Wales, too, the impact of events at Ely was felt in the same way. Korman and Glennerster (1990: 50), in their study of the closure of Darenth Park Hospital – the first actual closure to take place within the mental health sector in the community care era – conclude that earlier plans to upgrade the hospital were shelved as a direct result of Ely: 'It is quite clear from the Region's records that had it not been for the Ely scandal, its plans for "upgrading" Darenth Park would simply have gone ahead. Ely had both an impact on national priorities and on the perceptions of officers.'

Nationally, at least two other major changes can be traced to the Ely scandal. Firstly, the effect was to alter fundamentally the place which long-stay mental institutions occupied in official policy-making. As Martin (1984: 120) puts it, 'The catalyst which impelled policy changes was provided by the publication of the Ely Hospital Inquiry report... Nothing would ever be quite the same again.' The Post Ely Working Party which was now convened at the Ministry, chaired by Crossman himself, and attended by very senior officials and non-civil servants, including Geoffrey Howe and Brian Abel-Smith (one of the signatories of the original *Times* letter), was to lead to the 1971 White Paper, *Better Services for the Mentally Handicapped*. Martin concludes (1984: 127), that Ely had set in train the 'first systematic study of the problem since the Wood Committee of 1929.' Webster (1998: 119) agrees, identifying the Ely Report as the catalyst which meant that 'action on behalf of long-stay patients was no longer avoidable'.

The second major change which Ely brought in its wake was the establishment of what Richard Crossman, in his Statement to Parliament on the Ely Report, called 'a new system of regular visiting and inspection'. The Hospital Advisory Service, as it was to be known, was more contentious than might appear at first sight because of the implications it raised for the clinical autonomy of those in charge of institutions, an issue which was soon to loom large and directly in a number of subsequent inquiries, such as those at South Ockendon and Normansfield. Despite reservations, however, the force of revelations at Ely was so great that, as Martin (1984: 147) concludes, 'the impact of the Ely Report was such that the idea of such an (inspectoral) service could not be resisted'.

4

'Household Happiness, Gracious Children'

Children, Welfare and Public Policy, 1840–1970

Introduction

According to the Swedish feminist and political radical Ellen Key, the twentieth century was to be the 'century of the child' (Key, 1900). It is unarguable that in the last one hundred years there have been significant improvements in the material realities of children's lives. This is at least true for children in Sweden and Great Britain who have substantially benefited from the 'Golden Age' of European State welfarism. Key's vision encompassed more than material advancement, however. There was hope too for political progress. Now, the 'century of the child' is over and there is reason to doubt how far the 'cultural facts' (La Fontaine, 1979) of childhood have been transformed and how much progress along the road from 'marginality to citizenship' (Wintersberger, 1996) children have achieved.

The questionable success of children in achieving civil status in their own right, as well as being a theme of this and later chapters, is one of a number of factors that make the study of public policy affecting children particularly problematic. Because children have not been significant political actors, they have been unable to define a discrete policy 'space' of their own. Consequently, the responsibility for public policy affecting children, today as much as in the past, tends to be distributed across a range of administrative structures, departments and levels of local and central government. The fragmentary nature of public policy and the consequent discontinuities in professional practice are further recurring themes of this and succeeding chapters.

Other European countries have sought to ensure more effective coordination and development of policy that bears on children either by the appointment of ombudsmen or even through the establishment of whole ministries (as in Norway). In the United Kingdom, until the appointment of the Children's Commissioner for Wales early in 2001, the lack of any kind of sustained political presence for children, and the absence either of direct representation or of centrally placed advocates, has ensured that policy has often developed in a reactive way, frequently in response to a crisis or other 'special impetus', without which legislative programmes for children 'struggle' especially if there is 'the least hint of parliamentary controversy or of serious financial implications' (Hughes, 1998: 151; see also Drewry, 1988). As this chapter illustrates, the progress of legislation aiming to promote the welfare of children has very often turned on scandals, Public Inquiries and official reports which, in turn, makes thematic analysis a more discontinuous process than one might anticipate.

But perhaps the most difficult obstacle to providing an administrative history of policy affecting children has been the relative invisibility of children against the background of policy directed more broadly at the family. A subject in its own right (see Elliot, 1986; Van Every, 1992; Fox Harding, 1991, 1996), the family as a legitimate focus of interest by the State, especially the 'liberal dilemma' (Daniel and Ivatts, 1998) of how far public interest might intrude upon the private sphere of domestic life, is another theme that will run through this chapter and the inquiries for which it provides the context.

Notwithstanding the difficulties, this chapter seeks to gather the threads of an administrative history of public policy affecting children. It proceeds from a social constructionist point of view and recognises that the history of public policy is both a cause and an effect of wider shifts in the general understanding of what it means to be a child. In broad terms, the history of childhood has been described as a gradual process whereby the 'distance in behaviour and whole psychological structure between children and adults increases in the course of the civilising process' (Elias, 1939). This optimistic, evolutionary paradigm, developed in quite different ways by Aries (1960), de Mause (1976), Shorter (1976) and Stone (1977) and subsequently criticised, not least on historical grounds, by Pollock (1983) and MacFarlane (1986), still constitutes something of an orthodoxy (see, for example, Hayden et al., 1999). However, more recent writers on the sociology of childhood (especially, James and Prout, 1990; Quartrup, 1994) have sought to develop a more sophisticated paradigm for understanding both the historical and contemporary structural significance of childhood. For the purposes of this analysis, it must be sufficient to declare an appreciation of the plastic nature of childhood and to focus more narrowly on the nature of the child as an object of public policy (see also Butler, 1996).

At the turn of the century, then, as Key was writing, how did the child stand as an object of public policy? What were the interests of the State in children? And how far were these influenced by political and cultural ideas of the family?

The legacy of the nineteenth century

In responding to the circumstances of the factory child, the pauper and the delinquent, the nineteenth century made considerable progress in institutionalising childhood and in establishing a distinctive set of public policy discourses bearing on children. Driven by economic imperatives and necessary changes in the organisation of labour, factory legislation had, from the early years of the century, progressively removed the child from the workplace. In so doing it had served to identify children as a group requiring the protection of the State and coincidentally had accelerated the process of separating children from the daytime world of adults. This literal and social separation was reinforced by the development of universal schooling in the latter part of the century. The Elementary Education Act of 1870 originated free and compulsory education and the school leaving age was successively increased from 10 in 1876 to 12 by 1899. Not only would school literally and metaphorically further the process of removing children from a key area of socially significant activity (that is, work), it would also promote the idea of childhood as a very specific age-graded and age-related condition. School emphasised too the ignorance of children and their relative powerlessness and dependency, even to the extent that their extra-judicial corporal punishment was legally sanctioned.

Changes in the administration of the Poor Law after the Act of 1834 (see chapter 8), particularly the classifying of workhouse inmates which led to the physical separation of children from adults in different wards (Crompton, 1997), had already contributed to the functional differentiation of the State's response to the circumstances of pauper children. Building on the philanthropic enterprises of the previous century, at first 'barrack schools', then later experiments in family forms of care all served to define distinctive educative or reformatory regimes designed, in this case, to rescue children from poverty. In other areas of public policy more overtly concerned with the child as threat, rather than victim (see Hendrick, 1994: 7ff.) this Rousseauesque sense of the distinctiveness and malleability of children also found expression. The Youthful Offenders Act of 1854 and successive Acts thereafter encouraged the magistracy to see children differently from adults; as not always responsible for their actions and in need of care and protection as much as punishment.

By the end of the 1860s, the child had begun to emerge as a specific object of public policy. Increasingly, the child's individual nature was recognised as qualitatively different from that of adults and particular attention was accorded to the potential that was common to all children. The State's role was largely protective of that potential, but as yet was essentially confined to those public places (the street and the factory) from which it was intended that children should be removed. The concern with the circumstances of the child in the home (and in the family), which developed in the later years of the century has to be set against an implicit model of childhood that stressed the dependency and vulnerability of children and an increasingly optimistic view of the potential of the State to act in their interests.

Progress in expanding the State's interests to include those children who were the object of cruelty and neglect in domestic settings was to prove difficult in the context of the laissez-faire liberalism of the period (Fox Harding, 1991) and in the face of an acute sense of the inviolability of the family that was intrinsic to the Victorian conception of civil society. The challenge can be seen clearly in the oft-quoted reply Lord Shaftesbury, the foremost social reformer of the age, made in 1871 by way of response to a letter seeking his support for legislation to protect children from parental cruelty: 'The evils you state are enormous and indisputable, but they are of so private, internal and domestic a character as to be beyond the reach of legislation, and the subject, indeed, would not, I think, be entertained in either House of Parliament' (cited in Pinchbeck and Hewitt, 1973: 622).

The willingness and the capacity of the State to trespass across 'the sanctity of the domestic hearth and the decent seclusion of private life' (Taylor, 1874), had been foreshadowed, to some degree, in the factory legislation, judicial interest and sanitarian enterprises of the first half of the century but, according to Pinchbeck and Hewitt, up until the 1870s, the 'influence of philanthropists and philosophers' had resulted largely in 'local, rather than national, experiments in child welfare, and in piecemeal legislation' (1973: 612). Concerted social reform, especially in the absence of reliable and convincing data that might serve to prove the need for legislative action, was to depend on the advent of 'some particularly sensational piece of evidence … to rally a wavering public to the cause of the reformers' (Pinchbeck and Hewitt, 1973: 613). Considerable special impetus to the moral and political enterprises of the last thirty years of the nineteenth century was added by the scandal that formed around the practice of 'baby farming'.

Baby farming and the colonisation of the family

Baby farming, an emotive term in its own time, was defined in the 1871 Report of the Select Committee on Protection of Infant Life as 'where... children are put out for block sums of money, or small weekly payments, with an utter disregard as to what shall become of them, and possibly with the intention that their lives should be criminally soon brought to an end' (1871: para. 607). For many women, particularly unmarried women or widows, after the amendment of the Poor Law in 1834, the practice of placing their new-born infants with paid 'nurses', either temporarily or permanently, was simply an economic necessity. Despite a further amendment to the Poor Law in 1844 which enabled women to apply to the courts for maintenance orders to be made against a child's father, the circumstances of working-class mothers continued to be such that they had few means of support other than returning to paid employment. The death of infants in the care of paid nurses or even at their mother's hands, despite uncertainty over its extent, was, according to Hendrick, an inevitable and to some degree, accepted, consequence. He notes that in the early 1860s 'child murder had ceased *de facto* to be a capital offence: the popular view was that a newborn baby should not have the same rights as other people' (Hendrick, 1994: 45).

It was the case of Margaret Waters and her sister Sarah Ellis that would render such a position untenable. It began in May 1870 with the fascinating horror of finding the bodies of 16 babies in Brixton and Peckham, South London. This engaged the detective work of one Sergeant Relf (a character who might have come straight from the pages of a mid-century Wilkie Collins novel) and his secret surveillance of a private lying-in home on the Camberwell Road. The narrative of the events as reported in the press at the time, has all the stock characters, intricacies of plot, cliff-hangers and dramatic resolutions of many a popular drama of the time and of many modern child abuse inquiry reports.

Sgt. Relf observed a 17-year-old woman, Miss Cowan, whom he believed to have recently given birth, being collected from the home. After following her cab back to her own house in Loughborough Road, Brixton, he discovered that Miss Cowan's father had answered an advertisement in the local paper in an attempt to secure a home for his grandson, who had been conceived as the result of a brutal sexual assault. He had handed the child over to a 'Mrs Oliver' at Walworth Railway Station, paying half of the agreed fee of £4. After one frustrated attempt to trace 'Mrs Oliver' by placing an advertisement of his own, Sgt. Relf subsequently answered a further newspaper advertisement in which she offered her services. The woman who turned up to meet him, this time at Camberwell New Road railway station, was not 'Mrs Oliver', according to Miss Cowan's father, who was watching the meeting from a hidden vantage point, although she was wearing the same clothes. Sgt. Relf secretly followed the woman back to her house in Fredrick Terrace, Brixton and on the following day he called to be greeted by the woman he had met on the previous evening (Sarah Ellis). Sgt. Relf asked to see Miss Cowan's child, but Ellis denied that there were any children in the house. Eventually, Ellis' sister and the tenant of the house, Margaret Waters, was called. She led them into the kitchen where there were found ten babies, one of whom was the son of Miss Cowan. He was, according to the Medical Officer of Health for Lambeth, emaciated, dirty and had been drugged with laudanum. Five of the babies subsequently died, including Miss Cowan's son.

Initially, a verdict of manslaughter was reached by the coroner's court in respect of the Cowan child but the press kept the affair under a critical public gaze, occupying an important role as a secondary claimsmaker. The *Times* editorial of 4 July 1870 was far from satisfied with the coroner's verdict and in a manner which specifically elevates the particular into the general and understands the individual in terms of the type, it noted:

> Manslaughter appears a mild expression for the crime of a woman, divested of all the kindly nature of her sex, who has been proved to have traded for some miserable gain in the lives of unprotected infants. The evidence bearing upon the case of Miss Cowan's child conclusively proves foul play … and what we know from experience of human weakness, selfishness and cowardice, leave us nothing to guess at in the terrible tale …

On 26 July, Waters and Ellis were committed for trial on charges of wilful murder, manslaughter, conspiracy and obtaining money under false pretences. Despite popularly expressed doubt about the relative culpability of both women and evidence adduced at the trail concerning the mortality rate of hand-fed children, Waters was found guilty of murder at the Old Bailey in September 1870 and was hanged on 11 October, aged 36.

Ellis was sentenced to 18 months' imprisonment on the 'false pretences' charge.

One can see even in this abbreviated account of the 'facts' of the case how there might be necessary, if not sufficient, cause for this case achieving the notoriety that it did. As a melodrama or a morality play it could be told easily in the popular press. But this was not the first sensationalised account of baby farming to be taken up in this way. Five years earlier, the *Saturday Review* had reported how Charlotte Winsor had 'kept a regular establishment in which she had a tariff and even a 'familiar euphemistic language for the trade' of 'putting off' the babies placed in her care. Nor was it the last. In 1879 an Exeter woman, Annie Took, was hanged for infanticide and in 1896, more than a quarter of a century after the case of Waters and Ellis, the popular press reported the gruesome practices of a Mrs Dyer of Reading, who strangled the children in her care before throwing them into the Thames. In order for the Waters and Ellis case to become a scandal in the sense in which we are using the term, it had also to appear at the right time and to be serviceable to wider moral or political enterprises. In this instance, as Arnot (1994: 277) has convincingly argued, 'Waters became a sort of scapegoat for all infant death'.

Interest in infant death in general, and infanticide in particular, had been championed by a prominent group of London doctors from the mid-1860s. Conducted in part through the pages of the *British Medical Journal* but also reported in vivid terms in the press, the interest of the medical profession in infant death was, at one level, a continuation of public health concerns that had developed in the first half of the century. In this sense, infant death had become another area for professional colonisation. Arnot argues, however, that this was not simply a concern with infant death per se but was illustrative of a broader argument that all child care arrangements 'needed to be policed by medical men' (1994: 275) as part of the regulatory mechanisms of Victorian patriarchy.

The first attempt to formulate legislation to deal with baby farming was framed by the Infant Life Protection Society (ILPS) which had been formed, largely through the agency of Dr J. Brendon Curgenven, on 14 October 1870, three days after Mary Waters' execution. The Bill the ILPS drafted, which focused on the regulation and inspection of paid substitute care, was introduced into the Commons as a Private Members Bill in 1871 but was withdrawn in the face of government opposition and on the offer of a Select Committee to consider the issues involved. The Bill had also been opposed by some women's groups, including the National Society for Women's Suffrage, on the grounds that not only would it restrict opportunities for working women but that it also represented an unwarranted intrusion into family life:

> The responsibility for the child in infancy, as in later life, lies with [parents], and we deny emphatically that the State has any right to dictate to them the way in which it shall be fulfilled ... beyond such precautions against their exercising their right to choose a nurse, carelessly and wickedly, the State should forbear to limit their perfect freedom in this, as in all matters connected with the rearing and maintaining of their families. (*Committee for Amending the Law in Points Wherein it is Injurious to Women*, 1871: 3, cited in Arnot, 1994: 292)

Moreover, the Society for Women's Suffrage recognised how the scandal of baby farming divorced the issue of infanticide from its social and political context and as such dealt with the symptoms rather than the 'real and ultimate causes' (1871: 9) of child death which lay in poverty and the poor educational opportunities available to women. The decontextualising effect of scandal and the public policy consequences that they produce will be noted at several points in succeeding chapters.

The Select Committee did subsequently recommend legislation (*inter alia*) that would require the registration (but not the inspection) of paid carers looking after more than one child for a period of more than 24 hours. This was enacted as the Infant Life Protection Act of 1872. The provisions of the Act were easily evaded, however, and it was soon judged to have had little demonstrable effect on the practice of substitute child care, but its provisions were extended and revised only in 1897, shortly after the execution of Mrs Dyer, Reading's notorious baby farmer. It was not until the Children Act of 1908 that registration was extended to arrangements for singly placed children and proper arrangements were made for the administration of the law through the appointment, by the Poor Law authorities, of infant life protection officers.

Undoubtedly the baby farming scandals of the latter half of the nineteenth century did focus attention on the cruelty suffered by *particular* children and as such must be seen as contributing to some degree to the protection of *all* children. As such, their civil status was much enhanced, not least by asserting their right to life. Moreover, the several Select Committees that considered the issue did provide a national focus for debate in what was clearly a contested area. But the legislation was timid and ineffectual in its specifics. Opposition to the legislation revealed gendered and class tensions over the boundaries of the public and the private and especially over the State's mandate for intervention in the private arrangements made for the care of children, despite the fact that the focus of the debate was on cruelty suffered by children at the hands of substitute carers. Further difficulties lay ahead, as interest grew in the cruelty suffered by children directly at the hands of their own parents. The role played by scandal in the production of public policy affecting children to this point should not be over-stated therefore. The baby farming scandal had offered a site for the expression of other interests although it had, for a time at least, made the domestic care of children an explicit policy issue.

The prevention of cruelty to children

The scandal of baby farming and its legislative consequences were only a prelude to the larger struggle to rescue children from cruelty and neglect that developed in the last decades of the century. This struggle was substantially reinforced by the moral weight and political astuteness of the NSPCC, whose achievements, according to Behlmer (1982), the NSPCC's historian, were to amount to nothing less than a 'new moral vision in which justice for the young took precedence over the claims of parenthood'.

The proximate causes of the Bill which formed the basis of the 1889 Prevention of Cruelty to Children Act lay in the championing efforts of Benjamin Waugh and the London Society for the Prevention of Cruelty to Children which had been founded in 1885, two years after the founding of the original Liverpool Society. Waugh's Bill sought to make an offender of anyone who 'wilfully ill-treats, neglects, abandons, exposes [a child] in a manner likely to cause ... unnecessary suffering or injury to its health'. It sought also to exclude children from 'occupations' not covered by factory legislation (such as begging) and made changes to the laws on evidence enabling spouses and children to testify more easily. Moreover, the police were to have powers to enter a household upon receipt of a report of cruelty and remove the child to a place of safety and the courts would have the power to commit the child of a convicted parent to the care of a 'fit person'.

Opposition to the Bill in Parliament took a predictable form, typified in the response made at Committee Stage by the Attorney General on behalf of the government:

> In so far as this Bill does propose to deal with acts of cruelty committed upon children, we most warmly support the measure. At the same

time, we have to be most careful that we do not interfere with the legitimate conduct of parents and guardians with regard to children. (Hansard, 1889 CCCXXXVII, col. 227)

Yet the Bill did proceed to Royal Assent and so constituted, according to Hendrick (1994: 54), 'a turning point in social attitudes towards children'. Its success might be thought surprising but only if the Act is conceived of in such radical terms. In fact, the Act could be read as a deeply conservative piece of legislation in so far as its sponsors proceeded from the same unshakeable belief in the primacy of the family as did its opponents. Certainly, the NSPCC, in the writings of Samuel Smith, one of its founders, consistently stressed the 'culpability and responsibility of the individual family'. As Ferguson (1990: 31) reports, the York Society for the Prevention of Cruelty to Children was quite clear in its aims 'not to relieve parents of their responsibilities, but to enforce them by making … parents do their duty by their children'. If the State was to intervene in family life, it was to do so only in so far as it strengthened the family in question and enabled it to manage its affairs better.

More generally, by the time of the Bill's passage through Parliament, broader questions were being raised about the state of the family, especially the working-class family, and its capacity to realise and maintain the bourgeois ideal of civilised, domestic society. In this sense, the regulation of those families which, by treating their children cruelly, fell short of the 'golden mean' of 'household happiness, gracious children, debtless competence' ('Vastness', Alfred, Lord Tennyson, 1809–92), was a matter almost of national security. Towards the end of the century and into the next, the nation's and the Empire's fortunes were explicitly associated with the state of the family and the condition of the native stock. In 1906, the radical Tory, Sir John Gorst, introduced his far-sighted and humane *The Children of the Nation* in precisely these terms (p. 1):

> The object of this book is to bring home to the people of Great Britain a sense of the danger of neglecting the physical condition of the nation's children. These will form the future British people; and upon their condition and capacity will depend not only the happiness of our own country but also the influence of our Empire in the world.

Besides being a political imperative, preserving the 'true nature' of the family home, which, according to Ruskin, was 'the place of Peace, the shelter, not only from injury, but from all terror, doubt and division' (Ruskin, 1886: 122) was also a moral duty. In being a protection from the world, the family home was a defence against the mercantile, industrial, technological and spiritual revolutions of the age. In particular, it was the site for the further idealisation and sentimentalising of childhood, typically described by Froude in 1849, explicitly using religious imagery, as a 'Paradise ... all we have ever known of Heaven upon earth' (p. 116).

The 1908 Children Act

In one sense, the nineteenth-century interest in the welfare of children did not end until the passing of the 1908 Children Act. By stretching this account of nineteenth-century policy interests into the twentieth century, we make the point also that such chronological distinctions are, in reality, quite arbitrary.

Intended as a great consolidating measure, the Act saw the repeal or substantial amendment of 39 other pieces of legislation. *Inter alia*, it consolidated and extended the provisions of previous infant life protection legislation and extended the scope of the 1889 Act (as amended in 1904) principally by adding the crime of 'wilful cruelty' to that of 'negligence'. The Act also made changes to the administration of industrial and reformatory schools by allowing the transfer of children between them and in so doing substantially blurred the distinction between the delinquent and the non-delinquent child. This process, what has been called 'the conceptual integration of delinquent and deprived children' (Dingwall et al., 1984: 223), was further strengthened by perhaps the most well-known part of the Act, the establishment of juvenile courts. The jurisdiction of juvenile courts was not to be restricted to offenders. It was also to include those children under the age of 14 who seemed to be in need of 'care and protection'. The categories of non-offenders who could be brought before the court included beggars, the destitute, those in the care of drunken or criminal parents and children involved in prostitution. The court could place such children in industrial schools or place them in the care of a relative or other 'fit person'. In this way, the Act established that the courts, as was said during the passage of the Bill (Heywood, 1978: 109) would be 'agencies for the rescue as well as the punishment of children'.

Such a position shows the extent to which the confidence of the State was growing in its capacity to intervene usefully in the lives of children and their families. As Fox Harding (1991: 74) has put it:

> The State is seen as capable of beneficent, competent and unbiased action in removing children from inadequate homes and providing them with alternatives. Such a role for the State is seen as entirely

justified [and] not generally viewed as an unwarranted threat to civil
liberties...

It is important to stress the degree to which confidence in the legitimacy
(as well as the capacity) of the State to intervene in the lives of families
had grown by the turn of the century. The coincidence of interests
between the State, the child and the family appeared inseparable and
incontrovertible in a way that only a generation earlier might have
seemed unimaginable.

The prelude to welfarism, 1908–1945

It is perhaps surprising that the only piece of legislation directed towards
the welfare of children between the wars and consequent upon the economic depression of the 1920s and 1930s should have its immediate origins in concern with juvenile delinquency: specifically in the findings of
the Juvenile Offenders Committee, established in 1925 and reporting
in 1927. The Great War and its aftermath had witnessed a marked rise in
juvenile crime: from 37,500 under 16 charged with offences in 1909 to
51,000 by 1917. The industrial and reformatory schools were congested
and the number of birchings had risen from 1,702 in 1910 to 4,864 in
1916. The legislative response took the form of the 1933 Children and
Young Persons Act, which created an even closer link between the care of
the delinquent and the neglected child than that forged by the 1908 Act.
    Section 61 of the 1933 Act considerably broadened the category of chil-
dren who could be brought before the court as in need of care and protection and raised the age limit of all those who could appear before the court
to 17. The logic of bringing all children together before the one tribunal
was that there was nothing to choose between them either in terms of the
causation of their problems or in terms of how best to respond to them.
The *Report of the Departmental Committee on Reformatories and Industrial
Schools* in 1913 (para. 1029) had made the point very clearly:

> there is little or no difference in character between the neglected and
> the delinquent child. It is often a mere accident whether he is
> brought before the court because he is wandering or beyond control
> or because he has committed some offence. Neglect leads to delin-
> quency and delinquency is often the direct outcome of neglect.

Accordingly, the Act finally removed the distinction between industrial and reformatory schools. They all became 'approved schools'.

More importantly, the Act secured the pre-eminent position of the court in the implementation and interpretation of public policy directed at the welfare of children. As Parton (1991) notes in relation to much later legislation, it would be the courts which would hold the 'fine balance' between the protection of children and the 'unwarrantable interference' (p. 202) by the State into the private lives of families. This amounts to not only the creation of a new professional grouping within the 'political economy' of child welfare but also the intrusion of legalism into the discourse of child care practice. Legalism, with its emphasis on rules, rights, formal procedure and its particular conception of the 'truth' (the law admits of no uncertainties), would come to have a profound influence on the conduct of individual cases and, indeed, of later Public Inquiries.

The object of the exercise of bringing a child to court was set out at section 44 of the 1933 Act:

> Every court in dealing with a child or young person who is brought before it, either as being in need of care or protection or as an offender or otherwise, shall have regard to the welfare of the child or young person and shall in a proper case take steps for removing him from undesirable surroundings, and for securing that proper provision is made for his education and training.

In order to do their work effectively, courts needed to know more about the child appearing before them. Accordingly, the Act established a much more important role for the Local Education Authority (LEA) which was required to supply information concerning the child's health, character, schooling and family background. Moreover, the LEA was given the main responsibility for bringing children in need of care and protection before the courts and for running remand homes. The LEA was also now included in the category of 'fit person' with whom a child could be placed. In thus confirming an important role for the servants of the local State in the process of decision-making, the foundations were laid for the creation of a whole new cadre of child care professionals (besides lawyers, magistrates and doctors) looking for territories of their own to claim. Although less obvious at this point, the Act therefore also sowed the seeds of a tension between the administrative discretion of the child care professional and jurisprudential considerations that would emerge strongly over the next thirty years.

In terms of the responses available to the courts and the local authorities, Heywood (1978: 130) has noted in relation to the 1933 Act that: 'Although the emphasis on rehabilitation of the child is forward looking, the concept of care is still nineteenth century, based on removal from the degrading environmental conditions of squalor and poverty, and provides a substitute family for the home which has failed.' A concerted attempt to re-invest in the family as the means of rehabilitation was to await another world war. Not that the family was to be left entirely to its own devices since the late 1920s and the 1930s also witnessed the emergence of a corpus of popular childrearing manuals which were intended to reassure the domestically disadvantaged middle classes and to instruct the dangerously inept working classes of the period. Many of these continued the argument advanced by Gorst and others at the turn of the century that the national interest was intimately connected with the task of childrearing.

For example, the explicit purpose of Dr Frederick Truby King's popular baby care regime was, in the words of Mabel Liddiard, author of the *Mothercraft Manual* (1928), to engender 'self control, obedience, the recognition of authority, and later, respect for elders'. Such outcomes would be 'essential to the formation of the 'normal' stable personality that would form the bedrock of a strong nation' (Humphries and Gordon, 1993). The alternative seemed too awful to contemplate: 'The neglected toddler in everyone's way is the material which becomes the disgruntled agitator, while the happy contented child is the pillar of the State' (St Aubyn, 1935). It is important to catch the echo of these essentially functionalist justifications of childrearing practices as they emerge again in the socialisation theories of the 1950s and later.

Whilst the sheer physicality of the Truby King method of childrearing is striking to the modern reader (see Butler, 1996), it was not without its psychological grounding. The development of the 'psy complex' (Rose, 1985) clearly has its origins here, although it awaited its full flowering until the aftermath of the Second World War. The theories of Freud, Adler, Jung and others had begun to exert influence in the 1920s (Hernshaw, 1964; Armstrong, 1983; Ingelby, 1985), but it was not until they were placed in the hands of the professional cadres of the welfare 1950s that the maturational processes and transitional significance of childhood really came to be objects of broader social scientific interest. It is only after the child's nature had begun to be 'truly differentiated from that of adults and respected in its own right' (Heywood, 1973: 9) that it could be studied as such and begin to inform public policy.

Family problems, 1945–1969

In truth, the specific welfare of children played only a minor note in the monumental social policy shifts of the postwar period. The formation of the Welfare State that was part of the great postwar reconstruction drew its momentum from more powerful social and economic forces than a concern for the public care of children, except that the war did pose the particular problem of evacuation. The experience of evacuation had brought before the attention of a much wider public the existence of the slum child and there was concern about the possibility that not every child would be able to return home.

These concerns, which were not particularly well founded in that only 1,500 children were unable to return home to their families as a result of evacuation, coincided with a growing dissatisfaction with the nature and the quality of care provided for children in the approved schools and children's homes. According to an influential pamphlet, *Whose Children?* (1945), produced by Lady Allen of Hurtwood, consequent upon an earlier letter to *The Times* (see chapter 8), the staff of children's homes were inexperienced and insensitive; the children were grouped together for the convenience of staff rather than in response to their emotional and physical needs; children had nothing to play with and no personal belongings of their own.

Within a month of the government establishing a committee to examine the state of the public care of children in March 1945, the first major child care scandal of the century began to take shape and the first inquiry that can be seen to have a direct and substantial bearing on the development of policy in this area was convened. Thirteen-year-old Denis O'Neill had died of cruelty and neglect at the hands of his foster parents.

Denis, then aged 7, and his two younger brothers and sister had been removed from the care of their parents in 1939 by an NSPCC inspector. Denis' father had been convicted of offences of cruelty and in the intervening period, the NSPCC had made more than 200 visits to the home. Denis' sister was placed with her maternal grandmother but the boys were placed in a series of foster homes, the last one being Bank Farm, Minsterly, near Shrewsbury, in June 1944. Here, Denis was subjected to a regime of brutality and neglect and in January 1945 he died. The coroner's court recorded that his death was due to acute cardiac failure following violence applied to his chest and his back while in a state of undernourishment caused by neglect. The jury also commented sharply on the lack of supervision that had been carried out by the local authority. An immediate inquiry, led by Sir Walter Monckton, was established. In what makes depressingly familiar reading, the Monckton Report (May 1945) catalogues the 'small carelessneses, pressures of other work, difficulties of staffing and human procrastinations and failure to co-operate'

(Heywood, 1978: 142) that have echoed through so many other reports in the last fifty years. By the time the Report was complete, the Committee of Inquiry into the public care of children that the government had established earlier in the year had begun its work under the chairmanship of Miss Myra Curtis, the Principal of Newnham College, Cambridge. This committee, the Curtis Committee, which reported in 1946, was the basis for the Children Act 1948. The text of the Curtis Committee is deeply moving and is considered in more detail in chapter 8. The government accepted the recommendations of the Curtis Committee and gave them expression in the Children Act that passed into law in June 1948. Section 1 of the Act unambiguously placed with the local council the responsibility to receive into care anyone under the age of 17 (the maximum age under the Poor Law had been 16) whose parents were temporarily or permanently unfit or unable to care for them. Specifically, the Act required local authorities to establish Children's Committees and to appoint, at chief officer level, a Children's Officer whose Children's Departments were to assume most of the existing duties carried by local authorities.

The principle on which the Children's Department was to carry out its duties represented a significant break with previous enactments in so far as s. 12 of the Act required local authorities to carry out their responsibilities to a child 'so as to further his best interests and to afford him opportunity for the proper development of his character and abilities'. This made explicit a concern of the Curtis Committee that children had not hitherto been treated as though they were young people in their own right but rather according to type. This may be seen as foreshadowing the individualisation of children on which would turn much later legislation and which reflected growing popular and scientific interest in what Hendrick (1994: 1) has called a 'narrative of the mind' of children.

The second part of s. 12 required local authorities, in providing for children in their care, to 'make use of facilities and services available to children in the care of their parents'. This was an important recognition that separation was not an unmitigated good and that work was needed if children were ever to return to their former homes and communities. Support for such a view had developed from the first-hand experience of separation that evacuation had provided and from the particular influence of theories of maternal deprivation that were growing in force at this time. It is interesting to note that John Bowlby, the progenitor of the theory of maternal deprivation and W.D. Winnicot, the pre-eminent child psychiatrist of his day, both gave lengthy evidence to the Curtis

Committee. One should note also the significance of psychoanalytic theory (with its stress on the centrality of parental influence) in the early professional training of Children's Officers, which, according to Stevenson (1998), would ultimately prove to be a weakness but which at this time was 'an indispensable prerequisite of good practice' (p. 156).

The importance of the child's birth family had been established in s. 1(3) of the Act which required the local authority to 'endeavour to secure that the care of [a] child is taken over by a parent or guardian of his' so long as this was consistent with the welfare of the child. It has been argued that any commitment of the 1948 Act to family preservation and even to preventive work was more implied than expressed (see Donnison, 1954; James, 1998) but within a short time of the passage of the Act, evidence was available that suggested that almost 50 per cent of children who were received into the care of the local authority were returned home within six weeks. The rise in short-term cases that followed the Act, and the statutory requirement to assess children before admitting them to local authority care, increasingly forced the staff of the new Children's Departments into face-to-face work with families and encouraged an interest in preventive work that was to find full expression in the 1963 Children and Young Persons Act. Holman (1998) identifies this as one of the outstanding achievements of the first generation of Children's Officers. In contrast to the 'rescue motive' of prewar services, it was the Children's Departments, rather than the legislature, that 'restored natural parents to child care' through the exercise of emergent specialist skills and in a spirit of 'crusading zeal to improve the lot of deprived children' (1998: 206).

We should perhaps note just one further provision of the Act that was to have profound consequences: the responsibility for children's services at central government level was vested in the 'welfarist' Home Office (Hughes, 1998: 150). From this point on, the Home Office was able to build experience and develop expertise in the care of children that was to carry influence in succeeding decades.

Despite the fact that the State had learned some uncomfortable lessons about its capacity to deliver on all that it had offered for the care of children, confidence remained high, buttressed by the 'sense of optimism and challenge' shared by the 'home missionaries' (Stevenson, 1998: 154) of the Children's Departments. This confidence was maintained and strengthened by the development of a network of experience and expertise that centralisation and a revised service delivery structure at local level brought with it. With a revitalised interest in the family brought about by the war and its assumptions of the close association of the interests of parents and their children, attention soon coalesced around the idea of the family as a part of the solution as much as part of the problem, an idea which constituted the foundation of the 1963 and 1969 Children and Young Persons Acts, although it was once again a concern with juvenile delinquency which prompted legislative action.

Juvenile crime had begun to rise again sharply after the Second World War and throughout the 1950s. Whilst, at the time, this could be plausibly attributed to the upheaval of war, the absence of fathers, the loosening of discipline and the increased freedom for youngsters, such explanations were fast losing credibility in the postwar period. For the first time in nearly a century, the threat that young people posed as opposed to the threats to which they were subject, began to impose itself on the public consciousness. After pressure from the Magistrates' Association, the government in 1956 established the Ingleby Committee to review 'the working of the law in England and Wales relating to proceedings and the powers of the courts in respect of juveniles brought before the courts as delinquent or as being in need of care and protection or beyond control' (p. ii).

The Committee's response can be characterised in terms of its commitment to prevention rather than rescue and by its belief in the efficacy of the treatment approaches available to the welfare professionals of the day. Its belief in the capacity of the family to provide the child with the best possible upbringing it inherited from an earlier age. The duty of parents, for example, was to (pp. 5–6): 'help their children to become effective and law abiding citizens by example and by training and by providing a stable and secure family background in which they can develop satisfactorily. Anything which falls short of this can be said to constitute neglect'. Accordingly, the duty of the State in those cases where families are unable to meet those responsibilities was to (p. 6): 'provide through its social welfare services the advice which such parents and children need; to build up their capacity for responsibility, and to enable them to fulfil their proper role'. Ingleby firmly cemented the link established by the 1933 Act between neglect and delinquency. It is the early identification of such families by everybody from the school-teacher to the vicar to the social worker and their subsequent treatment which was the key to an effective response. As noted in the Report itself (p. 7): 'It is often the parents as much as the child who need to alter their ways, and it is therefore with family problems that any preventive measures will largely be concerned.'

The development of a unified preventive child care service was to await the 1969 Act. The 1963 Act, however, whilst primarily concerned with delinquency and the juvenile court system, did begin by granting local authorities specific powers to engage in preventive work (s. 1):

> It shall be the duty of every local authority to make available such advice, guidance and assistance as may promote the welfare of children by diminishing the need to receive children into care or keep them in care... or to bring children before a juvenile court; and any provisions made by a local authority... may... include provision for giving assistance in kind or, in exceptional circumstances, in cash.

At the end of a decade which saw increasing economic pressure brought to bear on the universalism of the Welfare State, it was to be the 1969 Act that would represent the final flowering, if not the highest point, of a family-orientated, preventive treatment ideology that had begun in the Children's Departments of the 1950s.

The main provisions of the Act itself involved raising the age of criminal responsibility from 10 to 14, voluntary agreements between parents and social workers to decide 'treatment' without a court appearance, the use of care proceedings for older adolescents, mandatory consultation between police and social services departments before prosecution, the replacement of approved schools (which were to be re-named 'community homes') and fit person orders by the care order and the vesting of powers in social workers to implement the orders of the court in ways which allowed considerable administrative discretion. The degree of professional discretion postulated by the 1969 Act, would, had it ever been fully realised, have presented a significant challenge to the centrality of judicial decision-making which had developed since the 1933 Act.

If the role of the court was to diminish and the numbers brought before it were to reduce, then additional preventive services would have to be provided. These would be achieved through the establishment of a new 'family service'. This service, at least as originally envisaged in the 1968 Seebohm Report, would have been a universal service, available to all families, rather than just those in trouble. Its practical implementation was brought about by means of the 1969 Act's twin, the Local Authority Social Services Act 1970, which came into force in April 1971. The scope of the new social services departments that the 1970 Act introduced was to include services to older people, those with disabilities, education welfare services and child guidance, mental health services, day care, home helps and some nursery provision. As such, social services departments were to have a broader 'community' focus as much as a family focus, and the voice of Children's Officers was now to be only one amongst many competing for attention and cash in the town halls of England and Wales. But, in 1970, the Labour Party lost the general election and the implementation of the 1969 Act was stopped in its tracks.

The age of criminal prosecution was not raised, the courts retained their powers to sentence directly to borstal or to detention centres, and it was for the court to decide whether it would order supervision by probation officers or social workers. Custodial sentences began to rise sharply and the courts began their lengthy struggle to regain their centrality in the management of juvenile crime.

Conclusion

In such a schematic review of almost two hundred years of public policy bearing on the welfare of children, in which the legislative outcomes of policy appear reactive, sporadic and opportunistic, one sees not so much an inevitable progress towards a rational consensus as, rather, the ebb and flow of several competing discourses around such matters as the boundary between the State and the family, the essential nature of the child, the balance of power between the courts and the agents of the local State and the competing claims of various professional or occupational groups. In particular, we have noted how children become a metaphor for the state of the nation from time to time and how their care has been constituted as a specialist area of expert knowledge and therefore of policy debate. We have suggested that critical realignments of these various discourses were sometimes signalled by the emergence of scandals which served to illustrate the failures of the old order and the possibilities of the new.

As the fate of the 1969 Act suggests, such a critical realignment was imminent. According to Clarke (1980: 95), 'an alliance' between the Conservative party and the representatives of the legal apparatus (notably the magistracy, but also the probation service) had made 'severe inroads' into the Fabian strategy which had informed the 1969 Act, long before it reached the statute book. As the ideological and economic retreat from universal welfare services (McCarthy, 1989) was gathering pace, the work placed in the 'secretive and impenetrable hands of the medical and allied professions' (Box, 1980: 121) was about to be made subject to scrutiny in an unprecedented manner. It was in this context that in January 1973, a little girl, just short of her eighth birthday, was beaten to death at the home of her mother and stepfather. Her name was Maria Colwell and out of her death was constructed the first child welfare scandal for more than a generation.

5
The Story of 'Cinderella'
The Report of the Committee of Inquiry
into the Care and Supervision Provided
in Relation to Maria Colwell

Introduction

The *Report of the Committee of Inquiry into the Care and Supervision Provided in Relation to Maria Colwell* was submitted to Barbara Castle, the Labour Secretary of State for Social Services, in May 1974. It was published on 5 September, at first only on a limited scale and in typescript form due to a strike (a contemporary characteristic) by printers at Her Majesty's Stationery Office. The Inquiry had been chaired by Thomas Field-Fisher, a judge, assisted by Olive Stevenson, a social work academic and Margaret Davey, a local authority councillor. It is a relatively short report containing 120 pages, including appendices, amounting to little more than 60,000 words. But it would be difficult to exaggerate the symbolic significance that this rather modest and much-delayed document was to achieve in succeeding years. According to Parton (1985), for example, it was through the case of Maria Colwell that child abuse, previously experienced by professionals as 'marginal to their everyday practice' and largely unattended to by the media and the general public, became established as a 'major social problem' (Parton, 1985: 69). Other accounts of Colwell (see, for example, Howells, 1974; London Borough of Brent, 1985; Merrick, 1996) make similar or even larger claims.

The emblematic nature of welfare scandals is an important theme of this book and it is clearly the case that the discursive consequences of Colwell extend well beyond the circumstances of one little girl's death at the hands of her carers. It is the purpose of this chapter, however, to recover some of the finer detail and contemporary significance of Colwell as a reminder that welfare scandals, whatever their subsequent fate, are founded on very particular events, inhabited by all too real people, and that the Public Inquiries which sometimes follow are very much products of their own time and place.

The events

Maria was born, in Hove, near Brighton, East Sussex on 25 March 1965. She was the fifth and youngest child of her mother Pauline Tester's marriage to Raymond Colwell. Within weeks of Maria's birth, her father had left home in circumstances which were complex, acrimonious and involved a large extended family network. Shortly after and before Maria was quite four months old, he died of natural causes. Faced with the care of five children under the age of seven, in the words of the Report (13), Pauline Colwell 'went completely to pieces'. She took Maria to Raymond's sister, Doris Cooper, and asked the Coopers to look after her. Pauline Colwell's care of the remaining four children became a cause for concern and in December 1965, the four children were removed from her care and subsequently made subject to Fit Person Orders (broadly equivalent to a Care Order under later legislation) in favour of the county council. For the next ten months, Maria continued to live with the Coopers.

In June 1966, Pauline Colwell removed Maria, then aged 14 months, from the Coopers, as she was entitled, given that no court orders had been made in respect of her. Mrs Colwell's resumption of the care of Maria coincided with her expressed intention to set up home with William Kepple, with whom she had begun a relationship and whom she would marry in May 1972. This arrangement for the care of Maria lasted less than a week and in August 1966, East Sussex County Council made a successful application to the Hove Juvenile Court for a Fit Person Order in respect of her and subsequently approved the Coopers as foster carers for Maria.

Maria continued to live with the Coopers until October 1971 despite the frequently expressed intentions of her mother to resume the care of her daughter. The relationship between Pauline Colwell and the Coopers remained strained throughout this period. Indeed, the nature of this relationship was to have a decisive effect on the subsequent decision to return Maria to the care of her mother. Its immediate effect was to place Maria 'at the centre of conflict' (36). A case conference was held on 26 April 1971 to consider Maria's position and in anticipation of Pauline Colwell's application to have the Fit Person Order revoked, the local authority began to plan for the transfer of Maria's care to her mother. If one is to judge by the tone of the court report (included as an appendix to the Report of the Inquiry), they did so with considerably greater reluctance than has been reported elsewhere (see for example, Reder et al., 1993: 153ff.).

From the point at which she was placed with her mother and William Kepple, on 22 October 1971, Maria's life was to be a sharp downward spiral of physical abuse, neglect, cruelty and unbearable distress. Under the intermittent and largely uncoordinated supervision of both the local authority and the NSPCC, the Inquiry found abundant evidence of a steady deterioration in Maria's condition over the next 15 months. Slowly Maria disappeared from view. She stopped attending school in the half term before Christmas and on the night of Saturday 6 January 1973, William Kepple came in at 11.30 p.m. to find Maria watching television 'and the events which formed the basis for the indictment against Mr Kepple then occurred' (146). On post mortem examination, the majority of the injuries found on Maria's body, described by the pathologist in the case as 'the worst he had ever seen', were judged to have resulted from 'extreme violence' (147). William Kepple was convicted of Maria's murder in April 1973 although, on appeal, the charge was reduced to manslaughter and he was sentenced to eight years' imprisonment.

'Cinderella': the myth of Maria Colwell

One might imagine that the bare facts of Maria Colwell's life and death would have been sufficient to engage widespread public and professional concern. However, then as now, child cruelty, although rare, was by no means unprecedented. In September 1973, Shropshire County Council had published the *Report of Inquiry into the Circumstances Surrounding the Death of Graham Bagnall and the Role of the County Council's Social Services*. As with Colwell, it too concerned a child removed from foster carers and returned to the care of his mother and stepfather, both of whom were subsequently convicted of his manslaughter. Indeed, during the course of the Colwell inquiry, the *Times* reported, in the words of the trial judge, 'a case of almost unbelievable cruelty to a three month old baby' who had been severely assaulted by his father such that 'one is almost tempted to believe that there was not a major bone in his body that was not broken' (10 November 1973). A few days later, Sir Keith Joseph, the then Conservative Secretary of State for Health, turned down a 'suggestion' made by Labour MP Jack Ashley that 'a public inquiry should automatically be held in all cases where a child is battered to death'. Joseph argued that 'such a course would pose considerable practical difficulties with doubtful value...The danger would be that a series of public inquiries would re-enforce the condemnatory and horrified attitude of society and prevent other parents from seeking help' (*The Times*, 13 November 1973). It was to take a considerable effort to secure Sir Keith's agreement to an inquiry in the Colwell case. The facts of Colwell's life, whilst undeniably tragic, were not in themselves 'scandalous', at least not intrinsically so. For them to become so they would need to be actively transformed from the domestic and particular into the public and symbolic and for that, sustained interest from wider constituencies of interest would be necessary.

As already indicated, a number of influential accounts of the Colwell case, in particular those produced by Nigel Parton (Parton, 1985 but see also Reder et al., 1993; Hendrick, 1994) construct Colwell as symptomatic of the 'profound misgivings about the nature of society' (Heywood, 1978: 196) that had arisen in the 1960s, as 'young men looked back in anger' at the rediscovery of poverty, the dissolution of established communities and the threat of increased violence, both on a local and global scale. Citing Chibnall (1977), Parton sees in Colwell (1985: 81): 'a focus for the expression of a range of social anxieties concerned with the "English way of life", the growth of violence, the decline in individual and social discipline and morality, and the need to re-establish the traditional family'. Such an account would have been instantly recognisable to Sir John Gorst or St Aubyn, a generation earlier. Both Parton and Hendrick (1994: 253ff.) regard the media as 'crucial' in providing a specific locus in which these anxieties could be exercised and exorcised. Parton in particular, (1985: 86ff.) has argued that the media in relation to Colwell was itself instrumental in the construction of the 'social problem of child abuse', a particular manifestation of the more general 'moral panic' (Cohen, 1973) he describes. He argued that before Colwell, 'any mention of the problem [of child abuse] in the media essentially reproduced the definitions of the experts in the field'. However, once the primary definitions of the experts are in play, 'the media is able to transform them into its own language'. Thus, the media 'can take on the guise of not only representing "public opinion" but of being "public opinion" (Parton, 1985: 86). In so doing, the media becomes a party to the production of the news and in the process, transforms and objectifies an 'issue into a real social problem that the general public is concerned about and [about which it] demands action' (however, see Fulcher and Scott, 1999). The suggestion would seem to be that it was the media that constructed the scandal of Colwell and, by implication, the 'social problem' of child abuse as a particular instance of more fundamental social stresses. We would suggest that the process was somewhat more complex and more subtle (see also Merrick, 1996). We detect little to support the view that the press 'campaigned in an independent way' (Parton, 1985: 98) around Colwell, at least initially.

At first, the media did what the media usually does; it went to 'the cuttings' (Galtung and Rouge, 1965). Accordingly, it reported Colwell in familiar and established terms, namely the 'tug-of-love' debate that had been carried in the national press from the mid-1960s (see Howells, 1974: 17ff.). On William Kepple's conviction, the *Daily Mail* (17 April 1973) reported neither child abuse, as such, nor moral outrage but 'Tragedy of foster girl sent back to mother' and the *Daily Express* (17 April 1973) another 'Tug-of-love error'. Understood in this way, Colwell was sufficiently intelligible and of sufficient interest to engage the passing attention of some sections of the national media. But much of what could be written about the 'tug-of-love' had already been written and, to judge by the space accorded by most newspapers to the story in its early stages, little more might have followed. By this point, the 'tug-of-love' and the debate about the significance of the blood tie on which it rested had lost momentum as a salient practice or policy issue and, more importantly, it struggled to be 'news' at all (see Wroe, 1988: 24).

'Tug-of-love' cases had involved the removal of children who had been placed with foster carers, often for considerable periods, and their reintroduction into their 'natural' families on the premise that a relationship based on the blood tie was stronger than any other. Public interest in such cases and evident sympathy for the position of substitute carers had been augmented throughout the late 1960's by increasing professional unease at the 'instability' of a wide range of foster placements (Thoburn, 1999: 122). Moreover, adoption law had remained unaltered since 1958 and voluntary adoption agencies were coming under strain (Rogers, 1980). Such concerns had led to the establishment, in 1969, of the Departmental Committee on the Adoption of Children ('Houghton Committee') (Home Office, 1972). This reported in October 1972, less than a year before the publication of the Colwell Report.

Houghton elevated the claims and interest of children over those of their 'natural' parents in the case of adoption and fostering. Hence, the report of the Houghton Committee, according to Heywood (1978: 204) marked: 'a final break with the old legal concept of children as the chattels of their parents and the presumption that parents are, the most appropriate people to represent their children's interests'. Such a judgement may bear some of the marks of hindsight, however, in that up until this point, the Houghton Report had not been debated in

Parliament and government had shown little interest in its conclusions. It was not until early in 1974, a few months ahead of the Colwell Inquiry's final report, that the Opposition Labour Member of Parliament, Dr David Owen, introduced a Private Member's Bill intended to give effect, *inter alia*, to the recommendations of Houghton. It was lost in the dissolution of Parliament, which followed in February that year although, as Minister of State at the DHSS in the next Parliament, Owen steered through a much-modified version of his original bill that received Royal Assent as the 1975 Children Act.

Some clues to the relative quiescence of the 'blood tie' debate as a professional practice issue can be gleaned from the conclusions of the Inquiry itself. In her minority report, exploring the decision of the local authority to work towards returning Maria to the care of her mother, Olive Stevenson noted, with scarcely concealed irritation, that 'the phrase is one which may trip off the tongues of lawyers much more readily than those of social workers' (315). As far as Stevenson was concerned, the social workers in this particular case, and the social work profession generally, had reached a more sophisticated understanding of what the blood tie meant in terms of a child's developing sense of its own identity. The debate had simply moved on in professional circles and it had all but disappeared off the policy agenda.

It was not because the private tragedy of Maria Colwell engaged with a topical and contentious issue in public policy or professional practice that it began its transformation into a public scandal. Nor do its origins lie in the independent moral entrepreneurship of the national media articulating and shaping fundamental strains in British society. It began in genuine popular sentiment that was firmly rooted in the particular and very local circumstances of Maria's death and where the struggle to make events public was itself a driving force. The scandal of Colwell was forced onto the policy and professional agenda and into the public imagination by a concerted effort, largely by those who might hitherto have had little claim on the attention of political, professional or wider national audiences. The 'outsiders' in this case were the 'mothers of Maresfield Road' (*Brighton Evening Argus*, 25 May 1973), Maria Colwell's neighbours.

It is important to note the one significant exception to the early reporting of Colwell at national level. On 16 April 1973, the *Sun* newspaper, possibly more familiar with scandal than policy or professional social work practice, carried a 'Special Investigation' under the headline **'Scandal of Murdered Step-Daughter'**. Explicitly using many of the narrative devices of the fairy story and with the same simple action and edifying purpose of the morality play, it is the popular and populist *Sun* that captures the moment and the tone in which the myth of Maria Colwell was begun:

> On a bleak Sunday night last January, Maria
> was brutally beaten to death by her
> stepfather. And she was only seven.
> Hers is a heartbreaking story. A story of
> crucial importance to parents, social
> workers, everyone concerned with the
> welfare of children.
> For it shows that the removal of a child from
> the care of her foster parents must
> ALWAYS be investigated with great care.
>
> *The youngster they all loved*
>
> ...
>
> Maria was nicknamed Choochie when
> she went to live with her foster parents, Doris
> and Robert Cooper.
> Mrs Cooper's brother had been Raymond
> Colwell, Maria's real father. But he died
> after an illness.
> Soon Maria was growing up happily at the
> home of the Coopers in Hove, Sussex.
> Everyone liked her. And she became the
> favourite of the sea-front traders at nearby
> Brighton.
>
> ...
>
> Maria was the inseparable playfriend of two
> of the Coopers grandchildren.
> Together they went on holiday trips to
> Newquay, Blackpool and Longleat. Family
> snaps all include Maria. "She was a part of
> us", they all said.
> *THEN came a sudden change ... a change*
> *that was to alter her life completely.*
> On October 2nd, 1971, Maria was taken
> weeping from the Cooper home.
>
> *Choochie became a Cinderella*

The mothers of Maresfield Road

From the time of Maria's death, the local press had reported the height-ened emotional temperature of neighbours on the Manor Farm Estate, Whitehawk, Brighton, where Maria had lived. Residents had organised a collection and had raised over £100, £20 of which was to be spent on wreaths for 'little Maria' (she is rarely referred to in any other terms). On the day after the funeral, the flowers around Maria's grave had been destroyed, 'torn up by rival factions of mourners'. At the funeral, Pauline Kepple had had to run a 'gauntlet of taunts' and cries of 'bloody mur-deress' (*Brighton Evening Argus*, 25 and 26 January 1973). After the trial of William Kepple some months later, Maria's mother had to move out of her home (albeit for a very brief period):

> The word 'murderer' has been scrawled on her front wall and as she edged open the door today, a crowd of neighbours shouted: 'Come out here and we will kill you. Let's get hold of you.' They stood by a car on which had been stuck a poster that read 'Bring back hanging – espe-cially for child murderers'. (Brighton Evening Argus, 17 April 1973)

The death penalty had been abolished scarcely five years earlier. At one level, the depth of local feeling is perhaps unsurprising, especially as the Inquiry would later hear details of 'the torrent of complaints' (80) that had been made by neighbours following Maria's return to the Kepple house-hold. Not all of these complaints related to the care of Maria, although many did. The subsequent evidence of neighbours to the Inquiry would testify to the avoidability of the tragedy that had befallen Maria. In weigh-ing this, the Inquiry acknowledged that the reliability of the neighbours' evidence could be questioned, not least because of a pre-existing antipathy to the Kepple family generally that had existed on the Manor Farm Estate and because of 'the depth of feelings aroused over Maria's death' (80).

It is not possible to determine at this remove what precisely motivated the emotional response of the residents of the Manor Farm Estate imme-diately after the death of Maria. Simple grief, a sense of frustration or collective guilt that more could have been done by them to have pre-vented her death; a wish by some to distance themselves from the image of the 'undeserving poor' represented by the Kepple family or a contin-uation of the family feud in which Maria had become inextricably implicated may all have played their part. Whatever the reason, the reaction of the 'ordinary, respectable people' of Brighton (*Sunday Times*, 22 April 1973) was powerful, increasingly articulate and sustained.

It might be supposed that some of the initial anger might have been deflected by the promise of a 'very full and careful investigation' of the Colwell case made by the Director of Social Services for East Sussex County Council, immediately on the conviction of William Kepple (*Brighton Evening Argus*, 17 April 1973). In fact, the emotional temperature noticeably rose once it became clear that the investigation would be carried out in private.

A panel of five – two East Sussex county councillors, a Brighton councillor, a magistrate and an academic – were appointed and announced their intention to begin work in May. Almost immediately, however, there was vigorous opposition to the idea of the investigation being held 'in secret' (*Brighton Evening Argus*, 26 April 1973). The local councillor for the ward in which Maria had lived, Danny Sheldon, attended a meeting of residents and made clear his intention to campaign for a separate and wider Home Office inquiry (*Brighton Evening Argus*, 28 April 1973). Letters in support of his campaign, with editorial endorsement, began to appear regularly in the local press, including one asking, in an age where such protests would not have been unusual, 'Why don't we protest in the streets?' (*Brighton Evening Argus*, 8 May 1973). The local MP, Andrew Bowden, was quick to lend his weight to the campaign and an approach was made to the Home Secretary, Robert Carr. A petition bearing 7,500 signatures was organised by the chairman of the East Brighton Residents Association and handed in on the steps of the Town Hall (*Brighton Evening Argus* 11 May 1973) which added substance to Councillor Sheldon's earlier claim that 'The public conscience has been aroused and demands that its views cannot be ignored' (*Brighton Evening Argus*, 3 May 1973). The *Brighton Evening Argus* made much of the 'public's right to know' (24 April 1973) and correspondents expressed fears of the 'old pals' act' (27 April 1973) were the inquiry to proceed in private. The MP, Andrew Bowden, insisted that justice had to be 'seen to be done' (8 and 12 May 1973) and declared that 'the people of Brighton and the nation have a right to know what went wrong'.

Nonetheless, the local inquiry began its work on Monday 14 May, although it did announce that its findings would be made public. This was insufficient to deflect the campaigners. Councillor Sheldon contrasted the 'cold and aloof' procedure of the inquiry with the depth of popular feeling and made explicit his concern that the inquiry should not only be impartial but public: 'People who have authority vested in them must always be aware that they are servants of the public. I believe that to proceed with the inquiry [*in private*] can only bring lack of confidence in those who administer the public's affairs' (*Brighton Evening*

Argus, 15 May 1973). On the next day, Wednesday, the *Brighton Evening Argus* published the 'evidence' of Ann Turner, Maria's primary school teacher, that appeared to confirm that Maria's death had been entirely preventable. In its editorial, the paper described the county council's reasons for proceeding in private, as 'utter nonsense':

> Nothing can possibly be considered confidential in a case of this kind. For the public need to arrive at a true picture of what really happened just as much as the inquiry panel. ... In a secret inquiry only the members of the panel will hear the explanations offered by the Social Services Department and the NSPCC. If the inquiry were open, however, the public would hear what took place in the words of the people who were there at the time, rather than in the official jargon of a carefully worded report published weeks or even months later.

The 'public's right to know' was now as much an issue as the circumstances surrounding the death of Maria. On Thursday 17 May, the local inquiry was adjourned, never to reconvene. By the end of the week, Brighton Council had also made a request to the Secretary of State for Health for the inquiry to proceed in public and Sir Keith Joseph had met local MP Andrew Bowden to discuss the situation. Although complicated by the fact that William Kepple had decided to appeal (successfully) against his conviction for Maria's murder, on 24 May, a government inquiry was announced by the Secretary of State. Perhaps inevitably, the announcement was welcomed by Andrew Bowden as a 'victory for public opinion' and by the local press as a 'victory for common sense' (*Brighton Evening Argus*, 25 May 1973).

It was not immediately clear, however, that the inquiry would be held in public, nor even in Brighton. A preliminary hearing was set for 28 August, in London, in part to decide how the full Inquiry should proceed. Representatives of the Maria Colwell Memorial Fund, set up initially by local residents, expressed their intentions to keep 'a silent vigil' at the London hearing, 'not only to assert our presence but also to represent the feelings of thousands of Brighton people who were moved by this crime. This may well be the last chance that Brightonians will have to express their feelings about this case' (*Brighton Evening Argus*, 7 August 1973). This demonstration by representatives of the Memorial Fund was perhaps the most bizarre and mawkish expression of popular sentiment to follow Maria's death. The Memorial Fund representatives took with them to London: 'a gaunt statue of Maria, dull-faced, scavenging from a dustbin. It was made by Brighton sculptor David Whipp. It rattled as the coach drove on. With a tattered metal arm outstretched, the model stared soundlessly from ghastly eye sockets...' (*Brighton Evening Argus*, 24 August 1973). The protest, the statue and the briefest account of the facts of Maria's life were reported in the *Daily Express*, the *Times*, the *Daily Telegraph* and the *Guardian* (25 August 1973) along with the news that the inquiry would indeed be held in public and based in Brighton. There had been scarcely any reference to Colwell in the national press between Kepple's conviction in April and the appearance of the statue on the streets of London in late August (see Chibnall, 1977: 22ff. for an account of the media's interest in 'events' and the importance of immediacy).

Through the Inquiry, the story of Maria Colwell's life would enter fully into the public domain and so constitute a space which could be occupied by a variety of new and more influential claims-makers. Already, the 'mothers of Maresfield Road' had been displaced by the representatives of the Memorial Fund who had taken it upon themselves to campaign for the restoration of the death penalty for child murderers. But here, the possibility of progress was limited. The death penalty debate had been resolved (at least for the political and journalistic classes) and the strength of their consensus would be sufficient to resist the intrusion of scandal. Even the Memorial Fund plays no further significant part in the events that had been set in train. It is interesting to note that of the twenty people who made the trip to London in August 1983, the men in their black ties, the women in their Sunday best (*Brighton Evening Argus*, 24 August 1973), none were from Whitehawk. But those who followed should be regarded as colonisers rather than pioneers. It was the anger, the indignation and the persistence of the 'mothers of Maresfield Road' that ensured that the moral landscape of the Colwell case was opened up to others.

As we will argue elsewhere too, scandals involve the *active* transformation of local events into national issues. Their escape velocity is provided by the persistence of often rather unlikely agitators for change in public policy or professional practice. However, whilst scandals often have to struggle to cross from the private to the public and from the particular to the symbolic, they also need to resonate with the time in which they are produced. In the case of Maria Colwell, the re-construction of child abuse and the practice of social work provided the terms in which the issues raised could be pursued.

The Inquiry and its Report

It is a central thesis of this book that scandals provide the opportunity and the momentum for a variety of moral, political and academic enterprises. But, as we have suggested, in the same way that the intensely local nature of scandals during the period of their genesis can be obscured when viewed in retrospect, so can the very specifics of Public Inquiries and the matters that were of immediate and contemporary concern be overwhelmed by the burden of historical significance that they come to bear. We would suggest that the actual terms of reference, composition and procedures of a Public Inquiry all have a direct bearing on the nature of the business they transact and on the conclusions that they reach. This is particularly evident in the case of Colwell where a number of professional and personal strains that relate to the day-to-day business of the Inquiry can be seen to have foreshadowed later events. It is important to note that the final outcome of the Inquiry comprises a majority and a minority report (written by Olive Stevenson) and it is in the differences between these two parts of the final report that much of the contemporary significance of the Inquiry is to be found.

The DHSS had appointed Thomas Field-Fisher, QC, as chair of the Inquiry Committee. Field-Fisher had been a Recorder since 1972, having been called to the Bar in 1942 and made a QC in 1969. He was a former Vice-Chairman of the London Council of Social Service and listed social welfare as one of his 'recreations' in *Who's Who*. As a barrister and as a judge, however, he had had very little experience of child care matters, having worked largely in the criminal courts. It is not clear how Field-Fisher came to be selected as chair of the Committee except to say that it might have been considered an appropriate step on the career ladder of a recently appointed judge (see chapter 3). His appointment preceded that of the two other members of the Committee, Alderman Margaret Davey and Olive Stevenson, then Reader in Applied Social Studies at Oxford University. Margaret Davey had experience as a former chair of Essex County Council's Health Committee and chair of the East Anglia Children's Regional Planning Committee. Her particular contribution to the process and the outcomes of the Inquiry is difficult to distinguish. Olive Stevenson, on the other hand, was running the social work qualifying course at Oxford and already had considerable experience of working as an advisor to government both as a member of the Royal Commission on Civil Liability and Compensation for Personal Injury and as an advisor to the Supplementary Benefits Commission. Her appointment to the Colwell Inquiry came in an evening telephone call from the DHSS. According to Stevenson (personal communication), prior to the call she had neither heard nor read anything of the case.

There was little opportunity for discussion between the Committee members of the terms of reference of the Inquiry which were: (1): 'to inquire into and report upon the care and supervision provided by local authorities and other agencies in relation to Maria Colwell and the co-ordination between them'. The specificity of the terms of reference is striking and has become familiar from many subsequent inquiries. In the majority report, written largely by Field-Fisher, the Committee is at pains to demonstrate the restricted scope of its mandate. For example, the Committee expressed itself 'chary' of criticising standard social work practice, except 'where any particular aspect of that practice may offend against ordinary standards of social or moral concern or even appears to go against accepted tenets of common-sense' but even then, it would only 'indicate at least a hope that the practice should be scrutinised anew' (45). Similarly, when the question of the uncontested court pro-ceedings which brought the Fit Person Order to an end arose, the Inquiry is quick to point out that it was not for them 'to consider the much wider and more radical proposition of independent representa-tion for the child' (68). In relation to the Coopers' lack of standing in those proceedings, the Inquiry is in no doubt that (228), 'It is not for us to pronounce generally upon matters which may go beyond mere pro-cedural rules into more complex questions of status and rights.' The two latter illustrations are important in that later commentators attribute to the Inquiry a particular interest in the much broader issues of the civil status if the child and the place of foster carers in the case of a 'tug-of-love' (see Merrick, 1996: 156ff. and 177ff.; Parton, 1985: 89), yet these were matters which the Committee itself explicitly did not consider in general terms. Similarly, the first illustration is important because it was precisely on the grounds of the practice of social work that the differ-ence between the majority and minority reports was to develop.

It is necessary to recall that there was no real precedent for inquiries of this sort in the field of child care. The Secretary of State had no statutory powers to convene such an inquiry (these were to be provided by s. 98 of the 1975 Children Act) and there was no established means of proceeding. It is important to recognise therefore that the form that the Inquiry took was a matter, to some degree, of choice. The choice made was to set the pattern for almost all of the child care inquiries that were to follow over the next quarter of a century. This applied not only to the composition of the Inquiry (a lawyer in the chair, a representative of 'local government' and a social work academic) but also to the procedure adopted by the Inquiry. Essentially, the Colwell Inquiry took the form of a quasi-judicial hearing. This choice was no doubt influenced by the principles established by the Royal Commission on Tribunals of Inquiry ('The Salmon Commission') that reviewed the procedures of inquiries set up under the

1921 Tribunals of Inquiry Act. This had reported in 1966 and, according to Blom-Cooper (1997: 5) had 'deliberately injected into the inquisitorial system a heavy dose of the adversarial system so beloved by English lawyers'.

The Report of the Inquiry records how, much in the manner of a criminal trial, (6):

> Witnesses were examined-in-chief by Counsel for the Committee or by their own Counsel if they were represented. All witnesses were open to cross-examination by all parties. At the end of the hearing we were addressed by representatives and Counsel for the Committee.

Proceedings on each of the 41 days on which the Committee heard 'evidence' (5) were begun with the formal entrance of Field-Fisher, followed by Stevenson and Davey, who took their place on a raised dais, as those present rose from their seats. The actual manner in which evidence was adduced was also often redolent of the courtroom. Counsel and the chair were heard to use the words 'defence and defendants' (Society of Local Authority Chief Executives, 1977: 28 cited in Hallett 1989: 120). In the following exchange between the advocate representing the County Borough of Brighton, the aptly named Mr Hidden, and Mrs Kirby, the NSPCC Inspector responsible for the later supervision of Maria, the forensic gaze is particularly intense:

> Q: ... but would you accept that in about two out of every three reports it is found that the child has physical injuries when the Society's inspector calls at the house?
> A: I suppose that would be about right.
> Q: But in your own experience it is less; you get very few cases like that?
> A: Yes.
> Q: So would Maria's case be unusual because you actually did find physical injuries?
> A: Perhaps not unusual.
> Q: But not a common occurrence?
> A: No.
> The Chairman: The words you used [in earlier evidence] were 'surprisingly few'?
> A: Yes
> The Chairman: Try to help Mr Hidden about that?
> A: I think in the last year I have seen only three children bruised, so that is surprisingly few.
>
> ...

> Q: Therefore, from April 1972, until now, October 1973, would it be
> fair to say that you have seen only four cases of bruising, one of
> the cases being Maria's?
>
> A: Yes.
>
> Q: You have said that if there is a battered child the one person who
> ought to be able to spot it is the NSPCC Inspector?
>
> A: Yes.
>
> Q: Obviously, when you saw Maria in April the battered baby syn-
> drome must have been in your mind when you called?
>
> A: Not particularly because Maria would not have come within the
> age range of the battered baby syndrome.
>
> ...
>
> Q: Did you at no time consider her to be a battered baby?
>
> A: Not when I knew her.
>
> > (Transcript of Evidence to the Inquiry, Day 12)

Another witness before the Inquiry (Jean Wall, an Area Director of Social
Services in East Sussex) describes her experience of being cross-examined
in these terms (Shearer, 1979):

> It was beyond one's experience to be a sort of pawn or puppet,
> pushed and pulled. It felt so totally unreasonable, so totally unjust, so
> totally untrue. The whole thing was unreal. One was unable to talk
> freely about what had happened. Because of the quasi-judicial set up,
> like a trial, the cross-examination, one had to answer only what was
> asked, with no opportunity to talk...

Crucially, for our purposes, Wall continued, that the Inquiry 'was
beyond our experience, because at that time nothing had been more private than social work'.

The Inquiry was conducted then in terms of the professional *habitus*
of its Chairman. It borrowed from the accepted discourses and manner of
proceeding of the criminal law. Whilst recognising the traditional
strengths of such an approach, particularly the way in which it induces
public confidence and the degree of forensic accuracy achieved, one might
argue that there exists a fundamental discontinuity between the form of
such quasi-judicial methods and the intangible truth of human relationships and the complex nature of child abuse. The process of child abuse is
usually cumulative, diffuse, slow-acting and insidious. This was certainly

the case in this instance. There is usually an intrinsic uncertainty about the nature, scale and timing of the possible outcomes of an essentially covert activity. In contrast to the 'elusive hazard' of child abuse (Kates, 1985), the law admits of few uncertainties in establishing either guilt or innocence. In the course of a hearing conducted somewhat in the manner of a trial, cause and effect may sometimes be simplified and a post hoc logic be imposed on what at the time was experienced as a much more fluid, dynamic and irreducible process. This is certainly the point of departure for Olive Stevenson in her minority report.

Perhaps with some impatience, she begins her account of the period from Maria's birth to the point in November 1971 when the Fit Person Order was revoked with the following observation (247):

> There is little dispute concerning the central facts of Maria's life during this period. My differences from my colleagues lie in the interpretation of those facts and the emphasis which should be given to them. ... Those who read the two reports dealing with this period are therefore free to choose whichever they find most convincing. As a social worker, my education and experience has taught me that in such matters, there is no one truth; in considering the subtleties of human emotions everyone is subjective. One's feelings, attitudes and experience colour one's perception. This is as true for me as it is for my colleagues.

Essentially Olive Stevenson's account, whilst far from exculpatory (see 323 and 332, for example), reintroduces some of the context and complexity of the circumstances in which critical decisions were made in relation to Maria. Her reasons for doing so contain possibly pointed references to the ostensible aims of the Inquiry itself. Without giving 'details of the [social workers'] attempts to cope sensitively with an extraordinary complex, rapidly changing situation' (312), Stevenson does not 'consider that justice can be done' (see also 248).

Much of Stevenson's account elaborates on the dynamics of the discordant family relationships in which Maria was embedded. For example, she is somewhat more critical of the Coopers than is the majority report. She is not prepared to see them as 'saints' (316) and, in terms that could easily be decoded by other social workers, makes explicit reference to the fact that the Coopers were approved *only* for the care of Maria (253). In reflecting on her colleagues' interpretation of the other two key actors in the drama of Maria's life, one cannot help but draw the inference that

Stevenson was of the view that her fellow Committee members (or rather Field-Fisher, who largely wrote the majority report) simply did not understand either the events or the lives and cultural contexts of the people who passed before them. She expresses herself 'at a loss' (328) at her colleagues' interpretation of the evidence concerning Mrs Kepple's capacity to care for Maria by virtue of her being the mother, by then, of nine children. Possibly with more than 'recreational' experience of large and chaotic families, Stevenson observes that 'one's attitude to this is much affected by one's social and cultural background' (329). In relation to William Kepple's 'attitudes' to the arrangements made for the care of Maria, Stevenson did not find these 'peculiar, given his cultural background' whilst she found the comments of her colleagues on this matter 'unhelpful' (286) and, in a further possibly ironic reference to the judicial scrupulousness of her colleagues, points out that there was 'no evidence whatever' to substantiate them.

Such comments may suggest that a degree of personal antagonism had grown up between Field-Fisher and Stevenson. This view is given substance by the fact that during the writing of the majority report, a certain amount of third-party brokering of the text was necessary by the Clerk to the Inquiry, Christine Hallet, then a civil servant, and later to become a distinguished Professor of Social Work. It would be unsafe to speculate further, although the point is made that the process of an inquiry remains a form of human activity like any other and with similar claims on human fallibility.

More seriously, the division between the majority and the minority reports arises from Olive Stevenson's explicit (but not uncritical) professional allegiances to the practice and the profession of social work. The credentials she offered to the Secretary of State in her letter explaining the submission of her report are those of 'a former social worker in child care' (p. 7) and her reasons include her belief that it would:

> ... be unjust to the social workers if a picture is presented which does not convey adequately the interaction of the many factors which were painstakingly considered in planning for Maria. This in turn may affect public confidence unjustifiably in those to whom Society entrusts children in care.

She goes on in the letter (and in some detail in her report) to elaborate the complexities encountered by the social worker in the case. Not only does she describe the intricacies of the family dynamics but she also addresses those difficulties which followed from the recent local and national reorganisation of social work and the 'stresses' that these produced (p. 8). It is not only Diana Lees' actions that Stevenson defends (where she thinks it appropriate), but also the capacity of social work itself to make claims to professional competence. For example, picking up on a comment in the majority report that a psychiatric opinion might have been sought in relation to Maria (60 and 61) before the application was made to revoke the FPO and the implication that 'too much emphasis [had been] placed on independent judgement' (61), Stevenson sees a direct threat to the very essence of her profession. According to Stevenson, to deny the social worker the right to make such an assessment as was called for (318):

> ... would be to deny her a basic tool of her trade. This is not an attempt to argue for professional omniscience, simply to point out that social workers in child care see, more than any other professional or lay group of people, children under this kind of stress. To deny them the right therefore, and indeed the necessity, to interpret such behaviour, and to make decisions in the light of the interpretation, is a contradiction of one of the very functions they were set up to perform.

At the end of her report, Stevenson asks that sympathy be shown to social workers – to 'those whom [society] employs to perform tasks of the utmost difficulty and complexity, under conditions of great strain' (333) – before she proceeds to dissociate herself from the 'hierarchy of censure' with which the majority report concludes (334): 'For one thing, it leaves a predominant impression of weakness rather than strength in the East Sussex social workers which is misleading. There was much that was excellent in their work ...'. The sense in which social work had been an explicit subject of scrutiny during the Colwell Inquiry was shared by others close to the profession. The General Secretary of the British Association of Social Workers writing after the publication of the Report noted (Andrews, 1974 cited in Parton, 1985): 'Apart from the individuals who have been pilloried, social work itself has at times appeared to be on trial. Basic assumptions have been questioned, as has the legal and judicial framework in which much social work is practised.' At the local level, too, animosity towards the particular social worker involved (not detectable in earlier local press reporting which warned specifically against any form of witch-hunt) may have been foreshadowed in the evident popular distrust of the local authority to examine Maria's death 'in secret'. It certainly emerged strongly once the Inquiry was underway. There was a 'minor disturbance' after which 'a woman was ushered out'

(*Brighton Evening Argus*, 8 November 1973) when Diana Lees first appeared to give evidence before the Inquiry on its twentieth day in session. (Lees was to give evidence for a total of six days.) Before the afternoon sitting of the Inquiry, the Chairman warned that in the event of any further disruptions, Lees' evidence would be heard in private. At the end of her second day of evidence, 'A crowd of women waited outside the inquiry office until Miss Lees left, and booed her as she was escorted to a car by the police and driven away' (*Brighton Evening Argus*, 9 November 1973). By the next day, queues of people wanting to attend the Inquiry had formed and 65 people had to be turned away. As with other dramas, the pace was quickening as the dénouement approached.

Stevenson does not dissociate herself from the general conclusions of the majority report; indeed, they would seem to bear the imprint of her particular view of events rather more than might have been anticipated. Pointing out the centrality of failures in communication between agencies involved in the care of Maria and recognising that it would be 'unfair' (240) to place the blame for the 'inadequacies in the care and supervision of Maria upon any individual or indeed upon any small group of individuals', chapter 4 of the Report concludes that it was the child care 'system' which failed her (242). The Report continues:

> Because that system is the product of society it is upon society as a whole that the ultimate blame must rest; indeed the highly emotional and angry reaction of the public in this case may indicate society's troubled conscience. It is not enough for the State as representing society to assume responsibility for those such as Maria. It must also provide the means to do so, both financially and by ensuring that the system works as efficiently as possible at every level so that individual mistakes, which must be accepted as inevitable, do not result in disaster.

In this sense, the Inquiry was centrally concerned, not just with the specifics of the death of Maria Colwell but generally with the practice of child care and significantly with the practice of social work. As Louis Blom-Cooper was to point out in recalling the Colwell Inquiry in his report into the death of Jasmine Beckford some ten years later (London Borough of Brent, 1985: 12):

> ... the [Colwell] Committee found itself ensnared by a public preoccupation with the fundamental question of the nature of the relationship between social work and society, social work and the State.

The interest of the public and of the media in the case of Maria Colwell...was fanned by a widespread feeling of a need to reassess the role of social workers in the community, and their role vis-à-vis some of the moral issues that are powerful factors in any culture – natural parenthood, fostering, adoption, child protection, delinquency and crime, deprivation and the freedom of the individual. ... The Maria Colwell Inquiry itself was conducted at a time when the social work profession had not yet come to terms with its relationship with the public.

Behind this commentary one can detect the echoes of a much older debate about the relationship between the State and the family and the legitimacy and the capacity of the State to intervene successfully in the care of children.

Before considering the importance to the development of public policy of social work as a central concern of the Colwell Inquiry, some final reflections might usefully be made on the process of the Inquiry. Irrespective of which account one favours, Stevenson's minority report makes its point that 'there is no one truth' (247), simply by virtue of its having been written in the first place. The 'facts' of this, as of any other inquiry, emerge through a very human and subjective process of selection and interpretation that will be influenced by the inquirer's professional habits of thought, life history and cultural context. These in turn will flow in and out of a particular human tragedy and a unique configuration of local interests. In doing so, every inquiry bears the impression of the immediate circumstances in which it is produced and every report the indelible mark of its authors.

Other truths

As indicated already, others have seen in Colwell deeper discursive roots. In particular, Colwell has been associated with the emergence of child abuse as a social problem (see Parton, 1985; Hendrick, 1994). We have suggested that it was social work, as much as child abuse, that emerged as the problem during the course of the Colwell Inquiry. The distinction turns out to be a subtle, but important one.

We would accept that the production of public policy is vitally concerned with the establishment and maintenance of social norms. As such, the 'moral issues' (London Borough of Brent, 1985: 12) which coalesce around child abuse might indeed constitute the raw material for a series of important and continuing moral, political and ideological debates (see chapter 4). But public policy is also more usually and more immediately concerned with the instruments and institutional forms of the State. The 'moral issues' arising from Colwell, we would suggest, have been debated less, as far as public policy is concerned, in terms of those factors which go to the heart of child abuse (for example, the nature of intra-familial violence, the civil status of children, social exclusion, race, gender and structural inequality) and much more in terms of the intermediary form and practice of social work. The years since Colwell have been filled largely with the rhetoric of child *protection* (that is, how to manage the 'social problem' of child abuse) rather than the discourses of child *abuse* itself. This is merely to reassert that in the realpolitik of policy formation, proximate consequences are of more immediate concern than more remote causes. For policy-makers 'How to put it right?' is often a more important question to answer than 'Why did it go wrong?' (see Drewry, 1988).

The distinction between these two very different kinds of questions would have been difficult to make even at the time of Colwell since by then child abuse and the practice of social work occupied exactly the same policy space, albeit uncomfortably. Parton (1985) has suggested that the emerging orthodoxy of the 'medical model' of child abuse offered support to Sir Keith Joseph's and the DHSS' theory of the 'cycle of deprivation' in that both were predicated on notions of personal pathology. The 'medical model' of child abuse (derived from the work of paediatric radiologists in the United States from 1946 onwards and accelerated by the work of Henry Kempe in the early 1960s) was hardly new, however, and had been thoroughly infiltrated into the United Kingdom during the late 1960s and early 1970s, via the NSPCC's Battered Babies Research Unit. Indeed, the 'battered baby syndrome' was sufficiently widely understood to have formed the basis of Mr Hidden's cross-examination of Mrs Kirby during the Colwell Inquiry itself, as we have seen.

We would also disagree with Hendrick (1994: 244), that in its 'medicalisation', the 'social and legal aspects' of child abuse had somehow been 'relegated' up until this point. Henry Kempe himself had advised in his landmark 1961 paper to the American Academy of Paediatrics in which he first identified and defined the 'Battered Child Syndrome', that all incidents of child abuse should be reported to law enforcement or child welfare agencies. By 1968 he had gone further (Kempe, 1968: 169):

> While many community resources may need to be involved in the management of abused children, welfare departments, through their protective services sections, are perhaps the *key* agencies in trying in an orderly fashion to co-ordinate the required steps which will provide

protection to the child and also safeguard the legal rights of the parents. (our emphasis)

In this, and in his qualified support of casework as an appropriate therapeutic response to child abuse, Kempe was being true to the perspective of the Children's Bureau which had funded his original research. Despite its apparent appropriation by the medical profession, child abuse as a social problem and as a form of welfare practice had been placed, not altogether securely, in the hands of the emergent social work profession by the time that Maria Colwell died. This sat less well with a Conservative administration which, in the context of a growing public sector wage bill that, it was argued (see Bacon and Eltis, 1975), put pressure on the productive sector through higher taxation, was looking for any opportunity for more targeted intervention that would reinforce the party and the government's ideological retreat from universal public services. This had already been evidenced in the field of child care by the failure to carry into effect the broader ambitions of the 1969 Children and Young Persons Act (see chapter 4).

The threat to social work (and possibly other forms of welfare provision) that Stevenson saw in the Colwell Inquiry might easily have been missed by others. At this point, neither Sir Keith nor the press were as strident in their criticism of social work as they would later become. We have noted Sir Keith's reluctance to convene a Public Inquiry in the Colwell case for fear that some would be reluctant to seek help. Even the *Sunday Times* 'forthright campaign' (Parton, 1985: 95) in response to 'The Battered Babies Scandal' expressed some equivocation, not fully reflected in Parton's account. In describing the failure to act or the lack of thought which informs the actions of those 'charged with the care of children', the lead article in the *Sunday Times* of 11 November 1973 notes: 'Very many are dedicated people doing superb work for little pay. They are struggling with agonising and deep rooted problems. Nothing in this article is intended to lower morale. But it has to be said that the co-ordination of their efforts is often fatally at fault.'

Even the tabloids were, as yet, less confident in their assessment of the place of social work than later accounts have suggested. Marjorie Proops, when interviewing Sir Keith Joseph in the *Daily Mirror* (29 November 1973), cites approvingly his measured expression of support for social workers generally, and comments:

I am glad he said this. I'd like to underline my total agreement with him. There are too many people who dismiss social workers as nosey-parker do-gooders. I often wonder how much real do-gooding their critics ever engage in. Or if they have any idea of what social work is all about.

However, the *Times* piece and Proops' column serve as further confirmation that it was social work as a response to child abuse rather than child abuse itself that was to provide the prime site of public and political debate after Colwell.

Social work had been a specific object of government attention before Colwell. It should be remembered that the Inquiry took place in the brief hiatus between two major reorganisations of social work services, both of which are referred to by Stevenson in her prefatory letter to the Report (p. 8) and in the Report itself (e.g. 333). The first of these, contained in the Local Authority Social Services Act of 1970, carried into effect the recommendations of the 1968 Seebohm Report to establish 'a new local authority department, providing a community based and family-orientated service'. Implementation of the Act had begun in 1971. In 1974, local government (outside London) and the health service were further reorganised as a result of the NHS Reorganisation Act 1973 and the Local Government Act 1972. These successive and extensive reorganisations are directly referred to in at least eight of the twenty or so inquiries which followed Colwell up to 1981 (see DHSS, 1982: 3.42). The DHSS (1982: 3.43) observed that: 'Many of the problems of supervision, staffing, accommodation, etc., ... were judged by the inquiries to have arisen out of reorganisations.' These reorganisations, far from making the practice of social work any easier on the ground or the role of social services departments any clearer in policy terms, had actually engendered further uncertainty and ambiguity. For example, in September 1975, the Committee of Inquiry into the death of Susan Aukland (DHSS, 1975) felt it necessary to offer its own 'text book' definition of social work in the light of the 'impossibility' of trying to encapsulate all of those statutory functions with which it had become associated (31) (see also Barker, 1975):

> Our conception of the responsibility of social workers is to contribute to the prevention of personal distress by the early identification of need, to provide support and help to clients within their homes, to arrange, where necessary, day or residential care, and to intervene, within statutory powers, where the clients' own safety or that of others demands it.

Some four years later, in the case of Darryn Clarke ('Darryn Clarke Report', 1979), it is suggested that confusion in the minds of family members (and the police) over the role of social services departments in the investigation of child abuse may well have contributed to the delay which surrounded the boy's death. The Clarke Report notes (175):

> An appreciation of the complexities of the social worker's task is important to a clear understanding of the responsibility of SSDs for children, particularly children who are at risk of injury or neglect, for it is in this field that skill and experience is at a premium, legal requirements are precisely drawn and public concern most frequently focussed.

A *New Society* survey in August 1979 showed that even people who had had contact with social services departments did not know how social workers spent their time – 24 per cent thought that social workers allocated council houses (*New Society*, 2 August 1979). Much of the substance of the Aukland and Clarke reports as well as Colwell and many others up to and beyond the Beckford Inquiry (London Borough of Brent, 1985) go to extraordinary lengths to map out the operational domain and practices of social work, especially where these overlap with the practices of other professional and occupational groups (see DHSS, 1982; DOH, 1991). It is in these 'turf wars' that the nostrums of inter-agency working, mapped out in the Colwell Report, are developed and which formed the substantive policy outcomes of so many child death inquiries in the 1970s, 1980s and 1990s. (For a discussion on the use of such regulatory mechanisms on the further bureaucratisation of social work, see chapter 9.)

However, in the period following Colwell, the press did grow inexorably more strident in its criticism of social work (Golding and Middleton, 1982; Wroe, 1988), particularly after the 1979 General Election and confirmation of the political ascendancy of the New Right. According to Greenland (1986: 164), dragging 'the reputation of social workers through the mire of the gutter press' had become part of a 'peculiarly British sport of social worker baiting'. Indeed, the 'unduly vindictive and sensational' accounts of social work presented by the media, especially in relation to child abuse cases, were several times cited by the Barclay Report (NISW, 1982: paras. 3.61 and 11.28ff.) as one of the reasons why it had proved necessary for a Working Group to be established by the Secretary of State, Patrick Jenkin, to inquire into *Social Workers: Their Role and Tasks*. Some three years later, the Beckford Report (London Borough of Brent, 1985: 5) noted the 'background of often virulent press hostility ... unbridled media coverage of an unpleasant, harassing nature' against which social workers had given their evidence to the Inquiry. The Beckford Report went on to note that since

Colwell (p. 13): 'social workers have become the butt of every unthinking journalist's pen whenever a scapegoat was needed to explain a fatality or serious injury...It is the height of absurdity for the media, or indeed the public to castigate social workers'.

Little was to change in the reporting of the Inquiries into the deaths of Heidi Koseda (London Borough of Hillingdon, 1986), Kimberley Carlile (London Borough of Greenwich, 1987) and Tyra Henry (London Borough of Lambeth, 1987) which clustered after the Beckford case. But the distinction that we have made between proximate consequences and more remote causes is not an absolute one, in that the press (and, by implication, the public) attack on social work which continued, with occasional lulls, from Colwell right through to the Cleveland Inquiry (1988) was not bereft of ideological content.

Martin's meticulous account (1988) of the press reporting of the Beckford case and the 'trial of social work by the Fourth Estate' (p. 117) is in no doubt that (p. 129): 'the intensity and selectivity of the press response to those criticisms [of social work] is not wholly explicable as a rational commentary on the conduct of the social workers in the case or even of the state of the whole profession'. She sees (Martin, 1988: 128), as one might have anticipated, that: 'two particular sources of moral ambiguity and social anxiety found a kind of temporary exorcism through the press outrage against social work. These concern the family and the welfare state.' The particular configuration that these two monoliths of public policy have taken up at different points in more than three decades since Colwell is too complex a narrative to be adequately condensed here. In short, the period between Colwell and Beckford, was, for Barclay (1982: 7), 'an age of disappointment' as confidence in the State's capacity to care for children (amongst others) began to founder in the face of too many very public failures and ever-shrinking resources. Parton, in his later work (1990, 1991), sees 'a whole range of different critiques which were: developing in the polity' throughout the 1980s and 1990s (Parton, 1991: 195) which built on the loss of faith in social work and what it could achieve, the net effect of which was: 'to dent the confidence of social workers and to undermine the political and public support for social work in the area of childcare'. These 'different critiques' (including feminist analyses, particularly of violence in the home, and libertarian objections to bureaucratic and administrative discretion) were to strengthen the force of 'legalism' in the political economy of child care, and we are invited to see in the Children Act of 1989 'an attempt to construct a new set of political and professional balances whereby public confidence could be re-established' (Parton, 1991: 196).

Conclusion

The immediate fate of the Colwell Report was left to the newly elected Labour government to determine. Barbara Castle had replaced Sir Keith Joseph as Secretary of State at the DHSS and her reaction, reported in the *Times* (5 September 1974), might not have been shared by him:

> It is right that we should feel shocked and angry at the social conditions which breed the circumstances in which [Maria] lived and died. Social work alone cannot solve these underlying problems. We as a society must recognise the very heavy burdens we lay on those whom we delegate to look after nearly 100,000 children in local authority care. We need to understand the very real difficulties they face and we need to help them to prevent this kind of tragedy.

As we have indicated, the most easily discernible consequence of Colwell (and succeeding child care tragedies throughout the 1980s) was the proliferation of guidance to regulate the conduct of child protection practice (see, for example, DHSS, 1982 and chapter 8) and to articulate the ground rules for the management of child abuse cases. Whilst this may have worked for the good of children and young people, other effects on social work practice are more in doubt.

As far as individual social workers were concerned, Olive Stevenson, in reflecting on the Colwell Inquiry some five years later (Stevenson, 1979: 3), noted:

> We must at least acknowledge that the launching of an inquiry is like casting a huge stone in a pond. The ripples spread outward often involving many who did not expect it and more important, in ways that they did not anticipate. The emotional cost is very, very high and can only be justified if the inquiries appear to play a constructive part in protecting the lives of other children.

More generally, Hutchison (1986: 180) reported how social workers: 'aware of their vulnerability, became more cautious in their practice and now looked more to "covering themselves". It has even been suggested that immediately following Colwell, more children came into care as a result of this "defensive" practice.' Whatever the benefits or otherwise, as Jean Wall had indicated in her account of her experience as a witness at the Colwell Inquiry, the previously 'private' world of social work was now very firmly on the policy agenda and, through the medium of the Public Inquiry, has remained so until the present day.

But both Stevenson's and Hutchison's observations are reminders of the ostensible focus of the Colwell Inquiry, the abuse of children. We have suggested that in much of the administrative and policy response which followed Colwell, at least as far as the early 1990s (see chapter 9), child abuse was constructed largely in terms of something else – namely as an aspect of social work. In this way, although under different guises, what followed Colwell was similar to what had preceded it. Some important questions about the nature of the relationship between the family and the State have occasionally been able to intrude upon the public conscious-ness, all be they refracted through the distorting lens of the public press. But, with social work as the point of reference, focus has been retained on the institutional arrangements for managing abuse. In this way questions which bear on the structures in which abuse originates and by which it is sustained have been largely avoided. In particular, the question of the civil and social subordination and relative powerlessness of children which lies at the heart of child abuse has almost been displaced by the public and policy interest in those whom the State has appointed to serve their interests. This is made more understandable if one recognises that child abuse is signalled to the general public only in terms of the excep-tional and sensational. One might be forgiven for thinking that only a few children suffer and that this could relatively easily be prevented if only someone else did their job better.

The dynamics of this particular scandal – the struggle of the primary claims-makers to receive an account of a personally felt and very real tragedy; the subsequent colonisation of the space that they opened up by different claims-makers; the working out of a particular narrative through the engagement of competing personal and professional world views and the participatory observations of the local and national press – have all helped to shape the truths that the life and death of Maria Colwell has come to represent. However, in aggregating the child death inquiries of the 1970s, 1980s and 1990s to build yet another meta-narrative, we recognise the dangers that we have located in other accounts. The death of children has much more than iconic value. Each Public Inquiry has a unique story to tell of a unique life. In the scandalising of such events, the very private, personal and tragic essence of those lives can become obscured or even lost. Were they not, public policy in this field might have progressed quite differently.

6

'Mere Oblivion':
The Fate of the Institution and the Advent of Community Care

Last scene of all,
That ends this strange eventful history,
Is second childishness, and mere oblivion,
Sans teeth, sans eyes, sans taste, sans everything.
Shakespeare, *As You Like It*, II. vii. 163–6

Introduction

The Ely Hospital scandal marks a historic moment. It captured public attention in a way which produced a deep and lasting impact. The Inquiry team itself, in the conduct of its business and in the Report which it produced, set the standard for those which were to follow. The impact caused by the publication of the full Report was felt both in the way in which social policy-making was conducted and in the development of policy itself. The Report marked the point at which it became established in the public mind that, as Jones and Fowles (1984: 11) suggest, 'institutions ... do not cure deviant behaviour, they perpetuate it, gathering marginal people into tightly segregated groups and reinforcing their sense of alienation from the rest of the community.' Yet, Ely marked the start, rather than the end, of an avalanche of scandal in mental health institutions which was to last for nearly 15 years. The purpose of this chapter is to trace the history of mental health policy during this period and onwards to the New Labour government of 1997. This will be history, however, with a particular flavour. The account which follows here concentrates upon the interplay between social policy and scandal, employing three further concepts – scandal inflation, scandal fatigue and policy hegemony – in an attempt to cast fresh light upon the relationship between the two dimensions.

Immediately after Ely

When it became clear that conditions at Ely were already known at the Ministry of Health, Richard Crossman noted in his diary (1977: 411) that, 'I am pretty sure they have a shrewd idea that there are a great number of unspecified long-stay hospitals with conditions not very different from those at Ely.' Within a very short period of the Report being made public he was to return to the subject again when allegations were made about the treatment of patients at South Ockendon Hospital in Essex: 'One mustn't be surprised that if one takes the lid off other evil spirits appear and we should have known after Ely we were bound to have more trouble. But this has come pretty quickly and in a hospital that has just had £1 million spent on it and where there is a young and vigorous staff.'

It tells us something about the importance of the personal qualities of claims-makers in scandal when it emerges that one of the significant sources of pressure for a South Ockendon Inquiry came from Barbara Robb, the chairman of AEGIS whose character had been so deliberately called into question in the *Sans Everything* Reports. As the Diaries of Barbara Castle (1983: 85) Richard Crossman's Labour successor as Secretary of State at the DHSS, explain, Crossman refused an Inquiry in 1969 because, 'Brian A-S. [i.e. Professor Brian Abel-Smith, Crossman's adviser] tells me Dick felt it would be too disastrous for morale, coming on top of Ely'. However, as the Diaries continue, 'in March 1972, Miss Barbara Robb, chairman of AEGIS [Aid for Elderly in Government Institutions], launched a campaign for a statutory inquiry into the death three years earlier of Robert Robertson, a patient at South Ockendon Mental Hospital, which policy enquiries had failed to explain satisfactorily. She was also disturbed by more recent incidents. In this she was strongly supported by Professor Abel-Smith and I took the matter up in the House of Commons.' An Inquiry was set up by the then Conservative Secretary of State, Sir Keith Joseph. It fell to Mrs Castle to publish the Report which she described in her Diary on 23 April 1974 as, 'horrifying and fully justifies my pressure in the House about R.R.'s death – a pressure for which all the credit must go to Barbara Robb and Brian A-S.' The Diary records the many improvements which Mrs Castle thought had taken place at the hospital in the meantime, largely as a result of the changes which Crossman had introduced in the aftermath of Ely. The whole business came full circle, on 15 May 1974, when the South Ockendon Report was published on the day of Richard Crossman's memorial service.

Having spoken at the service Mrs Castle immediately:

> Hurried into the House to prepare for my South Ockendon statement and the lobby afterwards. Both went well. At Brian A-S's suggestion I've sent a special message (and included a tribute) to Barbara Robb. I never thought when Brian and I had lunch with her two years ago that I would be making the statement on the report for which she was so directly responsible.

Learning from Inquiries

It is outside the scope of this chapter to provide detailed accounts of all those Inquiries which were published between 1968 and 1980 and in which allegations of maltreatment of patients in mental illness and mental handicap hospitals were investigated. A total of 18 were published during this period, seven of which related to the aftermath of *Sans Everything*. Overall, 12 Inquiries were held at psychiatric hospitals and four at mental handicap hospitals. A further two were held at hospitals whose inpatient populations consisted mainly of mentally handicapped patients with a minority of mentally ill patients – one of these being a special hospital. Based largely on the work of Kirkpatrick and Feldman (1983), it is possible to draw together some general conclusions, before looking in more detail at a small number of particular aspects in four different Inquiries.

Firstly, as already suggested in the case of Mr Pantelides, the institutional Reports of this period reveal the extent to which scandals relied upon routes other than official complaints procedures to bring them to light. The seven *Sans Everything* Reports were the result of a pressure group, AEGIS. Four others followed media exposure; three were the result of police investigations into malpractices; two followed strike action by staff; two came about as a result of allegations sent to the Minister of Health and other official bodies. Finally, only one Inquiry followed allegations by members of staff that were sent to their local area health authority, in accordance with internal complaints mechanisms.

Secondly, the establishment of Inquiries suggests something of the tension which is created in responding to scandal by public bodies. The majority of Inquiries were established by the Secretary of State at central government level. Four inquiries were set up by the local area health authority. In a number of the most contentious cases, local arrangements were attempted but proved inadequate to the task of investigation. South Ockendon, and Normansfield are both cases in point, where national action had to be taken following the failure of local efforts.

Thirdly, following Ely, the membership of most Committees of Inquiry adhered to a standard pattern. Terms of reference, however, differed in individual cases, tending to veer towards the very general, such as Farleigh's – 'to enquire into the administration of and conditions at the hospital' – or the very specific such as the remit provided to the Darlington Memorial Hospital Inquiry – 'to enquire into … the circumstances … surrounding the deaths of four patients'. Kirkpatrick and Feldman (1983) suggest that Committees were capable of taking a very different approach from their terms of reference. Some were prepared to go beyond an apparently narrow brief when emerging evidence provided a case for doing so. Others refused to stray beyond the narrowest of remits, even where specific, but new, allegations – for example of ill-treatment of patients – appeared to provide a compelling case for doing so.

Fourthly, once established, Committees conducted their inquiries in contrasting ways. The majority – twelve – were held in private, while only four were held in public. Two did not hold formal hearings or call witnesses. These early decisions provide an essential frame within which Inquiries set about their most fundamental task, the establishment of a master-narrative.

Fifthly, the essential raw material for such a narrative was provided, in all cases, by the testimony of witnesses and the analysis of documents. Only 12 of the Inquiry reports provide information about the number of witnesses heard. They ranged from 41 to 145, with an average of 71 witnesses per inquiry. The vast majority were hospital staff, relatives and people from outside the hospital. Only three Inquiries interviewed inpatients at the hospital and two more took evidence from former patients. Other Inquiries discussed in this book will give rise to discussion of the approach which investigating Committees have adopted towards evidence provided by children. In the mental health Inquiries under consideration here, Committees uniformly took the view that, whether interviewed or not, little weight was to be placed upon the testimony of patients.

Finally, the length of Inquiries varied considerably. Eight lasted between four and ten months. Nine took around a year. One – Normansfield – took nearly two years. The scope of final Reports varied accordingly, from the one and a half pages in which allegations at Springfield Hospital were dismissed in the *Sans Everything* publication, to more than 464 pages required after Normansfield.

Generating scandal

None of the Inquiries which followed Ely, many of which were highly notorious at the time, have obtained its emblematic status. Yet Ely is distinguished neither by the nature of the events themselves, nor the charges at the base of them. Rather, for those which followed in its wake, ever-more strident claims had to be made in order to attract the public attention which is a basic and necessary component in scandal. Three strands, drawn from just two Inquiries, must suffice here to illustrate this general argument – the charges of routine callousness and poor nursing standards which formed a central focus of the Ely Inquiry, the allegations of petty pilfering investigated in the same Report, and the emerging findings of indifference, incompetence and neglect on the part of the medical and administrative authorities.

Ill-treatment

In terms of incidents of cruelty, the 1968 scandal at Farleigh Hospital in Somerset came to light when officers from the Somerset and Bath Constabulary were called to investigate serious allegations of ill-treatment of patients by male nurses. Ely had been negotiated without recourse to the Courts, although Public Record Office documents now show how closely that issue had been discussed and debated before being rejected. Scandal inflation suggests that in order for events to attract public attention, an element of novelty and a further twist in the ratchet of disquiet has to be added to the raw material. At Farleigh, nine nurses were charged with offences relating to cruelty of whom three, a deputy charge nurse, a staff nurse and a nursing assistant, were eventually convicted of a number of offences and imprisoned for a combined total of eight years.

The Committee itself heard evidence (Farleigh Inquiry, 1971: 19) from one charge nurse who 'stated categorically that there are instances and occasions when it is essential and necessary to hit a patient who is violent and who is attacking a member of the staff or another patient. He said he did not care how such actions were construed by others, as he was doing his job, and doing it properly. Such treatment, we were told, was frequently necessary.' Against such a background it is perhaps less surprising to find that a member of the public who took her complaints to the then Chairman of the House Committee at Farleigh was met with the answer that, at the end of a very long spell of duty, it was perhaps reasonable for a nurse with a very difficult patient to 'turn round and give a punch'. The Committee concluded: 'The impression we gained overall was that the group of trained nurses who had been at Farleigh for many years belonged to a distinctly tough minded school of thought, and were probably unnecessarily robust in their handling of the patients.'

At Whittingham (1972) the immediate origins of the Public Inquiry were rooted in a police investigation of allegations of ill-treatment of patients, victimisation and maladministration. These investigations had already been concluded when a male nurse assaulted two male patients at the hospital, one of whom died. The nurse was charged with murder and causing grievous bodily harm, convicted of manslaughter and imprisoned. Martin (1984: 182) describes Whittingham as 'the only inquiry of which it could be claimed that campaigning or investigative journalism played a significant part in bringing the problem into the open'. The local paper, the *Lancashire Evening Post*, hearing rumours of difficulty at the hospital, set up what its editor described as a 'press desk' at a local pub, collecting sufficient material to publish a 'Big Probe into Allegations of Cruelty' on 7 February 1970. This story produced a reaction which was mostly defensive of the hospital and supportive of the staff, described by the secretary of the Whittingham Branch of COHSE as 'the finest nurses in England bar none'. Following the June 1970 general election, the editor of the newspaper travelled to London to present his dossier to the new Secretary of State for Health, Sir Keith Joseph. While the manslaughter trial delayed the more general inquiry into the affairs of the hospital, the newspaper maintained its interest, to the extent that its editor was named 'Campaigning Journalist of the Year', in the IPC National Press Awards (Martin, 1984: 182).

The argument we are making here does not, of course, suggest that these were not real events, or in any sense manufactured for the purposes of scandal. What we do suggest is that in the shift from the old-fashioned and unsophisticated nursing techniques at Ely, through the cruelty at Farleigh, and on to the death of a patient at the hands of a nurse at Whittingham, the *claims-making* for scandal also altered. In competing for media attention, in attempting to convince a wider audience that events at Farleigh and Whittingham were genuinely *scandalous*, the escalating nature of these events was crucial.

Dishonesty

Allegations of dishonesty of a quite different scale and order to those at Ely were made in a number of Inquiries of the 1970s. At Whittingham, for example, the Inquiry Report traces a complete breakdown in financial control in which 'cigarettes were appropriated from patients and sold back to them at high prices'. There was a general collapse in the system of ward records for patients' money and a large discrepancy between the total amount of money issued to patients and the amount spent locally. The Committee were given evidence by a charge nurse who made detailed allegations about organised thefts of patients' money and went on to say, 'it is a common belief that anybody that does not co-operate in corruption does not succeed.'

The Group Secretary of the hospital, in giving evidence to the Inquiry, quoted the words of two very senior nurses, who were both convicted of stealing: 'You know, everybody at the hospital is in the racket ... just every-one.' [15] The Committee drew its own conclusions (Whittingham, 1972: 38): 'It is clear to us that the system has been so open to abuse that it would be virtually impossible for unscrupulous staff to resist their opportunities. The facts set before us point towards large scale pilfering, if not more organised corruption.'

Chapter 3 discussed the cognitive dissonance upon which scandal, par-ticularly within institutions, relies for much of its impact. While pilfering at Ely was petty, its scandalous impact was the product of the fact that *nurses* were engaged in such un-angelic conduct. The distance between the minor thieving at Ely and the organised corruption of Whittingham pro-vides a second example of scandal inflation. Now, in order to generate an impact, the construction of scandal required a far greater gap between appearance and reality than had been necessary in the earliest incidents.

Medical and administrative neglect

As to medical and administrative staff, three different sorts of com-plaints, all discernible in Ely, came to regular prominence in later Inquiries. In the first place, Reports commonly protested at the level of resources available for the care of patients. Whittingham's 2000 patients were served by only five consultants although as the Report suggested, 'because of outside commitments there are in reality fewer than three ... Even more disturbing is the fact that little more than the equivalent of one whole time consultant's services is devoted to care of the 86% who are the long stay.' The position of one consultant, who was expected to cope with 625 long-stay patients during one session per week, was described in the Report (Whittingham, 1972: 41) as 'deplorable and almost beyond belief'.

Secondly, such staff as were available were often of questionable calibre. The description of Dr Knappe at Farleigh is worth repeating at some length, as the Report relies upon the cumulative detail of its account, rather than any more explicit assessment, to make its impression on the reader:

> Dr Knappe ... took a very restricted view of his duties ... His notes on patients' behaviour were unsophisticated and less revealing than

those of the nurses. He apparently last attended an outside course in 1958 ... Dr Knappe was closely questioned by the Committee about any wider interests he might have had in the activities of the hospital and the welfare of the patients. He said he had no knowledge of the training or practice of nurses in restraint. He had never been asked to advise on the use of mechanical restraint and could not say whether any changes in practice had taken place in Farleigh or elsewhere ...

He never saw any signs of ill treatment or cruelty during his 12 years at the hospital, and never received any complaints in this regard from either patients or relatives. He did not consider that it was within his province to concern himself with matters such as whether patients had private possessions, or visits from relatives. He only occasionally saw a relative ...

Dr Knappe did not know how patients on North Ward spent their day, nor had he inquired, as he considered this a nursing problem. He said he had nothing to do with nursing. He said he had nothing to do with the environment of Wards, and he did not make any recommendations if the wards seemed unsatisfactory for the treatment of patients. In fact he said he did not make recommendations about anything.

The benign neglect of Dr Cyril Wyn Jenkins at Ely was thus now replaced by a more culpable indifference and failure to discharge basic professional care.

Below managerial level, the Reports reveal a pattern of complaint about staff shortage and calibre of nursing personnel which would have been familiar to any Victorian Commissioner. At Farleigh, the chief nursing officer was so pressed that he employed two nurses who, two years earlier, had been dismissed for misconduct at a nearby hospital in an incident which the Report describes as 'cruel and sordid'. Both men were amongst those later arrested by police. At Whittingham it emerged that the ward around which many of the most serious allegations revolved had, until September 1969, been under the charge of a sister who, as the Report records, 'had served in the Ward continuously for no less than 47 years – ever since her qualification as a trained nurse, when methods of care in mental hospitals were very different. The deputy was an enrolled nurse from the continent who had never received any formal training or instruction and served on the Ward for 11 years.' Ely had contained a cast of ward-level staff who were clearly unsuitable for the tasks required of them. Professional isolation was a pervasive feature of the institution. Yet, the picture of physical and professional isolation which Ely had painted was, once again, writ larger in the Inquiries which followed. This phenomenon of scandal inflation reached its furthest point in events at Normansfield Hospital at Middlesex, to which this chapter now turns.

Normansfield

Normansfield Hospital was established in 1868, during the age of Victorian alienists described in chapter 2. Its founder was a Doctor Langdon-Down, after whom Down's Syndrome came to be called. At its outset, Normansfield was a model institution, designed to provide that separate but self-sufficient system of care for the mentally handicapped. Thus, on its greenfield site, in addition to wards and other accommodation, it contained a school, a church, a farm and a miniature theatre at which, a hundred years later, the original sets of the Gilbert and Sullivan operetta *Ruddigore* were found whole and intact. The original Dr Langdon-Down retired in 1901, handing control of the institution to his son. In one of those startling asides with which Public Inquiry reports are regularly studded, we learn that the Committee, during a visit, more than a century after the hospital's foundation, were introduced to a by-now very elderly lady who had been admitted to the hospital in 1898, by the original Physician Superintendent. In 1951, Normansfield was brought within the newly established National Health Service. By that time, the fabric of the institution already shared the physical decline which was characteristic of the Victorian asylum inheritance. It was, said the Inquiry, 'singularly ill-suited to modern concepts of the care of the mentally handicapped' (p. 25).

Dr Lawlor

By the time the third generation of Langdon-Downs had retired in 1970, the hospital had been continuously, since its foundation, under the control of the same family. It marked a sharp point of new departure in the history of an institution which had, until then, been characterised by a rather genteel decline and a benign paternalism. The single greatest cause of change was the appointment of a new Consultant Psychiatrist, Dr Lawlor. Although this was to be the only consultant post at Normansfield, the change of title was deliberately chosen. It signalled a move away from the single authority of a Medical Superintendent, in favour of a more team-based, multidisciplinary approach. A full appreciation of the Lawlor character and regime can only be obtained from a close reading of the Inquiry Report. Here it will have to suffice to say that Dr Lawlor proved to be an individual whose distrust of his fellow workers produced severe distortions in his own behaviour and profound difficulties in his relationships with others. Such was the scale of these difficulties that, during his tenure of office, he was made subject, in 1972, to the *Three Wise Men* procedure of the NHS, in which, as the Report puts it (p. 54) a doctor can be examined by three senior fellow clinicians, 'in order to ascertain whether by reason of physical or mental illness he was a danger to his patients.' In Dr Lawlor's case, the three doctors concluded that (p. 89): 'We believe that in view of the complaints made, as a result of our recent discussion with him, and in view of his demeanour at meetings of the Group Medical Advisory Committee, that Dr Lawlor may be suffering from a mental illness.' A further interview with an independent Consultant Psychiatrist found no evidence of any mental illness such as a paranoid psychosis and, as the Report (p. 89) puts it, 'His mental condition having been thus vouchsafed, Dr Lawlor remained in post at Normansfield. There was no marked or sustained change in his behaviour or attitude.'

What is certainly true is that Dr Lawlor's tenure produced a rapid deterioration in the conduct of the hospital. In an interesting example of the way in which scandals produce unintended consequences, Dr Lawlor was an avid reader of Reports into events at other mental institutions. In his statement of evidence to the Normansfield Inquiry he explained 'how he was "affected" by previous Inquiries, in particular the Inquiries at Ely Hospital, Farleigh Hospital and Whittingham Hospital' (p. 271). The impact of these Reports was further and further to restrict the range of activities in which he was prepared for Normansfield patients to take part, and the conditions under which even that limited participation might be conducted. 'Whenever a Report was published', the Normansfield Inquiry concluded, 'Dr Lawlor's preoccupation with the possibility of an accident increased ... A single misfortune in a hospital elsewhere in the country set off precautionary reactions on Dr Lawlor's part which were disproportionate to the real risks involved and were, more often than not, counterproductive' (p. 45).

Nor was his conduct of his office affected only by formal scandals of this sort. At an early stage of the Inquiry hearings, it became clear that he had imposed severe restrictions on patient outings at Normansfield, 'because he had read in a newspaper that a visitor to a safari park had been mauled by a lion' (p. 58). Dr Lawlor, presumably anxious at the prevalence of lions in the confectionery trade, thereafter forbade the long-established practice in which Normansfield patients had been allowed to visit a sweet shop just outside the grounds. As the Report puts it, thereafter, 'even a brief visit by patients in the company of nurses or teachers to the local sweet shop which did not necessitate crossing a main road (in itself a source of intense anxiety to him) needed his written approval on each occasion' (p. 45).

The sweet-shop edict was only a very small example in the changed nature of the Normansfield regime. Dr Lawlor's most significant drawback as a Consultant Psychiatrist was to be found in his intense dislike and distrust of nurses. In some of the staff at his disposal, and in some of the standards of nursing practice, the Inquiry makes it clear that he had grounds for concern. Strikingly, in terms of the case made in this book for the impact of landmark scandals, a Nursing Officer from the Department of Health and Social Security, who visited Normansfield in September 1975, described the state of nursing there as 'the gravest she had encountered since she had reported on Ely Hospital about eight years earlier' (p. 252). One case will have to stand as an example of the general state of relations between Dr Lawlor and his senior nursing staff, in particular. The Report records, in vivid detail, the particular feud in which he became engaged with an individual staff member, Nursing Officer Daphne Truman. In the early part of Dr Lawlor's tenure, both were leading figures in the organisation of the Normansfield staff club, he as its Chairman, she as its Secretary. Here their already abrasive relationship had ample opportunities for deterioration. To provide just two examples: in early 1973 Mrs Truman, acting as Secretary, wrote a letter to Dr Lawlor, 'requiring him to present himself before the Club Committee to answer a charge of causing a disturbance there' (p. 214), a course of action which he regarded as 'provocative and gratuitously insulting' (p. 214). A different sort of charge overtook Nursing Officer Truman herself when, in April 1974 she appeared – in the company of another senior nurse – on trial at Maidstone Crown Court, the petty pilfering at Ely and the organised corruption at Whittingham having, by this stage, become the subject of police attention at other institutions. Mrs Truman was accused of misappropriation of funds belonging to the Staff Club. She believed – wrongly, the Report concludes – that her arrest had been at the instigation of Dr Lawlor, an impression which he 'did little to disabuse her of' (p. 215) and which, not unnaturally, produced in her 'a lasting and smouldering resentment on that account'.

When both Nursing Officer Truman and Nursing Officer Smith were acquitted in January 1975, Dr Lawlor 'categorically refused to acquiesce in any decision which would allow her to return to patient care' (p. 216).

She was, as a result, 'forbidden to go on to the wards' (p. 250). The Normansfield solution was to appoint her to responsibility for 'personnel and in-service training' (p. 216), a capacity in which Dr Lawlor thereafter 'treated her with manifest contempt' (p. 214).

In this text we have argued, generally, that scandals at institutions are insidious affairs, in which long-term malpractices and corruptions of care break through the surface and are exposed to public view. While this was true of Normansfield, the precipitating event which produced disclosure – a strike by the nursing staff – was far more directly framed in terms of scandal by those who took part in it. Scandal production, scandal avoidance and the consequences of scandal for individuals and the institution itself were categorically discussed by leading protagonists and used as bargaining and threatening tools between them. Dr Lawlor, for example in his attempts to undermine the power of the Union, COHSE, suggested to one of his antagonists – a nursing officer – that, unless he assisted in promoting resignations from the Union, 'the information...would be given to the National Newspapers and scandal would develop' (p. 463).

Strike action

The connection between scandal and drama has already been explored on a number of occasions in this text. In the case of the Normansfield strike the Report itself adopts this approach directly in the account it assembles. Its treatment begins with a section titled 'the absent joiner', which describes the position of the leading Union official at the hospital. In it, the Report authors link the deplorable state of repair at Normansfield to the multiplicity of political, union and civic duties undertaken by the carpenter concerned. Thereafter, the text proceeds in classical fashion, by imposing a sense of chronological and intellectual order on a process which, in the accounts of those from which it is drawn, is always partial, error-strewn and which describes events which they uniformly regard as chaotic. By this time, as the Report sets out, the atmosphere at the hospital, and particularly that between Dr Lawlor and senior nursing staff, had become belligerent, provocative, angry and intimidatory. A vying for control was underway, in which accusation and counter-accusation were part of everyday encounters, conducted in front of staff, patients and visitors alike. By April 1976 nursing officers were refusing to meet with Dr Lawlor, unless accompanied by another member of staff. A series of attempts to bring the seriousness of the situation at the hospital to area and regional officials appeared to have little or no effect. In the same month a regular meeting of COHSE was – 'quite improperly', the Report notes (p. 318) – converted into an impromptu Annual General Meeting. A new chair was elected. Mr Vethanayagam is described in the Report as a 'quiet young man with a limited command of English' (p. 318). He was, the authors conclude, a 'puppet' in the hands of more powerful players. His deputy continued to be a Mrs Selby, a 'veteran vicechair' who, over her years in office' had become 'somewhat hard of hearing' (p. 318).

Into this atmosphere of escalating militancy was propelled the area's full-time COHSE official, Michael Somers. Normansfield is a Report which is notably short of heroes, although some exist amongst the more minor characters who do not make their way into the very truncated account provided here. The lack of heroes is made good, however, by a surfeit of villains, of whom Dr Lawlor is the most florid, but Mike Somers the one who attracts the particular disapprobation of the Inquiry team. He was, we are told, an 'ambitious young man' (p. 320) whose qualifications in labour relations at the University of Barcelona were to be put to good use in translating proceedings for the benefit of a group of Spanish cleaners who attended the final strike meeting. To health service management, and to the Inquiry itself, Mr Somers presented himself as 'confronted by a band of militants determined to strike' (p. 321) and over whom he struggled manfully to exercise a degree of control and restraint. To the union members he provided a source of eloquent encouragement in their growing anger and impatience, counselling against half-measures and propounding the advantages of bringing matters decisively to a head. As this challenging balancing act unravelled Mr Somers became, the Report concludes, a 'victim of his own conceit' (p. 321). His version of events, in which he was regularly at odds with almost all other major actors, was one which the Inquiry came to regard as not in the least convicing (p. 321).

The account provided of the strike meeting itself is essential reading for anyone interested in developing the necessary skills of deconstructing the text of Public Inquiries, separating the commentary which is so often implied in even the most apparently straightforward text. Spread over several hours, in order to accommodate the shift work patterns of COHSE members, conducted in different languages in order to meet the requirements of over 80 participants, chaired by more than one individual, the meeting was the subject of much dispute between those who provided evidence to the Inquiry. In Mr Somers' account, he wrung a 24-hour concession from a staff body hell-bent on strike action, in which he was to negotiate for the suspension of Dr Lawlor from his position at the hospital. In the accounts of others, the meeting was far more equivocal at the outset in its attitude towards industrial action, but swayed in that direction by the leadership provided by their full-time official. The volunteer organiser at the hospital, a Mrs Mott, recorded her impressions of the meeting in her diary:

> Mr Somers from COHSE was most eloquent. He made it clear to the members the points ... After the meeting he would go to the area if we voted him to and tell them to suspend Lawlor from now on. If they did not, or allowed him back before or after the enquiry, we would all *walk out.*
>
> He said this was the only way. No pussy-footing around. He managed to convince almost all the members ...
>
> How wonderful.

On the following day the Area Health Authority, by chance, was holding one of its regular meetings. The nature of events at Normansfield had sufficiently communicated themselves to the meeting to produce a pro- posal for action, which the Authority agreed. The complaints received were to be submitted to an Inquiry, set up by the Authority, but held in public. Mike Somers presented himself at the Health Authority and, although not allowed to address the meeting itself, met with a number of its members. He put the request for Dr Lawlor's suspension. Members replied that the Authority did not have the power to accede to the request and asked for more time to consider it. Mr Somers telephoned Mrs Truman, one of the most dedicated of Dr Lawlor's opponents, and informed her that the Authority had decided not to suspend, refusing their request.

The evening was spent in successive telephone calls between hospital staff and union officials, in which the Health Authority's response became more and more regarded as intransigent and provocative. An ad hoc meeting of night staff, and such others as could be summonsed, followed during the early hours of the morning. A move to immediate strike action was defeated, but a decision taken to place pickets at the hospital gate before 6 a.m. and to instigate a strike of day staff from 7 a.m. onwards.

Thus came about the only instance in the history of the National Health Service in which nurses abandoned their wards, leaving some very vulnerable patients without the care upon which their physical survival depended. The situation, according to the Report, was one 'fraught with danger', causing 'extreme risk to health and safety of patients' (p. 350).

At 10 a.m. a meeting was called, designed to take some of the heat out of the situation, and to produce at least a better level of emergency nursing cover. Informed, however, that there was no guarantee that Dr Lawlor would voluntarily agree not to attend the hospital, the position escalated and even those few nurses who had been allowed to go onto the wards to dispense essential drugs were withdrawn. Faced with this rapidly worsening picture, the Authority Chairman, Lady Robson, delaying her departure for the House of Lords, agreed shortly before 1 o'clock that Dr Lawlor should be suspended. Even then, a further hour and a half elapsed before he was informed of the decision, and it was not until 3.45 in the afternoon that the outcome was communicated to staff at Normansfield, and the strike called off.

Claims-making and Normansfield

In the immediate aftermath of the strike Dr Lawlor moved quickly to produce his own counter-claims-making, asserting – with the support of his own professional association and some national newspapers – that he had been victimised because of his determination to expose nurse cruelty at the hospital. In doing so, in the terms adopted here, he thus attempted to attach himself to the tide of scandal inflation in which ever-more extravagant examples of nursing iniquity appeared to emerge in successive institutional scandals. His success in all this was summarised by the Inquiry in this way (p. 365):

> So an impression gained currency that a dedicated Consultant had detected ill-treatment at his hospital, had made an issue of it and had been punished for his pains by concerted action on the part of the nurses who sought to protect themselves from further exposure of their wrong-doing by bringing about his suspension.

The extent of this currency went far beyond the local or general press. The Inquiry Report devotes nearly six closely evidenced pages in tracing the determination with which Dr Lawlor and his allies propagated his version of events. Molotch and Lester (1974: 107) argue that 'news assemblers' (by which they mean the newspapers and other media) 'commonly act upon the assumption that those with official authority are the most newsworthy'. Thus, within the professional press and beyond, for a time, it became accepted as an uncontentious fact that Dr Lawlor had been the victim of union militancy, fomented in order to distract attention from nursing abuse. A letter to that effect was sent to the Secretary of State by the Chairman of the Council of the BMA (of which body Dr Lawlor was not a member) on 7 October 1976. On 19 October the Joint Consultants,

Committee passed a resolution, condemning the suspension of Dr Lawlor, on the grounds, as the *Doctor* magazine reported in its leading article on 21 October 1976, that he had been 'suspended from duties in May for seeking an inquiry into unexplained injuries to his mentally subnormal patients' (p. 367).

In the event, the Inquiry itself uncovered a very different picture. It was Dr Lawlor's own practice which came in for detailed criticism, his prescribing habits described by the medical experts employed by the Committee as exposing some patients to unnecessary risk and, in one case, 'actual and unnecessary harm' (p. 55), his unlicensed experiments involving the forced starvation of overweight patients condemned as 'unethical' and 'unlawful'. As to the allegations of unexplained injuries, these were, the Inquiry concluded, 'wholly inaccurate' and had played no part in bringing about the strike. In this, and a wide range of other matters, the Inquiry's judgement of Dr Lawlor was straightforward and succinct (p. 49):

> Dr Lawlor showed himself to be a liar. He did not scruple to mislead us when he thought his own interests might be serviced by doing so…His adroit and frequently malicious use of words to conceal rather than reveal his true opinions took time to penetrate. But in the end, he was exposed as both untruthful and unreliable.

The Normansfield Inquiry team's recommendations in relation to those whose actions it was called to adjudicate upon was equally forceful. Less than a decade earlier, the Ely Report had gone to great lengths to conceal the identities of staff and patients and, dealing with incidents of palpable professional malpractice, had proved noticeably charitable in its treatment of them. Assistant Chief Nurse Edwards, so vividly described in action by Mr Pantelides, was described, in that Report's conclusions, as an individual who still had much to offer the health service. In the case of Normansfield, as we have seen, the Report was not preoccupied directly with charges of nurse cruelty. Yet, in dealing with the cast of senior staff, its proposals were bleak. It amply illustrated Peay's (1996b: 25) contention that, 'There can be little doubt that the Inquiry is a powerful means of labelling behaviour as good or evil and creating a forum for shaming'. Of the four Nursing Officers, two – including Mrs Truman – had already resigned from the health service. Neither, the Report said, should ever be re-engaged. The other two were deemed to be 'not fit to hold the post of Nursing Officer and should not be employed at Normansfield in any capacity' (p. 224). The Senior Nursing Officer was, the Report concluded, 'not fitted to hold the post'. His appointment 'should be terminated' and 'he should not be re-employed at Normansfield in any capacity' (p. 235). The Divisional Nursing Officer, who was not based at the hospital and whose duties, as the Report concedes, 'extended beyond Normansfield', faced the same fate. 'We feel compelled to RECOMMEND that his appointment as Divisional Nursing Officer be terminated. He is not at present fitted to hold the post of Divisional Nursing Officer. He should not be re-employed in any capacity which would involve responsibility for Normansfield' (p. 243). The Report's passion for the purifying effect of staff purgation did not even end there. Dealing with the most senior nurse with any responsibility for Normansfield, the Area Nursing Officer, the Report traces that individual's long and distinguished previous career, recording the fact that, in the period between the strike and the publication of the Report, she had retired from the profession. Its conclusion, however, was unswerving:

> she had no nursing policy for Normansfield as such. She set no objectives ... By her omissions she contributed substantially to the continuing neglect of patients at the hospital ... A substantial degree of blame for the state of affairs at the hospital must be laid at her door ... Had she not retired we would have recommended her dismissal (p. 254).

As to Dr Lawlor, the Report (p. 135) had already reached two clear conclusions. He was 'in serious breach of contract and duty and there are substantial reasons therefore to

Recommend that:

(1) Dr Terence Lawlor's contract as Consultant Psychiatrist in Subnormality at Normansfield Hospital be terminated forthwith.

(2) Dr Terence Lawlor be not re-engaged in any capacity in the National Health Service.'

On all three counts of cruelty, dishonesty and professional misconduct, Normansfield contained material which transformed the rather restrained and sober world of Ely to something far more surreal. Scandal had been inflated here to its limits and beyond. The Report which followed was infected by the same qualities. Ely had set new standards for thoroughness and determination in the conduct of its Inquiry. The losing battle to prevent publication of the full, 167-page, 80,000-word account of the Committee's findings had preoccupied Whitehall for many months in 1968 and 1969. By the time of Normansfield, the Inquiry itself had become a matter of dispute. Attempts by the Regional Hospital Authority to set up an independent inquiry came to grief amongst demands for a full Public Inquiry and the refusal of Dr Lawlor himself to cooperate with the Authority's arrangements. In a sequence of events which was to be repeated in the case of the Pindown Inquiry (see chapter 9), the Secretary of State intervened and, on 3 February 1977, appointed a Public Inquiry under Section 70 of the National Health Service Act 1948. The Inquiry team reported on 19 July 1978, more than 18 months later, and more than two years after the strike had taken place. By that time, as the Report makes clear, 'we were engaged for 124 days hearing the evidence, we visited the hospital on several occasions, we examined no less than 11,000 documents and records, heard 145 witnesses and read the statements of many others. There were 14,856 pages of transcribed evidence' (p. 3).

The end of the line for scandal?

In many ways, Normansfield represents the end of the line for major institutional scandals in the field of mental health. The gargantuan scale of the Report defied any further efforts to establish scandal-by-size. Public appetite for simple repetition of previously exposed discreditable conduct or disgraceful conditions was strictly limited. Tumber (1993: 50) suggests that, in media terms, 'scandal stories ... help to fulfil the audience-building strategies of the press'. By the time of Normansfield, the repetitive nature of such stories had ceased to meet such a purpose. In these conditions, even those most closely involved began to show signs of a second phenomenon with which this chapter is concerned – *scandal fatigue*. Tidmarsh (1997: 1) quotes Inskip and Edwards who had, respectively, conducted Inquiries at South Ockendon and St Augustine's Hospitals as writing:

> Major hospital inquiries burn up money that is desperately needed to improve the health service, disrupt the work of the hospital, and often have a devastating effect on individual and group morale, leaving in their wake a legacy of corrosive bitterness. They should be avoided wherever possible.

The scandal fatigue which set in during the 1970s was not simply a product of the unvaried diet of the events which successive Inquiries uncovered. Declining faith in the output, as well as the input of official

Reports, was significant in diminishing the part which scandal played during these years. When Eastman (1995) called for an uncoupling of the 'explanatory and disciplinary purposes' of Inquiries he was dealing with the mental health scandals of the 1990s which form the focus of the next chapter. However, the same criticism could have been levelled directly at Normansfield which, for all its efforts, produced an outcome which concentrated very largely on the *what* of scandal – its attempt to piece together an account of events – rather than the *why* of what had taken place. Its concluding prescriptions dealt rigorously with the disciplinary side of its remit, while leaving to one side what Peay (1996a: 7) describes as the 'more inaccessible issues of resources and management strategies'. Perhaps this is not altogether surprising. As earlier chapters have shown, the promise upon which Public Inquiries in social welfare are almost always launched is that, in this way, scandalous events 'will never happen again'. In practice, as inquiry followed inquiry, such a purpose proved unfulfilled and unfulfillable. In this text, we are interested in the ways in which the raw materials of scandal are ignited into something beyond themselves, and in the process by which that ignition results in the application of a Public Inquiry. The apparent failure of Inquiries to bring about improvement in the conditions of institutional care added to a sense of fatigue in the whole public engagement with these questions. Scandal inflation had exhausted itself in ever more flamboyant attempts to ignite interest in events described. Disillusionment with the consequences as well as causes of scandal added to a fatigue in which Public Inquiries were discarded as a method of response. Yet, even while the salience of scandal in this field was diminishing, it was on the rise again in a different dimension of social welfare. In child care, as chapter eight will demonstrate, interest in scandals involving children and social work was beginning to brew again, with a further crop of Inquiries to follow.

One final brief example serves to summarise the position which had been reached 15 years after Ely had taken place. In 1983, at St David's Hospital in Carmarthen, the local branches of the health workers' unions, published a report – *A Suitable Case for Treatment* – which, in the details of patient conditions and medical and administrative practices, would have been instantly recognisable to anyone involved in the Ely Inquiry. The two hospitals lay only some 60 miles apart, yet, in the reactions which followed, were at polar ends of the scandal and policy spectrum. If Ely is widely remembered both within the professional community and beyond, St David's has passed almost entirely from view. Indeed, even at the time, the public attention which allegations at St David's attracted was confined to brief and local notoriety. While Ely was resolved through a Public Inquiry, in which the Minister was directly involved at all crucial stages, the St David's allegations were pursued without any form of outside inquiry at all. Rather, the Hospital Advisory Service, the establishment of which had been one of the most direct consequences of Ely, was rapidly drafted in to investigate. Its report was described by Martin (1984: 61) as 'scathing' and largely bore out all the allegations which had been made. Yet, public reaction was short-lived and lacking in intensity. As Ridley (1988: 294) suggests, many affairs may seem scandalous to those most directly interested, 'but if they arouse little public indignation, they lack the particular driving force of a scandal'. That force was conspicuously absent in the case of St David's. As a result, the Secretary of State, far from inaugurating a policy response on an Ely scale, replied that it was not his intention to reward the poor performance of the hospital by bailing it out with additional resources in the form of cash or attention. And there the scandal ended, a last and feeble gasp in a series which had exhausted both itself and its public.

Policy development

The single most significant impact which scandal produced upon mental health policy during the years after Ely lay in the impetus it continued to provide to drive towards care in the community. Reform from within institutions appeared ever more unlikely. All the Goffmanesque critique had seemed to have been borne out at hospitals where every aspect of patients' lives were subsumed to the needs of the institution and placed under the unchallengeable authority of all-powerful staff members. At Whittingham, for example, the Committee found that, while the hospital had a nominal policy of unrestricted visiting on any day, and at any hour, in practice it was only possible to visit on Saturday, Sunday and Wednesday afternoons between 2 and 4.30 p.m. At the same hospital, conditions also illustrated the way in which institutional care militated against the prospects of recovery and reintegration. The Whittingham Inquiry were told that any attempt to employ social workers had been abandoned, because of the impossibility 'of getting applications'. As a result, one full-time untrained social worker carried the responsibility for the financial and personal problems of some 1,900 patients. By contrast, the hospital employed no less than 26 gardeners and groundsmen.

It is against this background that some brief account is needed of the way in which community care policy principles were translated into practice during the 1970s and 1980s. Richard Crossman, who had set up the Ely Inquiry and was heavily involved in its aftermath, had set in train within the DHSS a national plan to develop services for the mentally handicapped. It had reached the stage of a draft White Paper in 1970 when a general election was called. The incoming Conservative administration, with Sir Keith Joseph now Secretary of State at the DHSS, published the document almost unamended in March 1971, with the title *Better Services for the Mentally Handicapped*. As a policy document it was firmly in what has been called the 'central rationalist model' (Glennerster et al., 1983), a centrally directed social policy setting out goals over a 20-year period in which central government was – through spending allocations, encouragement and inspection – to implement its intentions by its own actions and through those of others in this case, principally, the new Social Services Departments of local authorities.

Despite the fact that, at the time, as Bayley (1973: 9) puts it, the White Paper was seen to 'mark a decisive switch from care out of the community to care in the community', actual progress towards that goal under the *Better Services* plan was modest. An incoming Labour administration in 1974, with Barbara Castle now Secretary of State, established a new National Development Group for the Mentally Handicapped and a number of other initiatives, designed to speed up progress. She was also responsible for a further White Paper in the field of mental illness, *Better Services for the Mentally Ill*, published in 1975 and characterised by Freeman (1998: 232) as 'the definitive White Paper'. The background to it, as the same author makes clear, was to be found in the additional resources which had been made available to the mental health services since the Ely Inquiry. Freeman's (1998: 234) figures show that between 1970 and 1975, psychiatric doctors and nurses employed by the NHS increased by 31 per cent and clinical psychologists by 64 per cent. Despite this, *Better Services for the Mentally Ill* gave expression to some of the frustration felt in policymaking circles at the slow progress which had been made towards deinstitutionalisation since the idea had first gained currency during the 1950s:

> although it is sixteen years since the Mental Health Act of 1959 gave legislative recognition to the importance of community care, supportive services in a non-medical, non-hospital setting are still a comparative rarity. In 1973–74 nearly £300 million was spent on hospital services for the mentally ill; by comparison just over £15 million was spent on personal social services of which some £6.5 million was spent on day and residential facilities. In March 1974, 31 local authorities, as then constituted, had no residential accommodation for the mentally ill, and 63 no day facilities.

The White Paper thus identifies a key policy issue which was to remain unresolved in the whole of the community care period – that of eliminating, or at least eroding, the boundary between health and social services. The separation between hospital-based medical care and community-based social care created a series of border zones – financial, professional and geographical – all of which militated against a smooth transfer of responsibilities. Financially, the balance of expenditure remained heavily weighted in favour of hospitals. This imbalance was further reflected within the field. Community-based services were to be provided by the new, unified Seebohm social services departments. The result, in Jones' (1983) suggestion, was that, 'integration of services often meant the disintegration of mental health provision' as mental health generally fared badly with the competition for resources within the combined social services.

Professionally, the medical establishment within mental health services were far from unanimous in wholeheartedly embracing the new imperatives. Hospitals, as the Normansfield experience so vividly illustrated, were capable of remaining the personal fiefdoms of their leading clinicians. If the sharing of power and responsibility *within* institutions had proved highly problematic, the cooperative and power-diffused set of relations demanded in working between services was even more so. Jones (1983) goes as far as to suggest that, most psychiatrists regarded change as disastrous for their work. From a social services perspective, too, the relationship was not an easy one. The anti-psychiatry critique of the 1960s and 1970s had been influential in parts of social work and the rights-based movement which was more generally felt in social welfare (Haines and Drakeford, 1998) was to be found in mental health, also.

The accelerating pace of change which was characteristic of the 1980s, therefore, has to find some additional explanation beyond the fact that existing plans were coming more rapidly to fruition. The facts of acceleration are plain enough, as hospitals were run down by reducing the numbers of people contained within them and then by shutting some altogether. Between 1986 and 1993, the number of patients in large hospitals halved from an average of 468 to 223 patients per hospital. In the decade 1980–90, 35 of the Enoch Powell 'water-tower' hospitals closed and by 1993 a further 89 were designated for closure. In the process, the number of beds in traditional institutions for mentally ill people fell by 36 per cent, from 96,350 in 1978 to 61,500 in 1993.

The essential explanation for this new pace of change is political and ideological. The reforms of the 1960s and 1970s were broadly bipartisan in nature. The advent of the Thatcher administrations in 1979 brought a different way of thinking to social welfare in which reductions in public expenditure and a 'rolling back of the state' combined to add a new edge to the assault on institutions. The physical state of the Victorian asylums made their upkeep resource-intensive. Their occupation of large, greenfield sites in what, through urban spread, had often become prime building land, also made their sale a potential source of substantial capital receipts. In their still near-monopoly supply of mental health services, such institutions also offended against the New Right's policy preferences for a dissolution of the power of the professions and a new pluralism in the supply of welfare goods and services. The reaction of the Tory Secretary of State, Nicholas Edwards, to events at St David's Hospital, described earlier, was based not simply upon scandal exhaustion but also upon an ideological determination that a mixed economy of community care was preferable to state-provided institutional solutions.

During the 1960s and 1970s, the grip which asylum-based policies had exercised over the provision of mental health services finally came to an end. The combination of left-leaning critiques and right-wing policy preferences meant that, during the 1980s, the community care approach had achieved the status of a policy hegemony. In their place a new certainty had closed over the surface of policy debate and disputation. 'Care in the community' had become a slogan from which few were willing to dissent. Tidmarsh (1995: 1), for example, draws attention to concerns about homicides by psychiatric patients which had been expressed as early as 1982 before concluding that 'incidents continued but public, or more accurately political, attitudes were slow to change'. The formal landmark of the policy was finally achieved in the 1990 NHS and Community Care Act, a crucial piece of legislation which provided a further endorsement of community care principles across a wide spectrum of need, of which mental health and learning disabilities – as they had come to be known – were only a part. The Act established a series of key principles:

- that local authorities were to be given the lead responsibility in provision of services which were to straddle the health and social services divide.
- that such services were to be provided, for the most part, from within the private, voluntary and independent sectors, rather than directly by local authorities themselves.
- that local authorities were to be placed under a duty to assess individual needs and then manage those packages of care which would enable people to live at home.

Taken together, the Act provided a new framework in which non-institutional provision was to be promoted and, it was claimed, a reality finally made of the community care ambitions.

Scandal and policy hegemony

Chapter 3 argued that landmark scandals take place at a time of policy flux, and particularly when the established order of a previous period may be giving way to new priorities and imperatives. Conversely, scandals in social welfare are far more difficult to establish at a time when particular approaches exercise a firm grip over policy-making. It is very important to emphasise that this is not to argue that the raw material for scandal is not occurring all the time. Rather it is to draw attention to the impact which an absence of precipitating conditions can produce upon the attempt to draw attention to this raw material and to make a claim for its scandalous condition. The next chapter will begin by exploring just such an event which took place during the middle years of the 1980s. In order to prepare the ground for that discussion, and for an understanding of policy changes of the 1990s, it is necessary to end here with an account of those issues which, during the 1980s, had begun to bubble to the surface of community care.

Even during times of policy hegemony, dissenting and questioning voices are to be discovered, submerged beneath the dominant discourse. Chapter 2 drew attention to the non-institutional practices which, even in Victorian times, were attempted in relation to the mentally ill. In just the same way, community care also attracted critical comment, from the outset. Titmuss (1963: 223), for example, had argued from the beginning that government was being too optimistic about the rundown of hospital beds. He pointed out that local authority expenditure on mental health services per head of the population in 1959 was less than in 1951 and warned that 'to scatter the mentally ill in the community before we have made provision for them is not a solution'. Campbell's researches in Sheffield had suggested, as early as 1968, that hostels instead of hospitals for the mentally handicapped produced no evidence that such placements led to a growth of contact with other residents in the same neighbourhood. Such concerns continued to be borne out during the 1980s. As Fotterell (1990) pointed out, by 1984, while nearly half the planned reduction in inpatient beds had been achieved in mental hospitals, the target for increased day hospital places had registered only a 17 per cent advance, while only 16 per cent of the number of day centre places had been achieved. During the 1970s, as this chapter has already suggested, the achievement of policy alignment between health and social services remained elusive and professional relations remained characterised more by rivalry than cooperation. These questions, and others, were to be repeated during the 1980s, even as community care was proceeding apace. Amongst the issues raised were the following:

Firstly, a continuing scepticism about the extent to which the system was able to provide a seamless service, in which individuals were to be enabled to remain, or resettle, in the community without falling foul of boundary disputes. Higgins et al. (1994: 270), for example, suggested that the reforms of the 1980s added to fragmentation and complexity, rather than reducing them. The same authors concluded that 'numerous research studies, official reports and inquiries have concluded that effective collaboration remains largely an elusive goal', if not a self-defeating illusion.

Secondly, a questioning of the wider social policy framework within which community care approaches were being pursued during the 1980s. If relations between different professional groups were characterised by conflict and stand-off, then these divisions were, it was argued, replicated and reinforced by the way in which different services – housing, social security, employment and so on – each had their own systems and regulations which, in practice, turned out to be inflexible, mutually exclusive or contradictory. The impact of changes in housing provision, for example, with the rapid reduction in the housing pool and lack of availability of council properties meant that more and more people were staying in unsuitable temporary accommodation and for longer periods. The fate of homeless mentally ill people, in particular, was influenced by such changes (see Bhugra, 1996). The questions raised suggested that care in the community was a policy which was actively made more difficult to achieve by other social policy practices of the same era.

Thirdly, a further critique suggested that the achievement of community care during the 1980s was undermined by the ideological impact of other social policy changes. Problems may not simply be administrative, or the product of misunderstanding. Put simply, such critics asked, what were the prospects for community care if the whole idea of community was under attack? Mrs Thatcher's often-quoted dictum that 'there is no such thing as society. There are only individuals and their families' certainly sat strangely alongside a policy in which a society-based solution was being sought for the mentally ill and those with learning disabilities. Less contentiously, other commentators noted the very variable set of conditions which the term 'community' glossed over. As Spicker et al. (1995: 30) suggested, ' "The community" to which people are discharged is not a single, simple set of circumstances; it refers to a wide range of different kinds of situations and relationships. If there is little sense of an ordered progress from "the institution" to "the community", it is at least in part because there is no definable situation to which patients can be directed'.

Finally, a set of practical criticisms were made of the actual conditions under which even apparently successful community care arrangements were achieved. At worst, some argued that such transitions masked a replacement of institutional experience with neglect and ghettoisation in the community. Others suggested that 'care in the community' had become care in mini-institutions which simply replicated a number of the unfavourable features of previous hospitals. For example, Gittins (1998: 27), in her narrative of Severalls Hospital in Essex, suggested that the history of postwar psychiatry had been one of:

> essentially transforming the control of hospital space, and control *by* hospital space, into control of patient body space by chemical means. One central result of this has been that patients can now be dispersed away from hospitals and yet remain, on the whole, controlled and restrained. Euphemistically, this has been called 'care in the community'.

Others suggested that the shift from hospital to community care had been accomplished through a move from expensive (trained, qualified) care, to cheap (untrained, unqualified) staff. Hatfield and Mohamad (1996: 216) suggested that, 'in comparison with professional qualified workers, lower remuneration means that mental health support workers are cheaper to employ, a crucial consideration in the costing of the service.'

The essential point which links all these criticisms and which has an important impact upon the production of scandal in social welfare is that, during the 1980s and well into the 1990s, while the *practice* of community care could be criticised, the *principle* of care in the community remained inviolable. Much might be done to improve the performance of the policy. Very few voices indeed were raised to question the policy itself. Scandal, which had played such a significant part in the early years which this chapter covers, had ceased to trouble either politicians or policy-makers. With community care under the spotlight only in so far as its performance might be improved, the scope for any more fundamental challenge had temporarily ceased to exist.

At the start of the 1990s the first cracks in this policy hegemony began to be discernible. Once again, scandal was very much a part of that process. In 1992, Emma Brodie, an 11-year-old girl, was killed in the centre of

Doncaster by a woman who had been released from a mental hospital only two days previously. At this stage, as the Health Committee of the House of Commons (1994) put it, reaction remained largely in line with previous responses that, whatever flaws might be found in the implementation of the policy, 'we wholeheartedly support a policy of community care for mentally disabled people'. The process by which the principle, rather than the practice, of community care came to regarded as flawed, and the part which scandal played in that policy reconstruction forms the focus of the chapter which now follows.

7
'Carnage in the Community'
The Christopher Clunis Inquiry 1993

Introduction

This chapter begins by retracing the steps from the start of the 1990s, to nearly a decade earlier. The previous chapter attempted to demonstrate the way in which scandals in the institutional care of those with mental health difficulties were extinguished in the years after Ely, both by the repetitive nature of events uncovered and by the grip which care in the community came to exercise over policy-making in this field. The purpose of this chapter is to trace the demise of that policy hegemony, and the part played by scandal in reviving public concern, not now about institutional conditions and practices, but about the release into the community of mentally ill people. In order to explore some important elements of scandal itself in this regard, however, it is important to look back at the first case, during this period, of a Public Inquiry involving a death caused by a discharged mental patient. In doing so, two major purposes will be pursued: firstly to consider the policy issues raised and secondly to ask the question, why did this not become a landmark scandal?

Isabel Schwartz

On 6 July 1984 Isabel Schwartz, then a social worker employed by Bexley Council, was killed at her office at Bexley Hospital in Kent. She had been stabbed to death by a former client, Sharon Campbell. Ms Campbell was arrested and charged with murder. On 22 August 1985 she was committed to Broadmoor, having been found mentally unfit to stand trial. Almost two years later, following extensive pressure from Dr Victor Schwartz, Isabel Schwartz's father, a Public Inquiry was appointed by the

Secretary of State. By the time the Inquiry reported in July 1988, fully four years had elapsed since the death had taken place.

The focus of this chapter moves from the institutional care of people with mental health difficulties to their care in the community. In 1984, Bexley Hospital itself was in a period of continuing transition. It was yet another of those Victorian asylums, set in 100 acres of largely open land whose patient numbers – 900 in 1984 – were in sharp decline. The Inquiry traces a large number of themes which were to become familiar in later years, despite its own failure to achieve landmark or emblematic status.

Revolving door

Sharon Campbell's behaviour first began to give cause for concern in 1980. The immediate series of events thereafter is worth tracing in a little detail, because it set in train a pattern which was to become familiar in the years which followed. In the first weeks of June 1980, immediately after the onset of Sharon Campbell's illness, medical and social services were quickly mobilised as continuing disturbances at home led to her moving to live away from her family. A brief weekend at a hostel for black adolescents in Brixton found her still 'disturbed and psychotic' (11). It was agreed, on 16 June, that she should be admitted to hospital on a voluntary basis. On 24 June, against medical advice, she discharged herself and returned home. On 25 June she was readmitted to Bexley Hospital, leaving once more on the same day before being returned for a third time in 24 hours, by the police, following a further domestic disturbance. On 30 June Ms Campbell discharged herself once more, before agreeing to return to inpatient treatment under medical supervision.

This acute pattern of discharge and readmission was to become characteristic of Sharon Campbell's history. It was one replicated far more widely. Rogers and Pilgrim (1996: 76) suggest that the pattern had already been established: 'by the late 1970s' they write, 'the new service pattern becoming discernible was one of revolving-door patients going in and out of acute psychiatric units but being backed up by sparse and unevenly distributed social service facilities'.

Compulsory treatment?

The medical management of Sharon Campbell's case was also, from the outset, dominated by a problem which the Inquiry identified as one in which 'a patient [is] unwilling to take medication and unwilling to go or to stay in hospital' (11). The events of June 1980 were resolved, at least temporarily, on 3 July when an order for compulsory detention and treatment was obtained under section 26 of the 1959 Mental Health Act. Resolving treatment-resistance by compulsory means remained a distressing feature of Sharon Campbell's case. More broadly, the problem of how to treat an unwilling patient was to continue to be a conundrum facing those responsible for mental health services and, according to Wells (1997: 333), 'treatment compliance of mentally ill people in the community has been a prominent issue in the United Kingdom' ever since.

Assessing seriousness

The Sharon Campbell Inquiry, while admitting the benefits which hindsight provided, nevertheless identified a series of matters which, it believed, were wrongly underestimated as factors in influencing the care provided to her. On one occasion a knife was found in Ms Campbell's locker during a period of inpatient treatment. There were other instances where evidence suggested that she was often in possession of such implements. Yet, the finding of the knife at the ward was not recorded in either the clinical or nursing notes. Given that the death of Isabel Schwartz was caused by stabbing, the view reached by the Inquiry was that the discovery had been 'played down' (22) when more serious attention might have discovered a pattern of behaviour which could then have been addressed.

In a more extended example, the Inquiry traces an interweaved set of events which had begun at Sharon Campbell's earliest admission to hospital in June 1980. On that occasion she had been driven by a male social worker from whom she had seized the steering wheel as he attempted to pull in to the side of the road. Other witnesses reported unease at having being alone in a vehicle with her. Yet, these incidents were not reported. On 5 October 1983, Isabel Schwartz was assaulted by Sharon Campbell while driving her car, an incident which led to her ceasing to be Ms Campbell's social worker. In the view of the Inquiry, the assault was evidence of the extent to which, by this stage, 'Isabel Schwartz had become a focus for Sharon Campbell's anger and violence' (40). The full significance of this development, however, was not fully appreciated at the time. Thereafter, a series of records suggested that the negative feelings of Ms Campbell towards her former social worker continued and gathered strength. On 9 March 1984, for example, hospital records suggested that threatening phone calls against Isabel Schwartz had been received from Sharon Campbell. Yet, these remained isolated straws in a gathering wind, rather than being regarded as connected and part of an emerging pattern.

On 25 May 1984 a further incident took place, at a hostel where Sharon Campbell was then a resident. A student nurse was attacked by her there with a knife with a four-inch blade. A housing welfare worker, involved in the aftermath, recorded that Ms Campbell, 'talked compulsively about her relationship with Isabel Schwartz, whom she alleged had hit and bullied her' (52). Other than this observation neither social services, police or medical services took any further action. Looking for a general explanation for this minimisation of difficulty, the Inquiry suggested that it rested upon the dislike by psychiatrists of 'labelling' patients, particularly where such labels might make more difficult the task of organising subsequent care.

Organisational arrangements

During the years in which Sharon Campbell was in receipt of treatment at Bexley Hospital, community services were provided to her by Lewisham Social Services Department. The Report notes that patients might move from one local authority area to another, but that 'this was not so in the case of Sharon Campbell'. Within Lewisham itself, however, services were organised on a district basis. Individuals were allocated social work services depending upon where they lived. The circumstances of individuals needing mental health assistance were often volatile, geographically and socially. The Campbell family lived in the Southern district. When Sharon Campbell first left home, in 1981 and 1982, she lived in the Central district. From November 1982 until August 1983, she moved to the Western district. From September 1983 she had moved again to the South-Western district. At different places, Ms Campbell also called herself by different names, using 'Bess' while in the Central district and 'Paulette' in the Southern. At each move, the potential for confusion, slippage in service, loss of records, boundary disputes over budgetary and clinical responsibility, differences in identification of problem issues and so on moved to the surface. As the Inquiry notes, at one point in its detailed account of these events, 'The effectiveness of communication between those caring for Sharon Campbell was one of our major concerns' (38).

Conclusions

The Sharon Campbell Inquiry makes a series of detailed recommendations about local service delivery, the content of social work training and professional practice. For our purposes, however, its views on what it straightforwardly called 'care in the community' are the most relevant.

It called for a clarification of statutory duties and better cooperation and multidisciplinary working between the services involved in providing care. It noted the financial problems facing health and local government bodies. It explored suggestions for a compulsory treatment order in the community, but reached no conclusion as to its likely effectiveness. All of this, however, was couched within the Inquiry's overall support for what it termed, 'the commendable policy of care in the community for mentally ill people [which] has been developing over many years.' In other words, the criticisms which the Report makes and the proposals which it advances remained firmly within the policy hegemony which was explored in the last chapter. The Inquiry concluded that, 'substantial improvements in the care of mentally ill people have continued in the years since Isabel Schwartz died'. More remained to be done, but the essential integrity of the policy itself remained unchallenged.

Generating scandal

From the perspective of this book, the Isabel Schwartz Inquiry contained many of the raw ingredients of scandal. It involved a history which, once uncovered, appeared to involve a dramatic pattern in which, had different actions been taken at crucial points, the final outcome might have been avoided. Yet, because that outcome was already known, and involved a matter of life and death, the Greek sense of tragic inevitability hovers over the whole text. In terms of character, the Report could be said to counterpoise the careers of good, in the shape of Ms Schwartz and evil, in the shape of Sharon Campbell. In Isabel Schwartz, the Inquiry reported on the career of an educated, dedicated young white woman who, while possibly out of her depth in the difficulties she faced, was motivated by a desire to assist others. In Sharon Campbell, the Inquiry reported the career of a failed, young, black woman, who consistently refused to help herself and remained a burden to her family and a danger to those who attempted to assist her.

Yet, despite possessing much of the raw material of scandal, this was a case which failed to make a substantial impression on the public consciousness. A number of contributory strands can be suggested in explanation. In the first instance, the contrast between good and evil outlined above was not as stark as that account might have suggested. Firstly, Sharon Campbell was *ill*. Her status as a patient, a sufferer from mental distress, complicates any simplistic attempt to portray her as a deliberate force for evil. Secondly she was a *young woman* and in the gendered world of archetypes upon which scandal draws so powerfully, was thus associated with innocence rather than guilt. The effect of ethnicity on her treatment was considered by the Inquiry and dismissed rather loftily: 'We accept that some have the perception that black people are disadvantaged. This may well be so from time to time, but, as we have indicated, it was not suggested to us that it had been a feature in the case of Sharon Campbell' (72). This chapter returns below, and in more detail, to the impact of race on the generation of mental health scandals.

In the case of Isabel Schwartz, too, some complexity arose in the public portrayal of her as 'heroic'. The treatment of social workers in the media has already been the focus of earlier chapters, particularly in relation to child care. There was no suggestion, in the case of Isabel Schwartz, that, other than a possible over-anxiety to remain involved in the help offered to Sharon Campbell, she acted in any way inconsistently with her professional responsibilities. Yet, she remained a social worker, and thus tainted by definition as a potential source of emblematic goodness.

That the death of Isabel Schwartz did not produce a public scandal is further evidenced in what Tidmarsh (1995: 1) describes as the 'extreme reluctance' and the two-and-a-half-year delay which preceded the setting up of the Inquiry into her death. Only a concerted campaign by family, friends and some parts of the professional press, orchestrated by her father, led to the eventual Report. The reluctance is explained by Tidmarsh as rooted in 'the prevailing dogma that mental illness could not lead to serious harm', or, in the terms adopted in this book, in the strength of the premise that community care remained the only way forward for mental health policy and that difficulties encountered in the implementation of that policy were only aberrations, scarring the surface of solid foundations.

Within the professional arena, the reaction to Isabel Schwartz's death was somewhat different. Muijen (1995: 148), writing a decade later in the social work magazine *Community Care*, suggested that:

> Until 1981, inquiries had addressed scandals in hospitals on behalf of an angry public, almost invariably showing patients as helpless victims and staff as abusers. In July 1984, when the first green shoots of community care could be seen, one shocking event had major repercussions for mental health care, and eventually, public attitudes. Sharon Campbell, a former in-patient, killed Isabel Schwartz her former social worker, at Bexley hospital. From then on, community care became associated with danger.

This view, and others like it (see, for example, Wells, 1997), suggests a further refinement of our understanding of the relationship between social welfare scandals and public inquiries. A distinction can be made between those events which produce ramifications which are felt within policy and professional communities and those which move beyond such circles and make an impact in the world outside. Muijen's contention that the Sharon Campbell Inquiry created an association between community care and danger is quite certainly premature as far as the public and politicians are concerned. Within the world of social welfare the death of Isabel Schwartz created a wider reaction, touching its audience more closely and leading to some change in practice and training. Even so, it was not until quite some time later, when community care scandals appeared to erupt on a far larger scale and with far greater impact, that the Campbell Inquiry began to be cited as the first important stirrings of a new policy tide (see Reith, 1998).

Chapter 6 ended with a reference to the death, in 1992, of Emma Brodie. It was in the following year, however, that the landmark scandal in community care took place. The death of Jonathan Zito is discussed in detail below. Many of the themes identified in the Public Inquiry which followed were familiar from the events surrounding Isabel Schwartz, nearly a decade earlier. It is important, therefore, before embarking on that account, to consider some of the contextual contrasts which surrounded both events and which contributed to the very different impact which each produced.

In the first instance, by 1992, the notion that community care was a policy which was problematic only in its implementation, rather than its conception, was beginning to come under pressure. For nearly thirty years voices had rumbled largely unheard in the background, warning against the premature closure of asylums, without adequate substitute provision already being in place. The radical measures of the 1980s, with the accelerating pace of institutional closure and the creation of a market in social care, drew new attention to the policy and practical consequences of reform. More generally, the first half of the 1990s was a period in which political stability itself came under increasing strain. There is a sense, we would argue, in which the robustness or otherwise of the general political climate produces an impact upon policy-making. The departure of Mrs Thatcher brought with it an end to the heady certainties of the neo-liberal agenda. The Major government of 1992 was very quickly mired in a series of difficulties in which its parliamentary majority, its support in the media and its reputation in the country were progressively eroded. In a general atmosphere of uncertainty and flux, policies which previously were regarded as fixed and immutable found themselves affected by the general climate of insecurity.

Christopher Clunis

It was within this context that, on 17 December 1992, Jonathan Zito was murdered by Christopher Clunis. On that day, Zito had set out for Gatwick Airport, to join his family who were flying in from Pisa. Having met up with them, he and his brother set off by train to Victoria and thence by tube to Finsbury Park. They were making for the flat where Jonathan and Jayne Zito had been living since 9 November 1992, following their marriage in the previous September. Jonathan Zito was a musician. Jayne Zito was a student at Middlesex University, training to become a social worker.

He never arrived home.

In the aftermath, an Inquiry was set up by the local Health Authority. Membership followed the usual pattern. It was chaired by Jean Ritchie, a QC specializing in medical law and negligence. Two additional members represented the social services[1] and the psychiatric profession. The terms of reference provided to the Inquiry were both specific, relating to Christopher Clunis, his care and its deficiencies, and general, relating to 'people in similar circumstances'. The method of Inquiry was described by its members in terms reminiscent of those employed by the authors of the Ely Report, as a 'bit like receiving bits of a jigsaw puzzle, in random order, and trying to find the next piece of the jigsaw so as to allow us to form the picture'. The Inquiry received both written and oral evidence from a total of 143 witnesses. It sat to hear evidence between 20 September 1993 and 11 February 1994 and included a visit to Christopher Clunis, then at Rampton Special Hospital.

Christopher Clunis himself was born on 18 May 1963. He is the only child of his parents' marriage, although he had stepbrothers and stepsisters on both sides of his family. In 1968 his family moved to Luton, where he received his education. He had a successful school career, obtaining up to six O-levels and studying economics and sociology at a sixth-form college. His main interest was in music. In 1980 his mother suffered a stroke and

---

1. In a sidelight on the influence of scandal upon social policy, the participation of Richard Linham, the Director of Social Services in Scilly Isles, was only possible because of an earlier social welfare scandal. The Stephen Menheniott Inquiry of 1977 had partly traced the death of Stephen, on the Scillies, at the hands of his father to the absence of a social work service on the Isles. Until that point, social services legislation had covered only mainland England and Wales. In the aftermath, the Labour government of the day passed a short act which extended the obligation to provide a social services department to the Isles. Without that decision, its director could not have been a participant in the Clunis Inquiry of 1993.

his parents went to live in Jamaica, their own country of origin. At about the same time, Christopher Clunis's own musical career took off. He played with a group called the Aqua Vita Showband and travelled abroad working with the group. He maintained contact with his family by telephone and, when in England, lived in Luton. In 1984 he moved to live in Hornsey and registered with a general practitioner, Dr Subrahmanyam. He then went abroad again, and while he was away in 1985 his mother died. He did not learn of her death until he returned to England and did not attend the funeral in Jamaica, as had the rest of the family. His sister told him of the death over the telephone, because he was too busy to visit her, as she had suggested. The Report draws particular attention to this event, suggesting 'that it seems to have had a profound effect on him. He would never discuss the matter with his sister and he never discussed his mother again with her' (9).

Thus before Christopher Clunis's illness he had both family support and a pattern of contact with mainstream services. Neither of these sources of possible assistance were ever called upon in the crises which followed. The implication that care in the community had become a policy divorced from the normal understanding of community life was highlighted in the Inquiry report (8):

Health and social services workers took few, if any, steps to contact members of his family, and thereby they lost touch with some of the basic realities of his personal history as well as losing the family's potentially valuable support in his treatment and its aftermath. They treated him as single, homeless, and itinerant with no family ties, and the more they treated him as such the more he began to fulfill that role. Too often his refusal to allow access to his family, those who were caring for him, was accepted without further question or investigation, even though family members had rights to be consulted regarding his detention under the Mental Health Act 1983.

Nor did ordinary services fare any better. Despite his frequent admission to hospital, his GP, whose name and address Christopher Clunis sometimes provided, never thereafter received any communication or discharge summary. The Inquiries of the 1970s and 1980s had provided dramatic illustration of the alienation from community which occurred within mental health institutions. Now, as Taylor (1995: 81) suggests, the alienation experienced within the hospital setting came to be reproduced in the networks of discharged patients. Mr Clunis began to show signs of disturbed behaviour in 1986, with a more serious onset in the following year. Between the end of June 1987 and the end of March 1988 he was admitted to hospital on six separate occasions. Diagnosis of his difficulties was disputed. He was variously thought to be suffering from schizophrenia, drug-induced psychosis, and organic illness or even faking symptoms in order to gain admission to hospital (12). On the majority of occasions his condition improved significantly following treatment and he was discharged with very little or no follow-up.

In 1988 the first significant episode involving the police took place. Christopher Clunis had already been admitted on two further occasions to two further hospitals when, on 25 May, he broke into the home of an elderly lady and was found in her bathroom. There was no suggestion that he was trying to steal or to commit any other offence. Arrested, he appeared in Court and was remanded in custody until 15 June 1988. Industrial action by prison officers meant that he was held in police cells in Doncaster. As a result no psychiatric report was prepared and, although visited by a probation officer, that report also could not be completed. He was remanded in custody again, this time to Brixton. A psychiatric report was now prepared, following a visit by Consultant Psychiatrist Dr Davies on 5 July. It had taken six weeks for that attention to be received. Dr Davies recommended a Hospital Order and said that he would make a bed available (18–19).

This Order was made by the Courts on 13 July 1988 and Dr Davies named as the Responsible Medical Officer. Christopher Clunis was admitted to Dulwich North Hospital. On admission he was noted to have poor self-care with side effects from medication. He was smiling constantly. His talk was monotonous with poor content. He had grandiose delusions and no insight. He was rude and abusive in the first days after admission. On receipt of medication, however, he improved rapidly and he was released from the Hospital Order on 11 August, being discharged to B&B accommodation on the following day. As the Inquiry report noted, he had been discharged within 16 days, 'far less time than it had taken to give him a psychiatric assessment' (19).

At this point, in the account which the Report offers, a number of running themes begin to be identified by the Inquiry team. These are set out below, broadly following the same categorisation adopted in considering the Sharon Campbell Report.

Revolving door

A pattern became established in the care of Christopher Clunis in which he was received into hospital following an incident in the community.

Such incidents were often linked, as in the case of Sharon Campbell, to difficulties in maintaining his medication in a way which provided for his care and met with his compliance and satisfaction. Once in hospital his medication was resumed, and the more difficult aspects of his illness came under control. A contradictory pattern then emerged in which either he appeared to be hardly ill at all or his behaviour became more outgoing and florid, to the point where he made, for example, inappropriate sexual references to staff or became quarrelsome with other patients. In either case, the result was the same: he was discharged rapidly again from hospital. In all this, the Inquiry noted not only the pattern itself, but the way in which, as the Report said: 'each episode of illness was treated separately, rather than as part of a continuing illness ... Christopher Clunis was treated almost as though he were a new patient, on each of his six admissions.'

While the pattern of hospital admission and discharge was common to both Sharon Campbell and Christopher Clunis, two important differences emerge in reading both Reports. In the first place, Ms Campbell was often the motivating force in the events in which she was involved – she took the initiative in leaving hospital, with staff requiring compulsory powers to retain her there. Mr Clunis, by contrast, was most often ejected from hospital, either without any initiative on his own part, or in the face of his own active opposition. In terms of scandal, the distinction proved significant. If it proved difficult to attach blame to a system which appeared to be doing its best to cope with a problematic patient, it was quite a different matter when it was possible to portray the system itself as deliberately refusing to provide the treatment which individuals and their families were determinedly seeking.

In the second place, the revolving door through which both Sharon Campbell and Christopher Clunis passed treated them rather differently. As the door opened on the community side, both found themselves facing a new set of circumstances on each occasion. As the door opened on the institutional side, Sharon Campbell found herself in familiar circumstances and amongst staff to whom she was known and at whose hands some sense of a continuity of care could be discerned. For Christopher Clunis, his hospital experience was as disjointed and unconnected as most of what he experienced in the community. Again, in terms of the generation of scandal, this difference was also to be influential. In Ms Campbell's case a sense of 'asylum' could still be detected in the institutional services which were, however unwillingly received, afforded to her. Ten years later, the fragmented remains of the hospital network, itself in the early throes of the 'internal market' of health care reforms, appeared quite incapable of delivering a sense of safety – either to patients themselves, or to the community at large.

Assessing seriousness

Although the Clunis Inquiry makes no direct reference at all to the Campbell findings, a directly parallel concern emerged in both cases, in what was believed to be a minimising of the problems faced and posed by both individuals. In Christopher Clunis's case, for example, the Inquiry cites an example in which a social worker responsible for seeking accommodation for him, in order that he might be discharged from hospital, took the view that he had not presented any behavioural problems on the ward, despite the contemporary written record of his violent and disturbed behaviour. Two different types of explanation for this sort of devaluation of difficulty are suggested in the Report. On the one hand, echoing the analysis of the Campbell document, the Inquiry said that it understood the 'humanitarian' impulse of workers not wishing to 'stigmatise a patient, or label him in any way as a violent or difficult person which might work to his disadvantage' (19). On the other hand, there is the clear implication that problems were not being communicated because these might lessen the chances of anyone else being willing to accept responsibility for care. Whatever the explanation, the outcome was the same: 'time and time again a failure to assess properly or to describe his condition properly did not present an accurate picture to those who came to care for him afterwards, which ultimately served Christopher Clunis very badly.'

In a further parallel with the history of Sharon Campbell, the Clunis Report found that the tendency to underestimate the seriousness of his behaviour was shared by more than one organisation. It records a series of concerns at the actions of the police in failing to take proceedings following incidents of violence. In 1988, as noted above, no action had been taken following a break-in at the home of an elderly lady. In June 1989, Mr Clunis had attempted to stab a police officer with a kitchen knife. No criminal charges followed. Rather he was detained again under section 136 of the Mental Health Act and admitted for a further period of hospitalisation.

In May 1992 an even more serious incident took place when Christopher Clunis made an attack upon another resident at Lancelot Andrewes House, a hostel for an itinerant population of single men where both were staying. The attack involved stabbing the other resident with a knife while that person was lying in bed. The case was ultimately abandoned by the Crown Prosecution Service some months later, when the police failed to trace the victim of the offence in order to provide evidence in Court.

The Inquiry Report summed up its explanation of these events in this way (22):

> The understandable desire to help him and perhaps not to stigmatise him was allowed to interfere with the process of law, which in our view was ultimately to Christopher Clunis' disadvantage. Since there was no conviction, the event tended thereafter to be brushed aside as a trivialised or minor incident.

Organisational arrangements

If institutional services were disconnected, preoccupied with boundary disputes and the avoidance of costs falling on their budgets, when discharged from hospital, matters were worse still. The idea of a 'seamless service' had no basis in reality. The Report identifies a continual series of occasions when information was not properly transferred from one organisation to another. From November 1989 to October 1990 Christopher Clunis enjoyed what the Report called 'the longest period of stability... since he became ill in 1986'. Even at this period, however, the picture which the Inquiry records is one in which there were (34):

> a number of people all trying to help and care for Christopher Clunis but doing so in isolation from one another. There was little effective communication between those who were caring for him and they each looked after him in the light of their own observations instead of as a team all working together to provide effective care ... Above all, no-one was co-ordinating his psychiatric care and treatment in the community.

Against this background, a further series of systemic criticisms, many familiar from the Sharon Campbell Report, were made. Hospital and medical services appeared determined by geography. For an often-homeless, and personally rootless individual like Christopher Clunis, the continual criss-crossing of boundaries resulted in endless delays in the transfer of information, countless opportunities for information not to be passed at all, and an open invitation for particular services not to accept responsibility because of disputes over boundary lines. At the same time, an analogous set of disputes emerged over money in which decisions were driven by financial considerations, rather than clinical need or best standards of care.

Conclusions

While many of the findings of the Clunis Report were echoes of those contained in Campbell, one of the differences between them is to be found in the directness with which Jean Ritchie and her colleagues were prepared to identify the blame for the conditions which they uncovered. Chapter 6 suggested that successive institutional scandals in mental health services moved in the same direction, from the determined refusal to find any service or individual at fault in the *Sans Everything* Reports to the series of dismissals recommended in the case of Normansfield. Something of the same shift can be discerned in these early community care reports. Dealing with the whole system, for example, the Clunis Report puts its conclusion plainly.

'It is abundantly clear', the Report says, 'that SE London has insufficient beds for the patients who need admission to secure facilities' (59). The result had been inappropriately early discharge of patients in need of continuing care and acute difficulty in securing admission at times of crisis. This sense of a system unable to meet the needs of its patients and the community, even when such needs involved serious threats to personal and collective safety, was powerfully communicated in the Report. It was to provide very effective raw material for those claims-makers who were already engaged in campaigns to characterise the policy of community care as in a scandalous state of crisis.

Nor did the Inquiry confine its criticisms to the hospital or medical sector. The chaotic nature of the care which Christopher Clunis was offered in the community has already been illustrated briefly above. The Report concludes that this was to be explained by whole-systems failure. Its verdict on one of the social services departments most closely involved was characteristic (88): 'Indecision and procrastination is the hall mark of the failure of Haringey Social Services.'

It was suggested earlier in this chapter that in the Sharon Campbell Report one of the difficulties in the path of scandal generation had been the ambivalent material which that Report produced in relation to social workers and social services. Put simply, it was difficult to mount an unambiguous attack on community services in the face of the death of one of those who had attempted to provide them. No such ambiguity stood in the path of the reporting of the Clunis case. Drawing on the well-established hostility to social work to which earlier reporting had made such a major contribution, a largely right-wing press was able to lay the blame for what had taken place upon one of its favourite targets.

The generation of scandal, as earlier chapters have argued, requires the simplification of guilt and innocence, of blame and exoneration. In the Clunis Report both systems and individuals were presented in terms which allowed its raw material to be presented in such lights. To provide just one example, the attack which Christopher Clunis made upon another resident at Lancelot Andrewes House had been investigated by DC Gwynfor Owen who, in his evidence to the Inquiry, emphasised the seriousness with which he had pursued that investigation. The Report's verdict was direct (57):

> We found DC Owen an unimpressive witness whose bearing and demeanour gave little cause to persuade us to accept his evidence. We are sorry to record our finding that we do not accept the greater part of his evidence. It seemed to us improbable that diligent efforts were ever made to obtain medical evidence or to trace the victim. We are concerned that DC Owen may not have investigated the matter in the way his training would require, perhaps because the attack had been perpetrated by someone who was mentally ill on a person who was homeless. When he assessed Christopher Clunis as very, very, dangerous, it seems to us that more effort, not less, should have been spent in ensuring that the case could be properly prosecuted.

Final sequence

In chapter 1 we attempted to set out some of the important connections which can be drawn between social welfare scandals and the archetypes of Western drama. In community care Inquiries, we know the tragic outcome. Some reports provide accounts in which the dramatic quality of events sits very close to the surface. Partly this is a reflection of events themselves, but it is also a reflection of the task of social construction in which report writers are engaged. The Christopher Clunis Inquiry is no exception to this rule. It takes an immensely confused and complicated set of events and circumstances and imposes upon that complexity a linear sense of order, in which the final outcome is infused with a sense of inevitability which cannot have been apparent to those involved at the time. In terms of the generation of scandal, however, that sense of events moving inexorably towards their tragic conclusion is fundamental to the transformation of ordinary lives, and everyday events, into something far more emblematic and resonant.

The weeks leading up to the death of Jonathan Zito were marked by a series of incidents involving Christopher Clunis which displayed almost all of the difficulties which had been identified in his care for a period of almost seven years. The Inquiry devotes nearly 20 closely evidenced and argued pages to this period. Amongst the incidents were two of actual or threatened violence to individuals in the street. These were reported to the police by individuals concerned and by other local residents. The casts of scandals involve minor as well as major actors and lesser as well as greater acts of heroism and betrayal. In these final days, the Clunis Report traces the tenacity displayed by those individuals who were concerned at his behaviour in attempting to obtain a response from the police. It also records the culpable failure of individual officers to respond to these inquiries. A senior police officer, Inspector Gill, denied having taken messages about these incidents or having passed the information on to social services.

The Inquiry Report concludes (96):

> We are very reluctant to say it, but we do not accept Inspector Gill's evidence ... Inspector Gill, we find, knew Christopher Clunis's name and where he lived. We find that he also knew that it was Christopher Clunis who had been waving a screwdriver in the streets and talking about devils ... He should have realised that Christopher Clunis was a danger to the public and probably to himself. It is our view that the police were not properly protecting the public from potential harm.

The incidents of violence in which Mr Clunis had been involved took place on 9 December 1992. By 15–16 December messages from the police had arrived at the Wood Green social services office. On the 17th and 18th that understaffed and inadequately organised office had also been contacted by a hospital-based doctor whose main concern appeared to be to resolve a further boundary dispute which had arisen as to responsibility for Christopher Clunis's health care. On Thursday 17 December a duty approved social worker, Ursula Robson, picked up the different messages and became concerned at the emerging picture. She agreed to call at Mr Clunis' address in order to make arrangements for a full assessment of his current condition. It was seven o'clock on the evening of the following day when, unaccompanied, she called at the address, receiving no reply. The reader, of course, knows that, by the time of that visit, at which a message was left, asking Mr Clunis to call at the social worker's office at 11 a.m. on the 18th, the murder of Jonathan Zito had already taken place. That realisation hangs over the account which the Report assembles. We know the danger into which the social worker could unwittingly have been placed as she made her way alone, in the late and the dark, to the door of a man whose condition had deteriorated to the point of murder. We know, even more strongly, the futility of her visit: the arrival of the cavalry, however vulnerable, taking place only after the battle had been lost.

As in any drama, the tension which communicates itself to the reader is heightened by the juxtaposition of the quotidian and the extraordinary. At this point, the Report's narrative returns to Jonathan Zito, making his way to Gatwick Airport on the morning of 17 December in order to meet members of his family arriving from Italy. While a friend drove most of the party back from the airport, Jonathan Zito and his brother Christopher travelled by rail. They reached Finsbury Park underground station at around 3.45 that afternoon, standing near the edge of the northbound Piccadilly Line. A number of witnesses subsequently described Christopher Clunis as 'shabbily dressed and acting in a strange manner'. A schoolgirl described how he approached the Zito brothers and took out a yellow/mustard-coloured knife with a four-inch blade. Although he knew nothing of the knife, Christopher Zito became concerned and stepped sideways, away from the edge of the platform. In the words of the Report, 'he then motioned discreetly to his brother to move away also'. At that point Christopher Clunis, 'swung out with his right hand extended in a circular motion, hard and fast, from behind and around Jonathan Zito's right shoulder, holding a knife in his clenched fist. He struck him fiercely in the face with a knife.' He then pulled the knife from Jonathan Zito's head and said calmly to Christopher Zito 'Come on then.'

In the panic which followed, Christopher Clunis boarded an incoming train on the Piccadilly Line and, 'without any sign of remorse or concern', sat down in the last carriage, sitting between other passengers as if nothing had happened. A member of the public on the station alerted the driver who had already seen Jonathan Zito in distress. He closed the doors of the train until the police arrived. A witness positively identified Christopher Clunis in the carriage and, without saying anything and without remonstrating in any way, he was arrested and taken away.

Transformation

Much of this text has been concerned with the process by which, through the generation of scandal, particular events are transformed into symbolic ones. The essential ingredients for scandal were clearly present, and highlighted, in the history of Christopher Clunis' life, care and actions, which the Inquiry assembled. The transformation of this material into a milestone event was very swiftly achieved. Clunis became the Inquiry which crystallised a changing set of attitudes in relation to the community care of the mentally ill, capable of being cited in a short-hand way, in the public and professional press, as symbolising the moment at which a policy change was set in motion. How was this achievement of iconic status brought about?

The construction of a master-narrative is, as earlier chapters have argued, one of the key tasks which Inquiries undertake. Even with a report which provides a powerful portrait of events containing every ingredient of scandal, the role of individuals and organisations in turning that latent potential into events of landmark proportions remains critical. Claims-makers must possess qualities of determination and persistence, personified in the *Sans Everything* Inquiries by Barbara Robb. They need either to be lucky – as chapter 3 suggested was the case with Mr Pantelides – or, as in the case of Dr Lawlor, to be capable of mobilising networks of influence. Beyond these capacities lie a set of personal characteristics which, in our argument, have a powerful part to play in the production of scandal. Questions of race and gender are at the heart of such considerations, as the two cases considered here amply demonstrate.

The connection between race and mental health issues has received renewed attention in recent years, as evidence has grown of the over-representation of black people within the more coercive systems of social welfare, including compulsory admission to mental health institutions. Explanations for that overrepresentation are competing and controversial. The conclusions of the Campbell Inquiry in relation to race were largely mirrored in the case of Christopher Clunis. Here the Inquiry specifically considered the part which racism might have played in the treatment he received, concluding that it had not been a factor. Its failure to consider the effects of racism in a systemic, rather than a specific, sense has since been criticised. What seems more certain is that the bald fact that in both the Campbell and Clunis cases, a white person had met their deaths was significant in the generation of scandal. Payne (1999: 187) traces the general shift in the discourse which surrounded discharged mental health patients from the mid-1990s onwards, concluding that during this period it came increasingly to portray 'the mad as alien and dangerous, [and] in which two distinguishing features, youth and masculinity, came to dominate the discourse through a variety of means'. Within the categories of youth and masculinity, the 'young, mad, black male' (Payne, 1999: 192) emerged with particular potency as an alien force, presenting heightened risk to the remainder of the community. The media presentation of the Clunis case drew heavily on this strand in the process of scandal generation. Pictures of the heavy, brooding and threatening presence of Christopher Clunis were, with great regularity, counterpoised with portraits of a blonde and attractive Jayne Zito. Payne (1999: 194) concludes that the presentation resulted in this being 'undoubtedly one of the central cases in the development of the pubic image of the mentally ill as young and dangerous'.

Even with these factors so vividly at play, the final pages of the Inquiry Report bring to the surface one further strand which distinguishes the Christopher Clunis Report from those which had gone before, and which was to become particularly important in shaping mental health policy in the period which immediately followed.

There is a sense in which, for a social welfare scandal to catch light in a way which embeds itself in popular consciousness, the individual reader has to be able to imagine her or himself as part of the drama which has unfolded. In the case of institutional scandals, chapter 3 suggested, the personal fear of becoming old and vulnerable, or of the care which might be afforded to a loved relation, produces in the reader not simply a general indignation at the treatment meted out in mental health asylums, but a capacity to identify vicariously with the possibility that this could be an experience met directly in the reader's own life. In the case of community care scandals, the personal connection is even more immediate. Unprovoked attacks in public places are the fodder of 'stranger danger' which, in the risk society of the 1990s, came so to permeate popular consciousness. The final sequence of the Clunis Report shares the sense of dramatic tension and tragic inevitability which was apparent in the Sharon Campbell Report and which was to become the stock-in-trade of so many community care scandals. An additional distinction here divides the production of scandal in these cases from those of the institutional scandals considered in earlier chapters. In the case of Ely, Farleigh and so on, the reader soon becomes aware that, had the clock been stopped at any time over many previous years, the same set of circumstances would have been uncovered by any Inquiry. In the case of Sharon Campbell, Christopher Clunis or many which were to follow, the opposite feeling is communicated. Here, the reader is made aware, the final outcome was not inevitable. Rather, the narrative contains a series of points at which, it seems clear, had individuals or organisations *acted otherwise* the death around which the Inquiry revolves would have been averted.

Even more strikingly, in terms of stranger danger, the Clunis Inquiry suggests the part which chance can play in events of enormous significance. It is one thing to be confronted with an account in which it is suggested that, were changes to have been made, outcomes could have been altered. It is rather different, if the circumstances described are portrayed as containing ungovernable elements of danger. In Clunis, the elements of stranger and randomness come together for the first time. The Sharon Campbell Inquiry rested essentially upon events which could have been altered had individuals or organisations acted otherwise. The relationship between the two central individuals involved was an established one: they were not strangers to each other. In Clunis, it is the combination of avoidability and unavoidability which produces the impact upon the reader – the sense that, even if everything had been done in the best possible way, the risk which he posed to strangers would still have remained.

Immediate aftermath and longer-term impact

Despite these powerful factors, the claims made in the immediate aftermath of the Clunis Report appeared to place it as simply the latest in a long series of suggestions that, here again, the practice, rather than the policy, of community care was at fault. The Inquiry chair, Jean Ritchie, accompanied her press releases and statements made on publication of the Report with an avowal that: 'Care in the community is the right policy. Nobody wants to go back to the old mental institutions with their locked wards and impersonal care and treatment.' These views were echoed in press reporting. The *Guardian* leader writer declared that:

> One tragic death must not be turned into a multiple tragedy... Mr Zito's death must not be compounded. Locking up much larger numbers of mental patients is not an answer... There are not large numbers of schizophrenic patients stalking the streets looking for murder victims... Reopening the Victorian mausoleums would be an irrelevance.

In this book, we have argued that scandal contributes to policy change only when that policy is already in the early stages of flux. The process of the 1990s was no different. Payne (1999: 191) quotes the Mental Health Commission in 1993 as describing a system 'which was on the verge of collapse, with too few beds for emergency admissions without the precipitous discharge of others, severely ill patients, and too little money to provide community psychiatric care for all those in need.' In 1995 Powell et al.'s detailed research concluded that London's inner-city psychiatric units were operating at 130 per cent bed occupancy. While the immediate aftermath of Clunis might have continued to emphasise the importance of community care as a policy, these underlying patterns provided the cracks through which a far more marked sea change in public opinion and social policy was beginning to gather pace. As this came about, so the Christopher Clunis Report came to represent a questioning not simply of the adequacy but also of the *legitimacy* of caring for severely and chronically mentally ill people outside institutions. The issue which came to occupy policy-makers was not whether community care was working properly, but whether the idea itself was the right one at all.

Policy, scandal and the media

The role of the media in this climate change was an active one. Rose (1997: 30) reported on her transcription and analysis of all prime time news, soap opera, drama and documentary on BBC and ITV for two months in 1992 and similar, but more restricted surveys in 1986 and 1993. She concludes that a fundamental shift had taken place between the first and second of her surveys. Dealing with mental health issues, she suggests that, 'in the earlier studies, stories about mental illness and violence and stories about community care were kept entirely separate. The links with violence and the coverage of community care were not woven into the story of community care's culpability for violent crime.' Thereafter, however, 'a new narrative has emerged' in which problems in community care and violent crime had been brought together in a 'relationship of causality' and a culture of allocation of blame and responsibility. According to Rose (1997: 31), 'Television has changed the way it represents poor mental health – and the new portrayal has had a powerful impact on policy and the public.' Citing the 'saturation coverage' devoted to the Clunis case, she suggests that 'the "community care is to blame" narrative has five central elements: an act of extreme violence, preferably random; a psychiatric diagnosis; the opinion of an expert; a quasi-explanation of the event focusing on prior contacts with the mental health services; and the allocation of blame to the NHS, the social services or the Health Secretary'.

Payne (1999: 192) has conducted a similar analysis of 'the main broadsheets during the first six years of the decade after two serious incidents involving people in receipt of community psychiatric care, in late 1992 and early 1993'. She makes the point that, while her research focused on the broadsheets, 'the tabloids were carrying the same stories with less temperate language'. It is all the more revealing, in that context, that the more 'respectable' newspapers also frequently resorted to language which was both extreme and sensational. When the *Times* used the phrase 'knife-crazy mental patient' (29 June 1993) to describe Christopher Clunis it was, Payne (1999: 192) argues, 'all the more powerful by contrast with other, more restrained articles in the same paper'.

Against this general background of media claims-making, the direct link between scandalous events and policy action is traced by Wells (1997: 335) who sets out a sequence of events in which television reporting, on 31 December 1992, of psychiatric patient Ben Silcock's entry into the lion's enclosure at London Zoo led to an immediate review of mental health law and a set of policy changes 'eight months later'. The part played by chance in scandal has been a theme of earlier chapters of this book. Ben Silcock's actions had been captured on amateur video and were thus available for television transmission. The events also took place on a day notoriously devoid of news, just as Ely hit the headlines in the dog days of August. Atkinson (1996: 124) describes the sequence of policy events which followed as an example of legislation being enacted to 'persuade a worried public, or at least a scaremongering media, that something is being done'. Given Rose's (1997) contention that one of the components in the new climate of scandal was a pointing of the finger of blame at government and its ministers, it is not surprising that, in August 1993, the then Health Minister, Virginia Bottomley announced the government's ten-point plan for the treatment of the mentally ill (H93/908). Among the measures suggested was the supervised discharge of mental health patients. Eastman (1995) described this proposal as 'fudged pseudocoercion', while to the Department of Health (1995: 19) it was a policy 'designed for so-called "revolving door" patients who go through a cycle of repeated admission to hospital under the Mental Health Act followed by the breakdown of arrangements for care in the community'. More generally, Davies and Woolgrove (1998: 25) describing a climate of 'widespread public anxiety', characterise general reaction to the supervision registers and the Supervised Discharge Orders of the 1995 Mental Health (Patients in the Community) Act as being 'poorly thought out', a 'waste of time' and the product of 'policy making on the hoof'. The ten-point plan was the start of what Sullivan (1998: 203) calls 'the almost constant stream of policy documents emanating from the Department of Health and the National Health Service executive which started with the Care Programme Approach'. This activity, however, did not serve to stem the growing tide which portrayed community care, as Fisher (1994: 453) described it, as 'a new financially driven dogma associated with a draconian decrease in the number of beds and an inevitable increase in suicide and homicide.'

Nor were media reports of these initiatives reassuring in relation to the policy stability of care in the community. Portrayal of the successive policy changes which followed after Silcock and Clunis drew on the same discourse as had come to dominate the community care debate. This language spanned the whole spectrum, from the *Sunday Times'* (25 July 1993) report of 'Bottomley unveils plan to protect public from mental patients' to the *Sun's* headline of additional community care money as 'Four million pounds to lock up schizos'. Ironically, however, it was another part of the same ten-point plan which contributed significantly to the growing sense that care in the community was a policy failure. In 1994, the Department of Health published *Guidance on the Discharge of Mentally Disordered People and their Continuing Care in the Community* (HSG (94) 27) which provided recommendations for the commissioning and submission of Public Inquiry reports. Paragraph 34 of the *Guidance* makes it clear that: 'after the completion of any legal proceedings it may be necessary to hold an independent inquiry. In cases of homicide, it will always be necessary to hold an inquiry which is independent of the providers involved.'

This requirement proved particularly important in relation to scandal, because it set in train a long sequence of reports which appeared to illustrate a growing tide of violent acts, perpetrated by the discharged mentally ill. Thus, over the months which followed the Clunis Inquiry, the number of Inquiries into individual cases accelerated. Many of the problems which Clunis identified were now to be repeated in other cases. Ely had been followed by a series of Inquiries in which the circumstances uncovered seemed to be repeated without any benefit taken from the lessons which it had drawn out. Now, too, Clunis was followed by a succession of Inquiries in which the same mistakes appeared to occur and reoccur, time and again. The *Sans Everything* contention that untoward incidents were the product of rare bad apples in an otherwise thriving system had been exploded in the reports which followed. Now, after Clunis, the evident inability of community care practice to remedy the difficulties identified began to erode the credibility of an explanation which suggested that these were simply practical problems, rather than anything more fundamental.

Thus, the death of Jonathan Newby, left alone in charge of a hostel in Oxford, was characterised, said the Report, by a lethal game of buck-passing between the 'seamless' services. Martin Mursell was discharged against

his own will, in July 1994, from a hospital bed to which he had voluntarily surrendered himself. Two months earlier, his records contained the following assessment by a worker preparing a Report for the Courts:

> his recent history catalogues a total failure on the part of health and
> social services to adequately support him, despite continued effort on
> the part of his mother who has borne the brunt of the responsibility
> for his care and indeed treatment. Should another hospital admission
> become necessary, I can only hope that something has been learnt
> from the catalogue of failure over the past year and that better
> discharge planning will occur as a result.

Martin Mursell was removed from hospital to 'care' in the community
which comprised a flat containing no furniture, no gas or electricity and
no cooking facilities. Three months later, he knifed his stepfather to death
and almost killed his mother, only seven days after she had received her
final letter from the social services department declining her long-
expressed plea that they should allocate her son a social worker.

The case of Martin Mursell was in the public domain at the same time as
Wayne Hutchinson, a 22-year-old single man who believed he was a tiger
and who was released from hospital in what police and lawyers privately
conceded to be a 'blunder' (*Independent*, 8 January 1996), to roam about in
that capacity, wounding three people and killing two others in the process.

Shortly thereafter came the Report of the activities of Darren Carr,
a case unique in crossing the boundaries between child care Inquiries and
mental health scandals with which this book has been concerned.
Darren Carr was a seriously psychopathic patient who was compulsorily
detained in a mental hospital following serious attacks on his mother
and her partner. Discharged from hospital, he found himself work as
a live-in child-minder in Oxfordshire, looking after two children who
had already been on the social services 'at risk' register because of concerns about the care provided by their mother. Local teachers accurately
reported that Carr was beating one child but a belated visit from a social
worker cleared him of this charge. A few days later, Carr poured petrol
outside the bedrooms of the mother and the two children and set fire to
the house. All three died. Nor was this the end of the line, by any means.
A string of other names – Andrew Robinson, Jason Mitchell and
Raymond Sinclair to name just a few – kept the issues of discharged mental patients, and the danger posed by them, in the public arena.

The media treatment of such events, and the Inquiries which followed
after them, now openly attacked the policy of care in the community – or

'Carnage in the Community' as it was called in *The Spectator* on 7 May 1994. It was in vain that figures such as Lincoln Crawford, the barrister who chaired the inquiry into Martin Mursell, suggested that, 'the public should not fear that the incidence of violent attacks by mentally ill people was growing and should not lose faith in care in the community. None of us believes the answer is to reopen the Victorian asylums' (*Guardian*, 8 March 1997). Press reporting, across the media spectrum, had set off on an entirely different track. Any new piece of information in the field of mental health was now capable of being reported within a framework which emphasised danger and policy collapse. The *Daily Mail*, with only a tenuous grasp of policy chronology, reported on 30 October 1995 that:

> Thousands of mental patients will pour into the community over the next few years as the Government accelerates its psychiatric hospital closure programme, it was revealed last night.

> This is despite the admission by Health Secretary Stephen Dorrell that the Care in the Community programme set up four years ago is already in chaos.

On 20 April 1997, under a headline 'Danger mental patients evade care', the *Sunday Times* drew on the journalistic cliché of a 'leaked report' to suggest that:

> Public safety is being put at risk by more than 5,000 severely mentally ill people who are being inadequately cared for in the community, the Royal College of Psychiatrists will warn this week.

> A leaked copy of the report – its most comprehensive analysis yet of the government's care in the community policy – says the system is on the verge of complete breakdown…

A BBC 'Panorama' programme in the autumn of 1997 produced a crop of headlines on 13 October, in which the *Daily Mail* reported that 'Freed mental patients kill two a month', and the *Independent* informed its readers that 'Mentally ill kill more often than we think'. The cumulative effect of this media attention, Porter (1996: 403) suggests, was to turn community care into 'an object of rampant public suspicion'. The practical effects of public attitudes were already becoming apparent. Repper and Brooker (1996: 290) report research into public attitudes towards the siting of mental health projects in the community which concluded that, by the mid-1990s, 'local opposition to community facilities has escalated over the past three years'.

Against this background, the Prime Minister of the time, John Major, wrote privately to his Health Secretary early in 1996 (Timmins, 1996). His letter expressed concern that existing policies in the care of discharged mentally ill patients were 'not working as well as they should' and had led to a 'growing public fear of the mentally ill'. The letter did not question the principle of community care, but did express the belief that the hospital closure programme 'may have gone too far'.

The result was a speech by the Health Secretary, signaling, for the first time, an official abandonment of the 'care in the community' slogan. It was no longer 'helpful' or 'accurate', said Mr Dorrell, to speak of 'care in the community', a policy which had come to be associated in the public mind with emptying mental hospitals before providing adequate alternatives. Instead, government policy was to move to the provision of a 'spectrum of care' ranging from hospital beds to independent living. Directly, in terms of what this book has been about, the Health Secretary provided the following characterisation of community care policies to a radio audience at the beginning of January 1996:

> They are unsatisfactory in a number of different areas for reasons that have been reasonably well-documented in the inquiries that have gone on into the homicides caused by mentally-ill people and, more extensively, in the quality of care available to mentally-ill people.

In the public mind, the positive image of care in the community with which the closure programme of mental health asylums had been launched had been supplanted. In its place, the policy had come to be associated with the emptying of hospitals before providing an alternative, and with the pursuit of savings in expenditure before the safety of the public. It was to be only a few short months before the election of a New Labour government, bringing with it an early halt to the programme of mental hospital closure (Department of Health, 1997).

'Goodbye' said the *Guardian* in its prescient comment column of 21 February 1996, 'to care in the community.' 'Community care has failed', concluded the incoming Health Secretary, Frank Dobson (Department of Health, 1998): 'it has left many vulnerable patients to try to cope on their own. Others have been left to become a danger to themselves and a nuisance to others … A small but significant minority have become a danger to the public as well as themselves.'

A new policy direction, in favour of 'assertive outreach' and compulsory treatment in the community, was announced, in which scandal had, once again, proved a powerful contributor to change.

Conclusion

During the period covered in this chapter, care in the community shifted in status from a policy which few could challenge, to one for which few would offer unqualified support. The part which scandal played in this remarkable turn-around was conspicuous. In the argument presented here, we suggest that, by the end of the 1980s, the apparently unruffled surface of policy hegemony was already being eroded from below. Through scandal, the surface itself was ruptured in dramatic fashion. The impact thus engendered fixed itself in popular as well as professional imagination with a strength and a durability which demanded a political response. Accusations of policy-making on the hoof, or simple opportunism, were largely swept aside, as primary and secondary claims-makers found a regular supply of raw material to act as grist to their scandal-generating mills. By the end of the period, with a new policy approach clearly gaining ground, the tide of scandal was, once more, in decline.

8
'An Ambience of Uneasiness'
The Residential Care of Children, 1834–1990

Introduction

Sir William Utting, in his 'special review' of residential care for children (DOH/SSI, 1991), asked himself two very particular questions: 'Is there any point in persevering with residential care? [and] Can it be revived?' (p. 8). Utting's review had been commissioned as a direct result of 'public concern about standards and practices in residential child care' (p. 3) following publication of *The Pindown Experience and the Protection of Children: The Report of the Staffordshire Child Care Inquiry* (Staffordshire County Council, 1991). We will deal with the Utting Report's answers to these questions in chapter 9 when we examine the 'Pindown' inquiry in detail. It is the purpose of this chapter to describe the policy and practice context in which such questions came to be asked in the first place.

We will suggest that despite the long history of residential care, such fundamental questions have been asked many times in the past. In fact, in one form or another, they have been raised at almost every point of transition between successive welfare ideologies and practices. They have been asked with renewed urgency in the period since the Utting Review, especially after the publication of the Waterhouse Inquiry (2000) into child care practice in North Wales. The frequency with which such doubts over the very continuance of residential care have been expressed may owe something to the actual failure of various institutional regimes and practices to meet their declared aims but possibly much more to the 'ambience of uneasiness' (Stroud, 1973: 98) that has come to inhabit the children's home in the four generations since its modern origins in the mid-nineteenth century. The persistence of negative attitudes hanging 'like a pall over residential care' (Walton and Elliot, 1980: 9), is a defining characteristic of both past and more recent practice.

This chapter locates the administrative history of residential care for children in the same policy context as that in which social work practice more generally has developed. The legislative history that was described in chapter 4 clearly bears on residential care as much as it does on other forms of child care practice. Moreover, it is important to remember that the particular experiences of children living away from home have to be understood in the context of the general experiences of children of the time. We have noted elsewhere (Butler, 2002: 201), that 'whilst one of the defining characteristics of institutional care might be the degree to which children and young people are removed from the wider community, institutional practices are embedded in the prevailing social construction of childhood and in the dominant professional cultures of the period.' We will also locate (in this chapter and the next) some of the causes in the particular dynamics of institutional life and the unique vulnerability of children living away from home.

'A sort of institution craze'

The nineteenth century was the great age of institutional solutions to social problems, producing the penitentiary and the asylum as well as the children's home (see Scull, 1979; Ignatieff, 1978). It was as if, according to a report of the Howard Association in 1896, a 'sort of institution craze [had] taken hold of the public fancy' (Howard Association, 1896: 6). Commonly, this 'craze' has been interpreted as a response by the State 'to the collapse of traditional forms of social regulation' (Parker, 1988: 3) through the introduction of controlled and controlling spaces in which new forms of disciplinary practices could be developed and effected (see also Mayer, 1983). As far as children were concerned, the early years of the century had seen social and political concern rise over the number of beggars to be found on the streets of England's larger cities. According to one estimate made in 1803, and referred to in the first of two House of Commons Select Reports made in 1815 and 1816, there were some 9,288 children begging in London alone. Excluded from the discipline of the workplace and not yet subject to the discipline of the school, the operation of the Poor Law seemed to offer little by way of answer to the growing public unease at the potential for disorder presented by the unemployed young person and the children of the idle poor. Indeed, according to the report of the central administrative body, The Poor Law Commission, the workhouse served only to confirm such children in 'idleness, ignorance and vice' (Poor Law Commission, 1834: 618).

The Poor Law was substantially amended in 1834 in ways that would have a direct bearing on the care of such pauper children. Firstly it required the proper classification of workhouse inmates and the separation of children from adults. Secondly, it required that workhouse children should receive a basic education. As described in the Orders and Regulations that followed the Act, this was to comprise 'for three working hours at least, every day, [instruction] in reading and writing and in principles of the Christian religion' (Appendix to the First Annual report of the Poor Law Commission, 1835: 60). Through the doctrine of 'less eligibility' introduced by the Act, it was intended that the education of workhouse children should be sufficient to enable them eventually to break the cycle of dependence on the parish and so look after themselves but not to provide them with anything like an advantage over the child of the respectable, working poor.

In fact, most Poor Law authorities were simply too small to provide the opportunity of even the modest curriculum required by law. Yet the zeal for the Christian education of the young had its champions, including some amongst the Poor Law Commissioners. In 1838, James Kay, an Assistant Commissioner, to some degree challenging the doctrine of 'less eligibility', argued that: 'Education is to be regarded as one of the most important means of eradicating the genus of pauperism from the rising generation, and of securing in the minds and morals of the people the best protection for the institutions of society' (Appendix B of the Fourth Annual Report of the Poor Law Commission: 145–6). It was not until ten years after the passing of the 1834 Act, however, that legislative provision was made to enable parishes and Poor Law unions to combine to create 'district' schools. According to Pinchbeck and Hewitt (1973: 508), the continuing reluctance on the part of Poor Law authorities to proceed to establish these 'vast State boarding schools' lay in local opposition to central government interference and additional bureaucracy, anticipated cost and a fear of breaching the widely supported doctrine of 'less eligibility'. Moreover, in London, the practice of 'contracting out' pauper children, permitted by the Poor Law, had led to the development of alternative provision, sometimes in the form of residential establishments operated for private profit. It was a scandal at one of these that finally released the pressure for change. As reported in the General Board of Health's Report on Quarantine in 1849, an outbreak of cholera in Mrs Drouet's Pauper Establishment in Tooting saw the death of 180 children and led to the trial of its proprietor for manslaughter. Confidence in the capacity of contractors' schools to provide for pauper children was undermined (at least for the time being) and several were closed or were placed under the control of the local authorities. Later in the same year, the first District School was opened.

Although never very numerous, it is to these District or Barrack Schools, sometimes containing as many as 1,000 children, born out of an Act designed to stigmatise and shame, that we can trace some of the persistently negative attitudes to the residential care of children. It is important to recognise how functional the 'deliberate cultivation of a repellent image' (Sinclair, 1988a: 8) was to the 'success' of the Poor Law. It served as a powerful deterrent to seeking parish relief and, in that sense, achieved one of the reformed Poor Law's central aims – to force the unwilling to find work. Hendrick notes the 'numerous scandals' (1994: 77) in the 1870s, and later, that revealed the wilful neglect and 'legal violence' of the regimes operated in some of the schools. The public attention drawn to these scandals served not only as a prompt to reform, but also played a part in cultivating a distaste both for this form of provision and, one imagines, for those who were subject to it. Sinclair (1988a: 10ff.) suggests that the 'scandals which from time to time erupted' (p. 10) were not necessarily any part of deliberate policy, however. They were regarded by the central authorities as attributable to 'a combination of the inadequate nature of their power to control what happened locally; cruel or ignorant staff; or brutal, incompetent and weak leadership'. Nonetheless, Sinclair argues, 'such incidents were also symptomatic of the contemporary rationales of institutions' (p. 10) which included punishment and deterrence as well as reformation.

Contemporary opposition to the District Schools drew strength from the supporters of the principle of 'less eligibility'. The schools were also considered expensive in that they did not cost any less than local provision. Moreover, the massing of children in badly ventilated and overcrowded workrooms and dormitories with little or no provision for exercise and fresh air produced physically weak children with little or no prospect of securing employment in adulthood (see Butler and Owens, 1993).

It is important to note that the end of the District Schools came not directly as a consequence of growing public awareness of their failure but rather as a consequence of the Elementary Education Act of 1870, which established (a degree of) universal educational provision. The availability of local schools was sufficient to persuade the Poor Law authorities that, on the grounds of economy at least, pauper children could just as easily be sent to school there. Alternatives to the workhouse and the largest District Schools were slow in developing, however, and awaited the considerable exertions of the philanthropic reformers of the latter half of the century, of whom Dr Barnardo was possibly the most energetic.

The democracy of the forgotten

According to his wife in her account of Thomas Barnardo's life, he began his work:

> ...when England was waking to the condition of the children of want. Laws were being unmade and remade for their protection; statesmen and philanthropists here and there voiced the long-stifled cry of the democracy of the forgotten. Some ministers...and even some churches...began to realise their duty towards those whose rights, ignored from the beginning, were now being recognised by the State. (Barnardo and Marchant, 1907: 94)

More precisely, Barnardo had opened his first home for destitute boys in Stepney in 1870, two years before the passage of the first Infant Life Protection Act (see chapter 4). This had attracted considerable public attention, not least through Barnardo's skilful use of the pulpit and the Christian press and also his keen eye for publicity. His conversion in 1872 of a public house, the Edinburgh Castle, into the 'People's Mission Church and the first Coffee-Palace in the country' had served to fix him even more firmly in the public eye. The accounts he published of his encounters with London's streetchildren rival Dickens both in terms of their poignancy and their sentimentality.

In 1873, Barnardo opened a second home, for girls, at Mossford Lodge, Ilford, Essex. However, his chance overhearing of a 'vile conversation' one night between girls at Mossford Lodge was to prove a turning point in his life and in the practice of residential care. Barnardo, 'in a moment realised' that 'our system of aggregating these girls...was but propagating and intensifying evil' (Barnardo and Marchant, 1907: 120–1): 'I saw that what I had done was not God's way. That was clear. The family life was His way; had He not from the first established it and blessed it? "He setteth the solitary in families" Ah! Then what had I been doing?'

Barnardo's answer to the despair he felt over his own experiments in residential care, and by implication other experiments elsewhere, was to be the founding of the 'cottage home'. Such 'little cottages' with their 'four or five rooms and under the influence of godly women' would be places where 'family life and family love might be reproduced'. Just as the infant life protection movement was doing at precisely the same time (see chapter 4), Barnardo found the inspiration, public support and finance to turn his ideas into reality in the contemporary idealisation of the family. His earlier rhetoric of the 'democracy of the forgotten' was to be realised, not in any action that might arise from a closer scrutiny of the more deeply embedded economic and social conditions that produced disadvantage, but in the removal of children into forms of care that would emulate and substitute for the family life of which they had been deprived.

An exploration of the form and origin of Barnardo's Christian philanthropy lie outside the scope of this chapter. Suffice it to say that the 'cult of benevolence' (Houghton, 1957: 274) which developed from the 1840s onward, owed as much to a concern for social order, at both ends of the social spectrum, as it did to the Protestant tradition of service to God. Houghton takes the view that the 'Puritan doctrine of work' would never have been stressed so much had its mid-century proponents 'not felt that aristocratic idleness had to be exorcised if society were to be saved' (p. 246). The work of Barnardo, Stephenson (who founded the National Children's Homes), the Church of England Waifs and Strays' Society, the Catholic Crusade of Rescue, Mr Fegan's Homes and the many other philanthropic enterprises that developed in the second half of the century provided many with an opportunity to take account of the fate of their own souls as much as those of the children for whom their charitable efforts were ostensibly joined. Such philanthropic efforts were not without their critics at the time. In 1850, Carlyle wrote of the 'blind loquacious pruriency of indiscriminate Philanthropism substituting itself, with much self-laudation, for the silent divinely awful sense of right and wrong' (Carlyle, 1850: 51). Later in the century, with increasing secularisation, even the most ardent philanthropy degenerated into mere sentimentality.

While Barnardo's own motives may have been authentic enough, the reality of the Barkingside Village was, as one might anticipate, somewhat less idyllic. The population of children with physical and learning disabilities who were admitted to the homes and who could not go on to paid employment grew rapidly and imposed a considerable strain on the financial resources of the Village. Staff employed at the homes were not always capable of dealing with the behaviour presented by the children, causing Barnardo to complain: 'I cannot but feel that if there was a larger amount of real loving godliness among the dear mothers who are my colleagues in the Village Homes, the necessity for punishment and the occasions of grave naughtiness would be immensely diminished' (Barnardo and Marchant, 1907: 136). Within months of the formal opening of the Village in 1876, rumours began to grow that children were being ill treated and ill fed. Barnardo was accused of having faked photographs of children dressed in rags and tatters, some of which were said to verge on the indecent, in order to secure charitable funds. Perhaps even more significantly at the time, there were accusations that Barnardo had misapplied funds for his own benefit. A formal inquiry was ordered by the court and for 38 days Arbitrators heard evidence on oath as to the conduct of the homes and its Director. The Arbitrators reported in October 1877. On the charges of financial impropriety Barnardo was cleared. The 'composite' photographs were allowed by the Arbitrators as 'artistic fiction'. The use of solitary cells had indeed been used for longer periods of confinement than was advisable but, generally, the 'Barnardo Institutions' were found to be 'real and valuable charities and worthy of public confidence and support'. However, the principal recommendation of the Arbitrators was that a 'committee of gentlemen' should be established to oversee the management of the homes and so bring some administrative stability and lines of accountability to what had hitherto been a largely personal enterprise.

The Barnardo Institutions prospered in the decades following the judgement of the Arbitrators. In the period 1867 to 1877, Barnardo received some 1,500 children; from 1877 to 1887, some 9,384. Other 'cottage homes' were opened elsewhere (see Young and Ashton, 1956: 133ff.), although their use never became very widespread.

In 1870, the same year in which Barnardo had claimed to have begun his work in earnest, a House of Commons Select Committee recommended that Boards of Guardians in England be authorised to allow the practice of 'boarding out'. In the same way as described in chapter 2, the boarding out of mentally ill patients had continued to form an unbroken, if subterranean, element in the range of choices available during the 'institutionally crazed' nineteenth century and despite a history dating back to Tudor times, in England, the practice of placing children in private households was not widespread at this time. In 1868, the Poor Law Board had found that only 21 unions in the whole of England were engaged in boarding out a total of just 347 children. Opposition to boarding out came, once again, most frequently from those who defended the principle of 'less eligibility'. Particular anxiety was focused on the fact that the 1870 Order allowed for the placement of illegitimate and deserted children. This could be construed as offering 'a reward ... to improvidence and a stimulus ... to immorality' (Fawcett, 1871; cited in Pinchbeck and Hewitt, 1973: 523) both real and present dangers to the preservation of decent family life.

However, boarding out did have its defenders. Mrs Nassau Senior (later to become the first woman Local Government Board inspector), in her report to the Board in 1874, established an antipathy between residential care and boarding out which was to resonate over the next 100 years when she wrote (p. 343): 'The enormous buildings that are erected for the reception of pauper children, seem to point to a belief that we are to have an ever-increasing race of paupers throughout the, centuries to come. Against such a belief boarding out is a protest.' Any real expansion in boarding out was to wait several more generations. In England, by 1905, still only 13 per cent (8,685) of the 65,579 children in Poor Law care were placed with families. Hence, the residential home remained the primary means of looking after children in the public care until well into the second half of the twentieth century.

Born out of not wanting to do more good than was strictly necessary and which would not make too many demands on the public purse, the essential nature of residential care for the deprived child was thus conceived in the nineteenth century. The attitude to the child in public care that it betrays is not one of deep concern but rather one of deep suspicion and routinised neglect. However, the most awful cruelties were to be found in the institutional responses to juvenile delinquency during the same period.

The terror of the law

In the early part of the century, the penitentiary movement offered some alternative to the contaminating effects of adult gaols and a considerable improvement on the 'floating bastilles' of the 'hulks', decommissioned warships, moored on the banks of the Thames. Here, boys as young as nine were housed in unsanitary, overcrowded conditions, subject to the predations of their guards and of older boys. For some, self-mutilation or suicide offered the only release. In 1838 an Act was passed establishing Parkhurst as the first specialist prison for juvenile offenders. In December of that year, 102 boys drawn from the hulks and prisons in London arrived to serve sentences ranging from two to 15 years. The regime was an explicitly punitive one. Inmates wore leg irons and prison uniform and were maintained on the most meagre of diets. The prison, according to those whose job it was to visit it and monitor its progress on behalf of government, was expected to exclude 'Every comfort and indulgence which was not essential to preserve health of mind and body' in order that there should be nothing in the arrangements of the prison which might tend to 'weaken the terror of the law or to lessen in the minds of the juvenile population at large, or of their parents, the dread of being committed to prison' (cited in Carlebach, 1970: 26). Criticism of Parkhurst was swift upon its establishment and was orchestrated by the supporters of the reformatory school movement, which shared the contemporary zeal for Christian education as the answer to delinquency as much as to poverty. Mary Carpenter, who published *Reformatory Schools for the Children of the Perishing and Dangerous Classes and for Juvenile Offenders* in 1851, castigated Parkhurst for its brutality and its high failure rates as evidenced by the number of whippings, escapes and transfer of boys to adult prisons as being beyond the capacity of Parkhurst to manage. The ideas of reform, expressed by Carpenter in her account of Kingswood, the school she founded in Bristol (1853: 474), was that by 'restoring' the child to 'the true position of childhood' and providing him or her with the care and control that a Christian parent might, the child will 'soon yield his own will in ready submission to those who are working for his good; [and] it will thus gradually be subdued and trained'.

Kingswood was a mixed reformatory, taking those who had offended and those who were in need of protection for other reasons. In practice, the distinction between the reformatory schools set up specifically for offenders after the Act of 1854 and the industrial schools set up three years later for those at risk, was soon eroded and formally abandoned by legislation in 1933. From the outset both the reformatory and industrial schools depended on regimes founded on discipline and hard work with 'brutal punishments, Spartan diets and austere living conditions' (Heywood, 1959: 189). Scandals are consequently not difficult to find.

For example, at a London Board Truant School in 1879 an inquiry found that the regime operated completely prohibited talking except to ask to go to the lavatory or in response to a question from a teacher. Play was banned completely and drill substituted instead. Dirty children were forced to lie naked on a stone sink in below-freezing temperatures while a cold tap was turned on them. Those who were sent to the school for a second truancy offence were given 12 strokes of the birch and kept in total silence for three weeks. At another inquiry in 1891 the captain of one industrial school training ship who had ordered 4,859 strokes of the birch over a three-year period was *cleared* of excessive cruelty. When a new captain was appointed, he punished boys found masturbating by painting their genitals with a liquid carbolic acid that left the boys in such agony that they could neither sit, stand nor lie down for the pain. After another scandal at a similar establishment, the Akbar Nautical Training School, in which it was found that sick children were caned, some were gagged before being birched and others were disciplined by being drenched in cold water and made to stand up all night, the Home Secretary ordered the establishment of a Departmental Committee on Reformatory and Industrial Schools, although its recommendations were never fully implemented because of the advent of the First World War. The date of the Akbar scandal was 1910 and the Home Secretary was Winston Churchill.

The point is that from the early nineteenth century until well into this, what characterises the residential care of children, offenders and non-offenders alike, is neglect, insensitivity and legally sanctioned violence. The truth is, however much it is obscured by philanthropic sentimentality or moral earnestness, that the child in the public care rarely excited the sympathies of anything more than a small number of individuals and behind the high walls of most institutional settings, children were subjected to the most stigmatising, brutal and harsh regimes with impunity.

Whose children?

From the turn of the century to almost the end of the Second World War, residential care both in form and substance proceeded, according to some, almost unchallenged and unchanged. Marjory Allen, in her letter to *The Times* of 15 July 1944, describes children 'under the guardianship of a Government Department' as having been 'entirely forgotten'. She continued: 'The public are, for the most part, unaware that many thousands of children are being brought up under repressive conditions that are generations out of date and are unworthy of our traditional care for children.' With remarkable prescience, the specific problems Lady Allen identified included the 'overworked, underpaid and untrained' staff, poor mechanisms for inspection, no clear standards, poor coordination of services, diffuse accountability and a lack of central direction. She argued that, 'A public inquiry, with full government support, is urgently needed to explore this largely uncivilised territory.' In setting the terms of such a Public Inquiry, which should address specifically 'how the use of large residential homes can be avoided', Lady Allen established not only the concerns of her own time, and those of the previous one hundred years, but also anticipated an agenda that is still being worked through today.

However, Lady Allen's use of the media to raise greater public awareness of the condition of children living away from home was not sufficient to secure the Public Inquiry she sought. As noted already, that required the death of Denis O'Neill (see chapter 4). There may be a more general point to make here about the nature of the subjects of scandal. There can be little doubt about O'Neill's status as an innocent victim. The status of children in residential care is more morally ambiguous. Either 'guilty' in a legal sense or 'tainted' by the unhappy experience of family life which brought them into care in the first place, they are unlikely to generate sympathy in the way that hospital patients might. Similarly, because such children remain largely undifferentiated, it is more difficult to generate a sense of the 'personal' (however spurious) that seems important to engaging public interest. The ambivalent status of children in the public care will re-emerge in our discussions of the Staffordshire Child Care Inquiry in chapter 9.

Nonetheless, in March 1945, less than three months after Denis O'Neill was killed and several weeks before the Monckton Report on his death was published, 'the first enquiry in this country directed specifically to the care of children deprived of a normal home life' was opened by its chairman, Myra Curtis (Report of the Care of Children Committee [Curtis Committee] – 'RCCC', 1946 para. 3). The inquiry was extraordinary in its scope. It met in full committee on 64 days; examined 229 witnesses; visited 451 institutions and numerous foster homes in 41 counties of England and Wales and spoke to officials of 58 local authorities.

The pattern of child care provision that the Curtis Committee investigated was still heavily biased towards residential care ('the persistence of traditional methods in the face of the changing attitude of the public towards social services'; RCCC, para. 129). Of the 124,900 children living away from home in 1945, 54,000 were accommodated in local authority residential care (including 13,400 in Approved Schools, Remand Homes or Approved Probation Hostels); a further 40,800 were accommodated in voluntary homes with only 27,800 children (22 per cent) 'boarded out' (RCCC, Table IV). The range of children who could be boarded was still cast in recognisable Poor Law terms (essentially reserved for orphan or deserted children), although it had been extended by the Public Assistance Order of 1930 to include those children over whom local authorities had assumed parental rights. These restrictions were finally removed in February 1945 in order to allow for the continuance of private care for children who had been billeted under the wartime scheme for evacuation.

Despite having to incorporate considerable technical detail, the text of the Curtis Committee Report presents a powerfully evocative picture of the daily life of children living away from home at the end of the Second World War. For those children still living in the workhouse (restricted since 1930 to a maximum of 6 weeks, except on medical grounds, for children aged between three and 16 but still numbering 6,500 children), conditions were particularly bleak (RCCC, para. 141):

> For the most part the children are housed in large gaunt looking buildings with dark corridors, high windows and unadapted baths

and lavatories. The best had been made of these forbidding buildings in a few of the institutions we visited, where admirable efforts had been made with the use of paint and pictures to brighten the rooms in which the children slept, and played. In others the traditional chocolate and buff paint remained, with bare boards and draughts, and a continual smell of mass cooking, soft soap and disinfectant.

Exceptionally, the members of the Committee discovered palpable neglect. Describing the children in one Poor Law nursery, the Report describes graphically how (RCCC, para. 144):

> Their clothes were not clean. Most of them had lost their shoes; those who possessed shoes had either taken them off to play with or were wearing them tied to their feet with dirty string. Their faces were clean; their bodies in some cases were unwashed and stained.

Conditions for children were generally better in children's homes outside of the Poor Law jurisdiction, even in the voluntary homes, those 'bare and comfortless' symbols of 'Victorian philanthropy' that had always been intended primarily 'to catch the eye and impress the passer by' (RCCC, para. 230). However, the conclusions of the Report are unequivocal in finding the standard of provision well below what was required:

> Where establishments fell below a satisfactory standard, the defects were not of harshness, but rather of dirt and dreariness, drabness and over regimentation. We found no child being cruelly used in the ordinary sense, but that perhaps was not a probable discovery on a casual visit. We did find many establishments ... in which children were being brought up by unimaginative methods, without opportunity for developing their full capacities and with very little brightness or interests in their surroundings. We found in fact many places where the standard of child care was no better, except in respect of disciplinary methods, than that of say 30 years ago; and we found a widespread and deplorable shortage of the right kind of staff, personally qualified and trained to provide the child with a substitute for a home background.

The Committee went on to note in terms of the emergent psychology of the day:

> The result in many Homes was a lack of personal interest in and affection for the children which we found shocking. The child in these

Homes was not recognised as an individual with his own rights and possessions, his own life to live and his own contribution to offer. He was merely one of a large crowd … he was without the feeling that there was anyone to whom he could turn who was vitally interested in his welfare or who cared for him as a person.

The Committee noted at several points how the younger, affection-starved children would clamour for their attention when members of the Committee visited a home and how the older ones seemed to have withdrawn into worlds of their own.

Despite the attendant difficulties of inspecting and regulating the practice of boarding out, the Committee came to share the view often expressed to them, that this was 'the best method short of adoption' (RCCC, para. 460; Recommendation 21) for providing the child with a substitute home. Indeed, 45 years before Utting would ask similar questions and 70 years after Mrs Nassau Senior had made her 'protest', the Committee did consider the possibility of the 'gradual elimination of the institution' (RCCC, para. 476) but despite the promise of 'family allowances and social insurance' the Committee doubted 'whether the next 10 or 15 years will bring us to the stage at which institutions can be dispensed with, or even in sight of that stage'. The question of how far it might be possible to prevent children being removed from home through preventive work was regarded by the Committee as of the 'utmost importance' (para. 7) but immediately excluded from their inquiry, as it was 'not the problem with which we have been asked to deal'. As indicated in chapter 4, the times were not yet right for asking such questions, but it is worth noting how, by defining the mandate of the Inquiry in this way, not only are some of the questions prescribed, but so too are the possible answers.

One should also note how many of the concerns of later inquiries into residential care are pre-figured both in Marjorie Allen's letter and in the Report of the Curtis Committee. The 'unsuitability' and 'inadequacy' of many of the staff and their training were the subject of frequent adverse comment; the opportunity that arose for 'individuals in charge of groups of children [to] develop harsh or repressive tendencies or false ideas of discipline, and that the children in their care may suffer without the knowledge of the central authority' (RCCC, para. 417); 'traditional inter-departmental antagonism which was thinly veiled by changes in organisation' (RCCC, para. 131) and the 'failure in co-operation between committees of the same area' which was illustrated to the Committee by 'the unfortunate results which may occur where one possesses information which is not available to the other' (RCCC, para. 135). Each of these observations would be made many more times in successive inquiries over the next 45 years.

The Committee went on to make a wide range of recommendations aimed at reforming the confused and confusing administrative infrastructure through which residential care was delivered. The Committee had also sought to extend the scope of those children for whom public care might be provided and to establish standards of accommodation and child care practice (see RCCC, para. 493). The government formally accepted the recommendations of the Curtis Committee (and the Clyde Committee which had reported on similar lines in respect of Scotland) on 24 March 1947 and began to give them immediate effect. In July 1947, the Transfer of Functions (Relief of Children) Order transferred responsibility for the 'child deprived of a normal home life' to the Home Office. In the same month, the Central Training Council in Child Care was appointed, although it was not until 1954, following two reports by Eileen Younghusband, that the LSE admitted its first graduates to train social workers in various settings, including child care, on a generic basis.

The Home Office continued about its new tasks with energy and enthusiasm and issued its first circular in September 1947 inviting local authorities to begin the process of establishing Children's Committees and appointing Children's Officers. These and other of the Curtis Committee's recommendations were to achieve legislative support with the passing of the Children Act on 30 June 1948.

Special pessimism

If the period between the wars could be characterised as a period of inertia in the development and practice of residential care, the period from 1950 to the time of the publication of the 'Pindown' report in 1991 could be described as a period of rationalisation and decline. A broad sense of the overall reduction in the numbers of children living in residential care can be gathered from Table 8.1. Despite a sharp increase in the early 1970s (discussed below), the downward progress in the scale of residential provision for children in the public care is inexorable and is matched by the growing use of foster care. In the space of little more than a generation, the number of children living in children's homes of various sorts fell both in absolute and proportional terms, from 35,400 in 1951 to 13,300 in 1991. (It should be noted, however, that the proportion of children looked after by the local authority as a proportion of all children under the age of 18 has altered little over the same period – from

Table 8.1 Patterns of placement for children in the public care, 1951–1991

	1951[1]	1956	1961	1966	1971	1976	1981	1986	1991
Number looked after[2]	62,700	62,300	62,200	69,200	87,100	100,600	92,300	67,300	59,800
Number in residential care – local authority	28,800	30,200	24,300	25,000	43,800	40,300	31,400	17,600	12,500
Number in residential care – voluntary homes	6,600	4,600	3,600	4,900	5,500	4,200	3,200	1,200	800
Total in residential care	35,400	34,800	27,900	29,900	49,300	44,500	33,600	18,800	13,300
Percentage in residential care	56.5	55.9	44.9	43.2	56.6	44.2	37.5	27.9	22.2
Number fostered[3]	24,300	27,100	29,100	31,800	30,200	33,100	35,700	35,100	36,700
Ratio of children placed in residential care to those fostered	100:69	100:78	100:104	100:106	100:61	100:74	100:103	100:187	100:276

Notes
1. Excludes remand/approved schools.
2. The term 'looked after' is used anachronistically.
3. The term 'fostered' includes those placed for adoption.

5 per 1000 aged under 18 in 1951 to 5.5 in 1991.) Similarly, for every 100 children in residential care, the number fostered rose from 69 to 276 over the same period.

The origins of this remarkable transformation can be traced, in part, directly to the 1948 Act. But the overall reduction in the scale of residential care was accompanied by, and is in part attributable to, a decisive shift in attitudes towards such provision, particularly amongst Children's Officers and the social workers who succeeded them that is not to be found, at least not to the same degree, in either the Curtis Report or the Act. As Heywood (1959: 160) has observed, following the 1948 Act, reception into the care of the local authority had become 'a judgement of need rather than a test of destitution' and it was to be in the exercise of that judgement that the future of residential care would lie. More precisely, it would be in 'the social work profession established by the 1948 Act and the ideas it came to espouse' that the challenge to residential care would draw its strength (Bullock, 1999: 162). We might note, as indicated in Table 8.1, how the provision of residential care became virtually the monopoly of the local authority between 1951 and 1991 with the almost total eclipse of the voluntary/charitable provider. The pre-eminence of the local authority both as assessor of need and as provider of service was to be central to the problematics addressed more than 40 years later by the 1989 Children Act.

How far such attitudes were to shift is evidenced by the report published by the DHSS in 1985, a little over a year after the practice of 'pin-down' had begun in a children's home in Staffordshire, which characterised the attitude taken by social workers to residential care as one of 'special pessimism' (DHSS, 1985: 16). This pessimism has a number of specific roots, some deriving from the history of residential care more generally, but others lying closer to hand in the intellectual tradition to which the social work profession made itself heir and in particular to the work of John Bowlby and Erving Goffman.

However, before the precipitate decline in the scale of residential provision indicated by Table 8.1, there was a brief period of expansion, although this may have been born more of necessity than out of enthusiasm for what residential care could offer. The number of children in the care of local authorities, estimated by Curtis to have been around 46,000 in 1946, had reached more than 55,000 by November of 1949. In the absence of sufficient field staff, children's committees turned to the 'tradition of institutional care' which at least had the benefits of being 'administratively convenient and largely understood' (Heywood, 1959: 161). But as numbers grew, so too did costs and in 1952, the government's

Select Committee on Estimates urged not only a greater use of preventive measures but also an expansion of arrangements for boarding out as not only the best but the cheapest option. The Select Committee's injunctions were to find a receptive audience amongst child care professionals, as witnessed by the fate of the residential nursery.

Curtis had envisaged a continuing role for such provision, albeit only where 'boarding out' or a voluntary home was unavailable or unsuitable (RCCC, para. 479) and in 1951, the Sixth Report on the Work of the Children's Department of the Home Office noted that there were 248 such nurseries provided under the Children Act and the National Assistance Act (Sixth Report, para. 70). By November 1954 that number had fallen to 215 nurseries looking after 4,812 children and by the time of the Eighth Report, in 1961, the number of children cared for in residential nurseries provided by local authorities had fallen to 3,543 living in 166 establishments (Eighth Report, para. 44). The Seventh Report (1955) had attributed the movement away from this kind of provision to 'recent developments in the practice of local authorities and voluntary organisations...based on advice tendered by the Advisory Council on Child Care' (para. 57), which had been established in 1951 in accordance with section 43 of the Children Act. Coincidentally, this was the same year in which John Bowlby presented his ideas on maternal deprivation to the World Health Organisation.

Echoes of Bowlby's work (which, according to Walton and Elliot (1980: 8), came to be 'bowdlerised' to mean 'that any family home in the community is better than institutional care') is distinctly echoed in the Home Office Memorandum of 1955 dealing with the care of children aged under 5 (appended to the Seventh Report). It confidently asserts (para. 3) that:

> It is accepted that every child should be brought up in his own home, unless separation from the family is unavoidable. The shock of parting even temporarily from the people he knows and particularly from his mother, and from familiar surroundings, is severe and may cause him lasting harm. Accordingly, those concerned with a child whose family is in danger of breaking up do all that they can...to keep the home together. ...It is particularly necessary that the young child should be able to find a substitute for the personal relationship that should have existed between him and his mother in normal circumstances.

The momentum towards the preventive, 'family first' strategies of the 1963 and 1969 Acts was clearly beginning to build (see chapter 4). It was added to by another important contribution from the 'literature of dysfunction'

(Jones, 1967: 14) which found its way onto the reading lists of qualifying social workers throughout the 1960s and 1970s, that of Irving Goffman. In the same way that Bowlby's work was reduced to a slogan, so too might it be argued that Goffman's ideas were simplified and reduced to the slogan that 'institutional life is depersonalising, intrusive, humiliating, dis-empowering and ultimately harmful to the inmate'. This was held to be particularly true of the larger institution (Goffman, 1961).

Serious attempts to reduce the size of children's homes, a particular source of complaint by Marjorie Allen, had followed immediately after the 1948 Act. As early as 1951, the Home Office had taken the view that 'the family group home is the best type of children's home' (HO, 1951: para. 56). Such homes, housing no more than around a dozen children were, by 1954, accommodating 9 per cent of the residential child care population whereas 34 per cent lived in homes for 12 children or more. By 1984, the proportions had altered to 25 per cent and 24 per cent respectively.

But the attitudes of social workers to residential care cannot be seen entirely in isolation. Both Bowlby's and Goffman's ideas and, to a lesser degree, Barton's work on institutional neurosis (Barton, 1959), became part of lay as well as professional received wisdom and as Bullock has noted, since the 1960s, there has been a more general and 'noticeable decline in all sorts of residential life' (Bullock, 1999: 161): 'Students prefer their own flats to halls of residence, soldiers and sailors rush home at weekends, monasteries are short of novices and residential "living in" is decreasingly attractive to staff.' However, there are two further particular examples of social work practice imperatives that we should note which were to be inimical to residential care; the permanency movement of the early 1970s and the broadly contemporaneous 'alternatives to custody' movement built around the 1969 Children and Young Person's Act.

As indicated in Table 8.1, the early 1970s saw a considerable and unexpected rise in the number of children in public care although the number of entrants to the care system continued to fall. Some of this growth was attributable to the transfer of approved schools to the control of social services departments in 1971. But the numbers continued to increase after this point and beyond the point that could be accounted for by demographic trends. It is difficult fully to account for this rise and for the proportionate rise in the use of residential care that followed. Kahan (1993) finds some of the reasons in the lack of adequately skilled child care specialists available to the new post-Seebohm generic social services departments and the fact that additional capital resources for building programmes were available. As an eyewitness, she comments that (p. 95): 'Competitiveness in building programmes took the place for a time of competitiveness in boarding out percentages when directors of social services met together.' Another contemporary account describes a growing sense that the 'early enthusiasm' (Ballance, 1973) for foster care appeared to have been 'to some extent misplaced' (p. 79), in that there was a 'worryingly high rate of breakdown' and a 'more cautious approach' was being taken to family placement. What was clear was that children were staying in care longer. These became, after the title of the book in which Rowe and Lambert (1973) published their research, the *Children Who Wait*; children drifting through local authority care, waiting for a suitable family placement. The publication of Rowe and Lambert's book coincided with the spread, from the USA, of the idea of 'permanency planning' (see Maluccio et al., 1986 for a detailed account of the origins of this set of ideas and Barth et al., 1994 for an account of their progress in the USA). As the phrase suggests, permanency planning was predicated on the idea that a child needed stability and continuity of relationships and that these were more likely to be provided in family forms of care. James (1998: 176) notes the 'paradox' whereby the role of 'families of origin was devalued and new families offering adoption was placed at a premium'. Nonetheless, foster care once again soon returned to became the placement of first resort, invigorated by the promise of new 'professional' forms of substitute family care deriving from Nancy Hazel's much-publicised innovations in Kent (Hazel, 1981).

However, the permanency movement was not, nor does it remain, without its opponents. Firstly there were those who argued that too little was being done to enable birth parents to carry out their duties, hence confirming them in their roles as 'incompetent' or 'uncaring' parents (Jordan, 1981; Holman, 1975 and 1988). Holman's work in particular was used, according to Thoburn (1999), by the British Association of Social Workers to inform their opposition to those parts of the 1975 Children Act which made it easier for local authorities to assume parental rights and more difficult for parents to remove their children from the care of the local authority after a period of two years had elapsed. In Thoburn's view, the effect of the 1975 Act was not so much to shift the balance away from parental rights towards children's rights as to increase the power of local authorities and foster and adoptive families. Secondly, research by Milham and others, reported by the DHSS in 1985, stressed how poor the decision-making processes were when it came to planning for children and how children too easily became *Lost in Care* (Millham, Bullock et al., published separately in 1986), isolated from their families of origin. The lack of adequate preventive services and the danger of more or less permanent estrangement fell particularly heavily on black children in care, who were being placed in white families in such a way that they were less able to preserve their cultural identity in an aggressively racist society (see *Black and in Care* 1984 and Small, 1985).

As important to the depreciation of residential care as the permanency planning movement but deriving from a concern with young offenders was the growth of 'intermediate treatment' (later 'alternatives to custody') that developed in the wake of the 1969 Act. Perhaps not surprisingly given the political fate of the 1969 Act (see chapter 4), which was intended to be 'the most definite decriminalising instance of postwar penal policy' (Muncie, 1984: 153), the number of juveniles committed to custody in the 1970s and 1980s rose substantially and far in advance of the increase in crime. Drawing on American ideas (in particular the 'Massachusetts experiment' of Jerome Miller), diversionary strategies were developed to keep young people not only out of the penal system but also out of the welfare system. Here, the administrative discretion of social workers had led, according to research centring on Lancaster University and the work of David Smith, David Thorpe, Norman Tutt and others, to injustices (such as de facto indeterminate sentencing and in relation to borstal training, de jure indeterminate sentencing) as great, if not greater, than any to be found in a court of law (see Jones and Kerslake, 1979; Morris, Giller et al., 1980; Giller and Morris, 1981; Harris and Webb, 1987). The fact that residential care in particular was understood as a prime target for the 'youth justice workers' of the period was precisely indicated by Spencer Millham (1977):

> I would stress to you that the residential tradition is very strong. It has been going for nearly 300 years and it is not going to be shifted by a few murmurs about intermediate treatment, particularly when children are often popped in institutions by an administrative elite who have been educated in similar places and whose idea of adolescent heaven is a whiff of Lifebuoy soap and sweaty socks.

What is of lasting importance in both the permanency planning and decarceration movements of the 1970s, however, is the fact that both intruded a new rhetoric of rights into the discourse of child care or, at the very least, began to postulate a new set of relationships between the child, the family and the state that would call into question the primacy in child care matters that had been acquired by the social worker. This was to have a significant influence on the development of the 1989 Children Act that was to come into force during the course of the Pindown Inquiry.

'Remarkably and depressingly constant'

Unmistakable evidence of these new currents running through the discourse of child care occurs in the work of the Social Services Select Committee which determined, in July 1982, to undertake an inquiry into children in care. Rejecting a call for a Royal Commission on the subject because 'past experience suggests that social work practice is more influenced by detailed and specific research than by broad philosophical discussions' (para. 11 of the Second Report from the Social Services Committee, later referred to as 'the Short Report', after its chairman, Renée Short) noted early that while the law changes slowly to meet new situations, 'society itself remains remarkably and depressingly constant in the way in which children are treated and mistreated' (para. 10).

First among the 'pressing reasons' given by the Committee for its inquiry was the 'continuing debate about the rights of children and the rights of parents, and the extent to which it was practicable to defend one without infringing the other'. Active discussion about parental rights, particularly the rights of birth parents, in the face of the protagonists of permanency planning had begun to be articulated by organisations such as the Family Rights Group and by the time of the Select Committee's discussions 'centred around parental access and parental rights resolutions ... a right to information and right of access to court' (para. 15). Similarly, the rights of children in care, defended by the youth justice workers initially and increasingly articulated directly through organisations like the National Association of Young People in Care (NAYPIC) (which was shortly to play an important part in the Pindown Inquiry – see chapter 9), were becoming ever more urgently expressed. As we have indicated (and indeed, as the Committee recognised), the tension between the interests of children and those of their parents and how these might be mediated by the State were not entirely new phenomena. The Committee had 'considerable sympathy with the advocates of family life' (para. 17) but recognised also that 'however young, a child is an independent person, with a complete and separate identity' (para. 16). The broader context in which the Committee and later the 1989 Children Act sought to achieve a balance between the rights of parents and their children through the rhetorical device of 'partnership' has been sketched in chapter 5 but we might note that the Committee clearly approved of the advocacy work of NAYPIC, which, according to the Secretary of State, represented the 'pure consumer interest in child care' (quoted in para. 18) and anticipated 'the growing conviction that children have or should have, enforceable rights as individuals, even within a general tradition of liberal paternalism' (para. 18).

As far as residential care was concerned, the Committee formally acknowledged 'a continuing and positive role' for it (para. 201), although there is something of a discontinuity in this sanguine hope and the terms in which such care is described elsewhere in the report:

> Residential care is going through an intensely difficult period, which may be optimistically typed as being a process of transition but less optimistically viewed sometimes looks like a gradual process of destruction. The current prevailing public preference for family placements and the perceived expense of residential care, together with the widely held belief that residential care for children can often be damaging in the long term, has led to deteriorating staff morale and to a sense of purposelessness in some residential homes. (para. 200)

> the Committee's visits and the evidence received confirm that there are indeed difficult if not intractable problems with residential care… (para. 201)

> residential care has both inherent and practical disadvantages… it is… apparent that a children's home is an undesirably artificial environment for a child to grow up in and that it does not and cannot provide the family experience which all children need. (para. 203)

> Residential care… has particular problems with discipline and control; with younger children boarded out, these problems will grow. The long-term emotional effects of growing up in residential care are perhaps even more serious. … The Royal College of Psychiatrists even went so far in evidence as to suggest that 'Prolonged residential care is likely to lead to abnormal psychological development'. (paras. 203 and 204)

In fact, the Committee made a number of recommendations that were to influence the specific provisions of the 1989 Act. These included recommendations on case management and the role of the keyworker, the provision of clear statements of purpose for residential homes, the management of admissions to care, post-placement planning, reviews, inspection record-keeping and research. These would be mediated by the DHSS *Review of Child Care Law* (1985) and the government White Paper, *The Law on Child Care and Family Services* (1987), as well as by the two influential papers from the Law Commission on *Wards of Court* (1987) and *Guardianship and Custody* (1988) but the Committee's influence was nonetheless a significant one.

In a broader sense, some of the currents with which the Committee was trying to contend were to await the 'catharsis' (Hendrick, 1994: 274) of the Cleveland affair (see chapter 5). At the time of the practice of pindown the new resolution of the 'liberal dilemma' brought about by the Children Act 1989 was still being contended. But the tensions were self-evident. As larger questions were being asked about the appropriate balance between the rights of children, their parents and the State, there was nothing to be gained, in the Committee's view, from concealing the problems of residential care (para. 229):

> There are problems over staffing, management, control and purpose. As the residential childcare population 'ages', these problems become ever more pressing. What must not be lost sight of is that the facilities are not there to serve the convenience of the staff, of social workers, of the children's families or of any other adults, but to serve the children.

Four months before these words were written, the practice of pindown had begun at a children's home at 245 Hartshill Road, Stoke-on-Trent.

Conclusion

As a form of welfare practice, residential care for children has proved remarkably resilient. The actual bricks and mortar of institutional provision as much as the ways of working and habits of thought of those who staffed them have proven almost infinitely adaptable to changing fashions in welfare practice and treatment ideologies. The 'large gaunt looking buildings with dark corridors and high windows' of the nineteenth century could easily be pressed into service to suit the moral and political enterprises of the Poor Law Commissioners intent on deterrence or the philanthropists troubled with the care of their own souls. Slightly adapted and given a coat of paint, they served the Children's Officers' missionary zeal and later, with the paint peeling again, they met the needs of social workers looking for places in 'community homes with education'.

Behind each of these transitions the same larger forces that we have described earlier were at work. But there is one particular and enduring characteristic of residential provision made for children and that is its relative 'invisibility'. Almost by definition, residential care is an activity which takes place behind the literal or metaphorical walls of the institution, away from public attention other than when revealed through the reports of 'scandals'. Children in care are accordingly relatively isolated. Largely unobserved, children placed in care are also uniquely vulnerable through whatever experiences brought them into institutional care in the first place. These factors accentuate the powerful positions of adults under whose authority children are placed. Such adults are routinely in a position to make life-changing decisions for the young people they are looking after. As Westcott (1991: 12–13) has observed, children in institutions are a 'voiceless population, having no control over decisions affecting their current and future placements, and no influence over the quality of care they receive'. Central to the very concept of abuse is the relative powerlessness of the victim, which may be accentuated in an institutional setting. It is the relative powerlessness of children that makes them particularly vulnerable to abuse and which prevents them acting for themselves or engaging others to end it. It is this perhaps, more than anything else, that lies behind the 'ambience of uneasiness' that came to occupy certain Staffordshire children's homes in the 1980s. As in hundreds of other children's homes over the previous 150 years, children in Staffordshire appeared to have no voice, no control, no influence. In short, they were not in possession of even the most fundamental rights of citizenship. Scandalising their circumstances would prove hard work.

9

'A Narrow, Punitive and Harshly Restrictive Experience'

The Pindown Experience and the Protection of Children. The Report of the Staffordshire Child Care Inquiry

Introduction

The report of the Staffordshire Child Care Inquiry was published on 30 May 1991 under the title 'The Pindown* Experience and the Protection of Children'. The term 'pindown' was used to describe practice in a number of children's homes in Staffordshire between April 1983 and October 1989. It was said to have its origins in the phrase 'we must pin down the problem', used by Tony Latham, 'the architect and leading exponent' (1.4) of pindown, 'whilst he gestured with his forefinger pointing towards the floor' (paras. 1.4 and 12.18).

The Report identifies several variations on both the practice of pindown and the terms used to describe it, including: 'basic pindown'; 'total pindown'; 'full pindown'; 'heavy pindown'; 'strict pindown'; 'negative pindown'; 'nasty pindown'; 'relaxed pindown'; 'sympathetic pindown'; 'positive pindown' and 'therapeutic pindown'. As the Report suggests, the words 'give us a clue as to the approach used in the practice of pindown' (12.15) but it is important to recognise how the central term, 'pindown', suggests a meaning in advance of any particular definition or explanation. It might seem to tell us all that we need to know about the practices it describes and the people involved.

---

* The term 'pindown' is variously found written as one or two words, hyphenated and or capitalised. In this chapter 'pindown' is used to refer to certain practices carried on in children's homes in Staffordshire. 'Pindown' (capitalised) is used to refer to the scandal that followed their discovery. All references in parentheses throughout this chapter are to the relevant paragraph or page of the Inquiry Report.

As well as the practice of pindown, the Inquiry's terms of reference also included scrutiny of the 'participation by young persons in care in the activities of undertakings not owned by the County Council and known as Fundwell' (1.7). Fundwell was the name given to a 'network of voluntary organisations and private companies' (13.2) set up by Tony Latham to provide services to Staffordshire County Council. As a name, it seems to permit of a variety of ironic assumptions about the motives, character and actions of those involved. If part of the task of any inquiry is to simplify complex phenomena and to make them accessible to a wider audience, such headline-friendly and emotive terms as 'pindown' and 'Fundwell' might be considered an advantage. Inevitably, the underlying reality is more complex and considerably more ambiguous but as one journalist (Christopher Hitchens, *The Observer*, 12 November 2000) has commented, the 'perfect scandal' has to have a name. The journalistic attraction of such names may offset the difficulty mentioned in the previous chapter of scandals involving the residential care of children struggling to engage public interest without the appeal of a named individual such as Maria Colwell.

The practice of pindown

The practice of pindown would appear to have developed, rather than to have been designed, as implied by the repeated references to Tony Latham as its 'architect' (both in the Report and subsequent media coverage) as a response to circumstances at 'The Birches', a children's home/family centre in Stoke-on-Trent, Staffordshire. The local Social Services Department had reorganised its residential services for children during 1983, introducing the concept of the family centre, which was 'fashionable in the early 1980s' (4.4). Such family centres, in the case of The Birches and other former children's homes in the county, retained their residential function as well as acquiring new sets of roles and tasks. In the view of the Inquiry, the reorganisation was under-resourced from the outset (4.5, 4.6):

> the emphasis on budget reductions required in 1983 led to staffing establishments which were unrealistic in relation to over ambitious objectives for the centres … The whole scheme also ignored the reality that a complex list of tasks many of which required considerable skill, knowledge and experience, would in the main inevitably be carried out by inexperienced, untrained and unqualified staff.

Buildings were not adapted to their new purposes and the numbers of children accommodated in the various centres throughout the county were considerably higher than the plans for reorganisation had allowed. For the staff at The Birches, 'How they carried out their new role and tasks was left largely to their own initiative and no guidelines were issued from social services headquarters to assist them' (4.10). There was a threat of industrial action in the county and by July 1983, 'stealing, fighting, defiance, shouting, crying and non-school attendance, which were problems made worse by overcrowding and understaffing, were affecting staff and children alike' (4.26). From April through to September, The Birches' logbook recorded five instances of children being made to put on their pyjamas as a 'measure of control' (4.16) and a similar number of other instances of children being 'off privileges' (4.20). On 3 November, the police picked up three boys who had absconded from The Birches. In evidence to the Inquiry (4.40–4.42):

> Each recalled that after being handed over by the police, they had their clothes removed, probably at The Birches, and were then taken to 245 Hartshill Road in their underpants without shoes … The boys were all put into the same room. This had initially been empty but after … they moved the furniture, it contained a table and upright chairs. They were required to have a cold shower, then $\frac{1}{2}$ hour to keep fit … They were given cheese on toast, tea and 'even a fag' … They then went to bed, sleeping in a second room on mattresses on the floor with no other bedding … the next morning they were required to do physical exercises outdoors in their underwear … the boys were told … they would have to earn back their clothes.

This account reveals many of the elements that came, in the view of the Inquiry, to characterise the practice of pindown as well as identifying the principal site used, 245 Hartshill Road. This was another children's home, approximately two miles away from The Birches, used partly as a semi-staffed 'independence unit'.

In seeking to define pindown, the Inquiry decided that at least four features were usually present (12.15):

> Firstly isolation for part of the time in a children's home cordoned off as a 'special' or Pindown unit; secondly removal of ordinary clothing for part of the time and the enforced wearing of shorts or night clothes; thirdly being told of having to earn 'privileges'; and fourthly being allowed to attend school or a 'school room' in the unit, and changing back into shorts or night clothes after returning from school.

As well as at The Birches and Hartshill Road, pindown came to be practiced at two other sites in Tamworth and Stoke-on-Trent, although to a much more limited extent. In total, the Inquiry determined that 132 children had been subjected to pindown between November 1983 and October 1989. They noted that the longest continuous period in which a child had been subject to pindown was 84 days whilst the longest overall period was 129 days (four episodes). The youngest child subject to the regime was aged nine and the oldest 17 (12.32).

The Report includes extracts from a variety of 'documents' drawn up at different points during the currency of the regime in which attempts were made to explain the 'philosophy' which lay behind the practice of pindown. The Inquiry gives little credence to such explanations and justifications as they contained and notes in any case that the 'actual use of pindown…wandered far from its so-called philosophy' (12.12). They go further (12.5):

> We have…no doubt after considering the totality of the evidence that in the vast majority of cases the children perceived pindown with its supposed panoply of meetings, reviews, contracts and attempts to establish a structure of understanding and trust, as a narrow, punitive and harshly restrictive experience. We think that their perceptions are correct.

In considering the impact of pindown on those children who were made subject to it, as well as calling on the evidence of a series of experts in social work, psychiatry, psychology and penology, the Inquiry took a 'commonsense approach' (12.34) to understanding the 'likely negative effects' on children of the regime and came 'firmly' to the view that (12.56): 'Pindown in all its many manifestations was intrinsically unethical, unprofessional and unacceptable…fall[ing] decisively outside anything that could be considered good childcare practice.'

Fundwell

The Inquiry's scrutiny of the activities of Fundwell has not lived so long in the professional or public imagination as pindown. This is in part due to the acknowledged complexity and lack of accurate records kept of the 17 'organisations and activities' (13.7) that were associated with the company which bore the name. In essence, the many schemes operating involved children and young people in work experience or training, originally developing out of Manpower-Services-Commission-funded Youth Training Schemes. The Inquiry casts considerable doubt on the efficacy or merits of the provision made for children through Fundwell (13.28):

> Much of the work, in our view, was not educational or generally beneficial in other respects. Some of the young people who were interviewed by the Inquiry resented being used as a 'general dogsbody' and working very hard for little or no reward and without any choice.

Although usually omitted from later commentaries on the events in Staffordshire (see, for example, Berridge and Brodie, 1996; Corby et al., 1998; Stanley, 1999), the Fundwell strand to the Inquiry is important for our purposes for two very particular reasons. Firstly, it was the activities of Fundwell and not the practice of pindown which first came to the attention of local media and hence wider political and public interest, and secondly because the activities of Fundwell significantly modify both the presentation of the central characters involved in pindown and also problematise the distribution of blame. We consider the question of blame in more detail below, but it is important to note that Tony Latham had been appointed in July 1987 to the post of Voluntary Bodies Co-ordinator, specifically to manage the operation of Fundwell with the apparent support of his line manager and the Director of Social Services. The Director's report to the General Sub-Committee of the Social Service Committee, which approved the establishment of the post, noted that it 'would be a considerable loss to the county if [five named companies operating under the management of Fundwell] ... were to fold because of absence of direction and leadership' (8.60). How far elected members believed they had been presented with the full picture of how Fundwell operated was to become an issue later but it would appear, at least in 1987, that Tony Latham and several other key figures associated with the practice of pindown enjoyed considerable prestige amongst colleagues and superiors. Even the Inquiry is moved to comment on Latham's (and others') activities with Fundwell that they 'worked long hours and with enthusiastic commitment' before adding, however, that 'from the children's point of view this sometimes meant that there was scarcely any aspect of their lives which was not under the control of Tony Latham and those working closely with him' (13.33).

Other matters

The Inquiry had its terms of reference extended in October 1990 to include a consideration of whether any child in the care of the local authority had been the victim of a 'gay sex circle preying on young boys' (14.3). Concerns had arisen as a consequence of the conviction of a number of men in November 1989, two of whom had been visitors to children's establishments in Staffordshire. The Inquiry found no evidence to substantiate concerns in relation to either man, although it did feel able to make recommendations to improve procedures in relation to staffing and the recording of visits to children in care. The Inquiry also considered the case of a young man who had been placed in rented accommodation operated by a convicted sex offender and who had subsequently been abused by him. The Inquiry notes the confused policy operating in Staffordshire in relation to checking the suitability of private landlords and made a number of recommendations not only in relation to local practice but also in terms of inadequate notification procedures operating between the Home Office, the police and local authorities. Neither of these matters was considered by the Inquiry to have a direct bearing on pindown or Fundwell and no further consideration is given to them in this chapter.

'Business as usual?'

The Inquiry Report contains many examples of the indignities and deprivations experienced by the children who were subject to pindown. A separate chapter is devoted to seven individual accounts of those who experienced its 'rigours' (11.1). In the light of such accounts, it would seem reasonable to ask how could such 'intrinsically unethical, unprofessional and unacceptable' practices have gone apparently undetected and unremarked upon for so long? In fact, it is hard to escape the conclusion that the practices associated with pindown (and Fundwell) were widely known as well as tacitly or directly supported by the senior management of Staffordshire County Council for much of the period of their operation.

There is direct evidence to support such a view contained in the Report itself. Correspondence between Fred Hill, Senior Assistant (Child Care), a member of headquarters staff, Elizabeth Brennan, Principal Area Officer (Latham's line manager) and Peter Crockett, then Assistant Director of Social Services, beginning in February 1984 and continuing at least until March 1985, discussed doubts expressed in writing by Hill concerning the legality of pindown following a visit he had made to The Birches. Practice at Hartshill Road appeared to him 'to be in contravention of the Community Homes Regulations on control' (5.22). The Inquiry notes that interest in the matters raised simply 'petered out and major potential issues were unresolved' (12.71). Similarly, the Report notes numerous 'statutory visits' both to The Birches and to Hartshill Road between 1983 and 1989. A few of these also raised concerns over the methods of control used, although most did not. Where such concerns were raised, they were expunged from the record submitted to the District Advisory Sub-Committee of elected members who received the reports of statutory visitors (e.g. 7.40; 7.42; 8.20; 8.36; 8.47; 9.27). One might note the capacity of most bureaucracies to filter out or absorb any indication of a possible failure or deficiencies in its operation. This tendency may be particularly strong in the semi-closed world of residential care, which may explain why determined outsiders play such an important part in the generation of scandals in institutional settings.

Other evidence presented to the Inquiry suggested that senior management actively promoted the activities of both Latham and his team. Pindown was extended to another children's home, The Alders in Tamworth, following a request by Crockett, now Deputy Director of Social Services, 'to advise and assist wherever necessary' in March 1989 (10.15) and to Heron Cross House in September 1989 (10.48). Latham seemed to enjoy privileged access to senior managers, especially Crockett, which caused his immediate line manager (Brennan) some difficulty (7.67ff.) on occasions.

Perhaps most surprisingly, The Birches and Hartshill Road were both visited in December 1987 by the Social Services Inspectorate. Their programme included a discussion on 'philosophy, staffing, rotas, procedures etc., child care practices, work loads, case work, shared programmes etc., files' which took place at a meeting in The Birches. Inspectors also attended a 'family meeting' at Hartshill Road (8.40). It might seem implausible that the topic of pindown would not have arisen, especially during the course of the 'family meeting' at Hartshill Road, yet the Inquiry announced itself to be 'quite satisfied that the Inspectors were not told about Pindown and its workings or shown a unit in action. Had they been told we cannot believe that they would not have investigated further and fully reported on the Pindown unit' (12.75). Such a view has not been questioned by subsequent commentators (see, for example, Corby et al., 1998: para. 4.64), although a slightly less sanguine view of the role of the SSI was to be taken in the later Inquiry into events at Ty Mawr, in Gwent (Williams and McCreadie, 1992).

It is not possible, at this remove, to make any definite judgement as to who precisely knew what about either pindown or Fundwell during the period in question nor seriously to question the conclusions of the Inquiry on this point. However, we note that the Inquiry does not report any evidence to suggest that any sustained attempt at concealment was made during the currency of pindown (other than in relation to the sanitising of reports of 'statutory visits' in some instances). The practice of pindown affected almost 140 children over more than six years and the activities of Fundwell considerably more. A number of senior managers, 'statutory' and other external visitors entered the premises in which both activities took place on a regular basis. Copious documentary evidence, including 400 'logbooks', were readily accessible to the Inquiry and so, one imagines, to others. It would seem to us that, at the time, far from being considered scandalous, both pindown and Fundwell were very widely understood in terms of 'business as usual'. Indeed, in respect of Fundwell at least, local practices were regarded positively. What cannot be in doubt, as noted in relation to Ely Hospital (chapter 3), is that the circumstances and practices that were the focus of the Inquiry were of long standing. How then could a 'scandal' be made of what must have been accepted, even approved practice to some and common knowledge to many others?

An explosion of public inquiries

Before considering the events and processes that secured the transformation of the facts of pindown into the scandal ('Pindown') it was to become, some consideration should be given to the general context of policy and practice in the field of child protection as it had developed in the 25 years since Colwell.

In the intervening period, there had occurred, according to Reder et al. (1993: 17) 'an explosion of public inquiries'. Various estimates of the scale of this 'explosion' have been made. Reder counts 35 between 1973 and 1989 (1993: 30), the DHSS/DOH, 37 between the same dates (DHSS, 1982: 4 and DOH, 1991: 115ff.) and Corby, 27 between 1973 and 1981 (2000: 38). Whilst mindful of the caution that we entered in relation to the Colwell case not to lose sight of the unique nature of each inquiry, the degree of similarity in terms of their findings became the subject of comment in several Reports themselves. For example, the Report of the Carly Taylor Inquiry (Leicestershire County Council and Area Health Authority, 1980) noted:

> ...the plethora of recommendations in the various reports of similar inquiries in recent years; we have studied nine of them, and while we agree with the majority of their general recommendations many of them are largely repetitious of others, it would be pointless of us to repeat them.

The DOH, in its review of inquiry reports, noted the 'remarkable' coherence of their findings, at least in those reports published up to 1980 (DOH, 1991: para. 3).

As already indicated, the most obvious consequence of these inquiries in policy terms was the development and progressive refinement of a more systematic and bureaucratised formal response to the management of child abuse. Despite the terms in which social work was increasingly cast by inquiry reports, the responsibility for child protection remained firmly placed with social workers, all be they now 'faced with the daunting task of sharing [the territory] with physicians, nurses, teachers and other reluctant members of the "helping" professions' (Greenland, 1986: 170).

In practice terms, the degree to which social workers became increasingly 'authoritative and decisive' (Parton, 1985: 127) in carrying out their mandate is uncertain. Dingwall's research (Dingwall et al., 1983) would suggest that practice remained predicated on a cautiously optimistic view of the possibilities of working with abusing families that had formed such an important part of the profession's cultural and technical inheritance from the Children's Departments. Such a view was directly challenged by the Beckford Inquiry in 1985. Here, social workers were criticised not only for not acting with the full authority given them by the courts but also for 'regarding the parents of children in care as the clients rather than the children in their own right' (London Borough of Brent, 1985: 294). The effects of the Beckford Inquiry seemed to have been demonstrated in a sharp rise in the number of children placed on child protection registers and/or made subject to Place of Safety Orders, from 17,622 in 1985 to 29,766 by 1987 and 41,200 by 1989.

The sense in which the interests of children was being differentiated from those of their parents (at least in extreme situations) was evident too in the Short Report (see chapter 8) and reinforced in the *Gillick* judgement of 1986 (*Gillick* v. *West Norfolk and Wisbech Area Health Authority*, 1986 AC 112). The courts had, from at least 1970 and Lord Denning's judgement in *Hewer* v. *Bryant* (1 QB 357), begun to establish that the legal right of a parent: 'is a dwindling right which the courts will hesitate to enforce against the wishes of the child, the older he is. It starts with a right of control and ends with little more than advice.' Lord Scarman's judgement in the *Gillick* case, went further in establishing that 'parental right yields to the child's right to make his own decisions when he reaches a sufficient understanding and intelligence to be capable of making up his own mind on the matter requiring decision'. Public reaction to the *Gillick* judgement suggested that this principle was far from uncontroversial. Hutchison (1986: 180) notes that while the mid-1980s saw a 'growth in the Children's Rights lobby, apparent in the proliferation of organisations which seek to establish and uphold the rights of children', such 'emancipation of children' was taking place against 'a prevailing political ideology [which] calls for a return to old values whereby the family is recognised as the cornerstone of society'. The invidious position of social workers operating as intermediaries between the family, the child and the State was explicitly recognised in the 1987 Inquiry into the death of four-year-old Kimberley Carlile (London Borough of Greenwich, 1987: 144):

> Mindful of the dilemma facing social workers, between the duty to pay full respect to family life and to observe scrupulously the rights of parents to bring up their own children without unnecessary interference from authority, and the duty to protect children from risk of abuse by their parents, we have paid particular attention to the fine balance that needs to be maintained between the two … Here we are at the crossroads of competing social policies – parental rights and the interests of children.

In its review of inquiry reports, the DOH also noted, with perhaps a degree of understatement, that (1991: para. 6): 'The proper balance of judgement between respecting family privacy and intervention to protect a child must always be difficult to achieve.'

The degree of difficulty had been demonstrated in the Cleveland Inquiry which sat for 74 days between August 1987 and January 1988. Although set in the as yet unfamiliar territory of child sexual abuse, the Inquiry's Report criticised social workers for their 'strong focus on the needs of the child in isolation from the family' ('Cleveland Report', 1988: 75). This had amounted, according to Corby (2000: 44), to social workers having 'rushed in overzealously to rescue abused children'. In the view of the Minister of State at the DOH in his statement to the House of Commons on the publication of the Report:

> The whole House will be united in its condemnation of sexual or other abuse of children, and in its support for proper action to protect children from it, but it will be no less united in insisting that this must be achieved in a way that does not trample on the rights of parents … It is clear from this Report that this balance was not achieved in Cleveland during the period in question. (Hansard, 6 July 1988, Col. 1061)

Whilst the pendulum between the primacy of parental or children's rights had swung dramatically in the late 1980s, one constant remained, the failure of social workers to 'get the balance right'. The practice of pindown would provide another case in point.

The beginnings of a scandal

Scandal begins with 'discovery' and the preparedness of a claims-maker to pursue the matter. On 2 October 1989, a local solicitor, Kevin Williams, telephoned the Deputy Director of Staffordshire Social Services (John Spurr), reporting his concern over a 15-year-old girl for whom he was acting in care proceedings. She had told him of her experience in pindown. In subsequent discussions with Spurr, Williams made it clear that he saw pindown as 'a matter of public concern' (10.60). Minutes of a meeting of the North Staffordshire divisional management group on the 4th indicated that pindown had ceased to operate at Hartshill Road and Heron Cross on 3 October, although a log entry to this effect did not appear at Hartshill Road until the 13th, the day on which Williams had made his original client and another 15-year-old boy, wards of court. He had also secured on that day an injunction in the High Court 'to prevent any further use of pindown and any employment of a child of school age in school hours other than in circumstances agreed in consultation with the Education Welfare Service' (10.61).

The possible consequences of Williams' interest and actions did not seem to register at this point. The team leader at Hartshill Road remained confident on 13 October that 'at the end of the day an official approval … will come out of this' (10.62). The Director of Social Services, in his report to the Social Services Committee on the court cases, seemed to suggest that there had been little more than an administrative error when he explained that 'the main weakness of the project was … that it had never been incorporated into the department's approved practices'. In his view, pindown had 'not been harshly repressive and has not entailed ill-treatment. It has been aimed solely and directly for the good of the young person' (10.65).

Indeed, we have found no tangible evidence of the 'very considerable public concern' noted by the Inquiry 'over the next few months' following Williams' telephone conversation with John Spurr. In order for a scandal to develop, after discovery must follow sustained and focused attention by a wider audience. The opportunity for this was to be provided initially by the local press but in relation to Fundwell rather than pindown. The first mention in the local newspaper, *The Sentinel*, of any matter related to pindown or Fundwell came not until a full six months after Wiliams' telephone call, on 18 April 1990. This followed the decision by the Council to end their support for Fundwell, following the government's decision to end the Community Programme Scheme on which several of Fundwell's activities had come to rely for funding.

The Chair of the Social Services Committee (Michael Poulter), responding to requests for an investigation into the activities of Fundwell, is reported to have accused Liberal Councillors Jebb and Thomas, who had initially raised a question over the scale of the local authority's financial commitment to Fundwell, of making political capital out of the issue and of a 'cynical attempt to denigrate the imaginative provision of services by the Labour administration which could not otherwise have been provided' (*The Sentinel*, 18 April 1990). The original claims-maker (Williams) now found himself with two powerful secondary claims-makers. On the following day, the newspaper carried a story under the headline 'I'm just a political pawn', a quotation from Tony Latham, who went on to claim that he had become a 'pawn in a political point scoring game' (*The Sentinel*, 19 April 1990). The same story reported that councillors Jebb and Thomas were also calling for 'a second investigation' into the 'operation of a behavioural control method known as pindown'. Throughout the remainder of April and all of May, no decision was made on either 'investigation'. But by now, fuelled by local political antagonism and in the hands of politicians with ready access to local media, the transformation of pindown, the practice, into Pindown, the scandal, had become inevitable.

On 8 June 1990, the National Association of Young People in Care, an organisation with claims of its own to make, announced that it would hold a public meeting in Stoke Town Hall to consider the possibility of legal action for false imprisonment in respect of young people who had been subject to pindown. At a meeting of the General Purposes Committee of the County Council on 12 June, held *in camera*, it was decided that an independent, internal inquiry would be established to look at both Fundwell and pindown. This decision was informed by the County Council's Chief Executive, possibly reflecting a primary concern to protect the Council, who advised the Committee to reject any calls for a public inquiry. Councillor Jebb, who had first raised the issues in public, is reported as saying that the proposed inquiry would 'go part of the way to what we asked for. At least they have taken it seriously. When we first raised the issue it was dismissed as innuendo' (*The Sentinel*, 13 June 1990). Kevin Williams, who had made representations to the Committee meeting, was less satisfied, claiming that this was 'too little too late … The gravity of concern demands a formal inquiry which should be held, as far as possible, in public' (*The Sentinel*, 13 June 1990). Opposition to the idea of a private rather than a public inquiry was also expressed by two members of the controlling Labour Party on the County Council to the point that, subsequently, they were to have the Labour Whip withdrawn from them and would need to take action in the High Court to challenge disciplinary proceedings instituted by the local Party. One might note that in the hiatus between the announcement of the inquiry and the publication of its findings, the local press continued to focus on the fate of these 'rebel councillors' who were, perhaps inappropriately, reported as 'facing a pindown' of their own (*The Sentinel*, 24 July 1990).

Any attempt that might have been made to 'contain' the developing scandal became futile when a Granada Television 'World in Action' programme, called 'Pindown', was shown nationally on 25 June 1990. The programme immediately catapulted pindown from a local to a national phenomenon and drew in more powerful voices to the growing chorus of concern around events in Staffordshire. There were immediate calls from influential local MPs for a public inquiry. Both Jack Ashley (Lab.) and Nicholas Winterton (Con.) were reported as intending to 'press the Secretary of State' for such an inquiry. According to Winterton, 'The only way this matter can be cleared up and a number of minds put at rest is to have a public inquiry to which everybody can give evidence' (*The Sentinel*, 26 June 1990). The government, in the form of the Minister of State for Health, Virginia Bottomley, appeared content with the arrangements made locally and a Staffordshire County Council spokesman is reported as saying that 'the DOH is satisfied with what we are doing and we also understand that any ministerial inquiry will only be considered if the adequacy of the local inquiry was in doubt' (*The Sentinel*, 2 July 1990). The Minister did, however, set in motion a series of Social Services Inspectorate investigations that reported at intervals during the currency of the Inquiry. The effect of these was, in the absence of any substantive reporting of the proceedings of the Inquiry, to maintain the local political temperature at a very high level. Over the next 12 months, there were repeated calls for the resignation of both the Chair of the Social Services Committee and of the Leader of the Council.

On 29 June, according to the Report (1.6), Alan Levy QC, who had latterly represented the DOH and the SSI at the Cleveland Inquiry, and Barbara Kahan, the former Children's Officer and possibly the leading figure in child care social work of her day, were appointed by Staffordshire County Council to commence their inquiry.

The Inquiry and its Report

Process

Whether to make a virtue of a necessity or not, Levy and Kahan, acknowledging the 'considerable debate' that had taken place during the build-up to their Inquiry, 'concluded that it was necessary in the particular circumstances to proceed in private' (1.13). Of 'overriding importance', according to the Inquiry, was that 'children should be protected from any possibility of identification and publicity'. In the absence of statutory powers, the Inquiry took the view that cooperation was more likely to be secured if they carried on proceedings in private. Moreover, they wished to avoid the 'formidable practical problems' that would follow from the 'full panoply of a public Inquiry held under the scrutiny of the media'.

Even after the Inquiry had been established, calls for it to conduct its business in public did not abate. A residential social worker, who resigned in protest at the continuing poor standards of care in the county's children's homes, was reported as saying that he would give evidence to a public inquiry but not the 'internal review' 'because he fears it will be a whitewash' (*The Sentinel*, 29 June 1990). Other calls for a Public Inquiry came from the National Council for Civil Liberties whose local group was reported as being concerned 'that difficult and disturbed children in the care of the County Council may in some respects have fewer rights than convicted prisoners in jail' (*The Sentinel*, 10 July 1990). The Inquiry was sensitive to accusations that, as a private, 'internal' review, it might be seen to be too close to the local authority, especially as it conducted most of its hearings in the main offices of the County Council in Stafford. It arranged for evidence to be heard in Stoke, directly in response to the suggestion that staff and others might be intimidated by having to appear at the County Council's headquarters.

Nonetheless, the Inquiry proceeded in private, sitting for 75 days between 23 July and 29 November 1990. The Inquiry heard from 153 witnesses and considered the contents of 150,000 pages of documentary evidence, including the 400 logbooks referred to above. In terms of process, it was Levy and Kahan's aim that the Inquiry should be conducted as 'informally as possible but with fairness and thoroughness' (1.17). Witnesses were seen separately but were allowed to be accompanied by legal representatives, union officials, friends and, in the case of children, by their parents. Witnesses were 'urged ... to deal constructively with the issues arising and the improvement of practice'. In several senses, then, the Inquiry was inquisitorial rather than adversarial in style.

How far the tension between 'public' and 'private', 'voluntary' and 'statutory', 'inquisitorial' and 'adversarial', 'informality' and 'thoroughness' were resolved in this instance must remain matters of speculation. We know of no accessible record of proceedings and we can never know what other outcomes, other arrangements might have produced. Ultimately, the Inquiry declared itself 'reasonably confident that [it] received a very comprehensive picture indeed of the relevant events' (1.19).

The Report

The Report of the Inquiry consists of 23 chapters, mostly written in short paragraphs of 6–8 lines and 15 appendices, including extracts from material taken as evidence. The central narrative (chapters 3 to 10) sets out the history of events in chronological order. Each chapter is divided into five parts: national events; local characteristics of Staffordshire and its social services department; County Council financial policies; social services reorganisation; the career of Tony Latham.

This particular structure produces its own effects. Beginning each chapter with an account of national developments tends to invite a comparison between the ideal and the actual, with the actual, represented by Staffordshire County Council, falling very far short. For example, in one of its longest paragraphs the Report (3.9) lists various circulars, reports and guidance issued by central government before noting that these publications were 'sent to all local authorities, including Staffordshire' (3.10). It then proceeds to characterise Staffordshire in these terms (3.13):

> ... we received considerable evidence suggesting that both [Stoke and Staffordshire] were insular and inward-looking communities, reluctant to seek new ideas or new people outside their boundaries ... Other witnesses referred to Staffordshire being in a time warp and believed this acted as a barrier to development of new concepts and methods ...

The gap between the world 'as is' and the world as 'ought to be' and the inadequacies of the County Council in particular, are further reinforced by the Report's inclusion of verbatim extracts from logbooks and other records produced by residential care staff during the currency of pindown. Undoubtedly, these reveal instances of callous indifference (at best) but they also reveal countless spelling mistakes and grammatical infelicities that accumulate in the reader's mind. Each one is scrupulously pointed out in the text by the use of the Latin abbreviation '*sic*' and is thrown into sharper relief by the polished prose of the Report itself. The contrast in style further works to discredit the staff involved in the operation of pindown and to make them appear, if not actually illiterate, then in some other way falling below reasonable expectations, not so much of literacy as of common humanity (see, for example: 6.36; 6.40; 6.44; 6.46, all on pages 58 and 59 of the Report). Similarly, the facsimiles of various documents contained in the Report setting out the 'philosophy' of pindown provide an ironic self-commentary, given the Report's findings.

In one sense, the account of the context of local practice in which pindown was developed is not unsympathetic (see Berridge and Brodie, 1996: 183ff.), but the effect of its presentation in the Report is to render events in Staffordshire as entirely atypical as well as simply deficient. We are invited to see Staffordshire as isolated from better regulated, better funded, better managed and more intelligent practices elsewhere. In fact, this was far from being the case. Much of the plethora of regulations and guidance cited by the Inquiry Report were developed on the back of the Short Report which, as noted in chapter 8, saw little to celebrate in the practice of residential care anywhere in the UK. Indeed, Staffordshire was one of the four local authority social services departments that Renée Short and her colleagues chose to visit in order to inform her Committee's work, presumably on the advice that it was either better than some or no worse than many others. While the degree to which practice in Staffordshire differed from practice elsewhere is open to debate, the conditions in which such practices developed would appear to have been far more common.

Closely associated with the process of particularisation, which is intrinsic to the scandalising process, is the matter of explanation or, more usually, of blaming. The ambiguity, complexity and subtlety of the events which form the substance of a scandal not only need to be simplified and securely located in time and place in order to connect with the world outside of the private world of the institution and the particular discourse of those who inhabit that world, they also have to be cast in such a way that the wider audience know whose fault it was. One device is to reduce the narrative to reflect an elemental struggle between good and evil, to a contest between heroes and villains, perpetrators and victims. This was not an easy proposition in this case.

As indicated, Tony Latham and his closest colleagues proved rather more difficult to blame than the 'villains' of other scandals. Despite having a section devoted to him in every chapter and repeated references to him as pindown's 'architect and prime practitioner', the Inquiry was 'prepared to accept that' (22.2):

> Tony Latham, with an excess of enthusiasm and energy, hoped to control those he saw as difficult adolescents by use of a system

designed to provide individualised programming and the development of social skills. The grim reality, however, was quite different. ... We can only think that Tony Latham, a person of drive energy and ability, who had contributed much in other areas to Staffordshire, lost sight of [the] minimum standards of behaviour and professional practice which are essential to a fair and sympathetic approach to children in care. ... It is a matter of great regret, in our opinion, that so many were prepared to be enthusiastic practitioners of Pindown. We would hope that the frank and explicit nature of the records and comments in the logbooks only represent a temporary aberration on their part.

The ambiguity surrounding Latham's blameworthiness was also echoed in the media. On the day of the publication of the Report, the local paper carried his picture on the front page with the strap line 'The man behind Pin down' and a headline 'A Brutal Regime' (*The Sentinel*, 30 May 1991). Within a week, the paper was asking 'Who copes when others can't?' (*The Sentinel*, 4 June 1991). The story casts doubts on the culpability of Latham himself, the adequacy of the management arrangements which surrounded pindown, the responsibility of government and ends with the reminder, 'But don't let's forget either that in most cases where children are in care, the real culprits are their parents.'

By early July, when the disciplinary procedures instigated by the County Council were underway and before a report by the District Auditor on the affairs of Fundwell was published, an even more sympathetic picture of Latham is drawn by the paper. Under the headline, 'I am just a scapegoat', the paper reports how 'the child care scandal drove him to consider suicide and "wrecked and ruined" his life'. The newspaper continues:

> Speaking for the first time about his part in the discredited regime, Mr Latham, 47, said he had been abandoned by politicians, colleagues and some of his friends ... 'I am just a pawn in a political game and I'm the only one likely to lose my job at the end of it. Everyone is now saying they never knew anything about it but they did'. The father of three described how the Pin down affair transformed him from being a bundle of energy to being 'depressed and listless' ...

Latham, along with several of his colleagues, did indeed lose his job. He was, in fact, the most senior figure to do so. The Director of Social Services (O'Neil) and both Assistant/Deputy Directors (Spurr and Crocket) were allowed to resign. It is not clear from newspaper reports whether Brennan 'jumped' or was 'pushed'. No local politician either resigned or was forced to step down.

In so far as there were few obvious 'villains', so too was the Inquiry unable to report on any very credible heroes. Fred Hill appears at several points in the narrative raising his quite proper concerns, but his influence on events seems to have been slight. There were, of course, victims and the report does devote a whole chapter to the experiences of seven of them. The accounts of their experience in pindown do make distressing reading, but it is not clear how far these were typical of the more than 120 other children involved. They do not appear to be typical by age or gender. Although the Report does not describe the general age profile of children subjected to pindown, the impression gained from the body of the text is that they were mainly in the 13–15 age range and mainly boys (81:51). Of the seven selected profiles, five relate to children aged under 12 and four were girls. This is not to argue that the pindown regime did not operate in relation to these children and many others exactly as described in the Report, but it is to remind ourselves that a very considerable process of selection and interpretation preceded the accounts that find themselves in print. What these examples do achieve, as a narrative device, is to dramatise events and to add considerably to the emotional content of the Report in a way that again both localises and personalises the events and which invites a response at a human level. The question which arises in the mind of the reader at the end of this chapter is more likely to be 'Who did this?' rather than 'Why/how did this happen?'

One might note that the status of the children and young people as victims was not always certain either. In a speech to her party's National Conference in September 1990, Councillor Jebb is reported to have accused Michael Poulter, the Chairman of Staffordshire County Council's Social Services Committee, of having held the belief 'that children in care are naughty by definition and that society needed to be protected from them because they are delinquents and putative prostitutes' (*The Sentinel*, 18 September 1990). Although denied by him, there is little evidence to be found either in Poulter's comments at the time or in the political leadership that he showed of his having advocated hard in support of children's interests. Within weeks of the publication of the Pindown Report, *The Sentinel* was running stories on children running amok in children's homes now that strict measures of control were not allowable and within months, the local press was carrying accounts of drugs and drink being bought out of the compensation that children and young people received as a result of civil actions begun against the

County Council, largely by Kevin Williams, acting on the instructions of former residents of Staffordshire's children's homes. Far from the 'Cinderella' of Colwell, the 'victims' of pindown were regarded by many as little better than 'Artful Dodgers' at best.

Beyond Latham and his immediate colleagues, the Report does allocate blame to the management of the Staffordshire Social Services Department which is described as 'inadequate for its task and lack[ing] many of the essential characteristics required to ensure good services to the public' (22.5. (i)). More concerned with cost-cutting, 'excessive tinkering' with the organisation of the department (17.25) and 'so long as there was no trouble', willing to turn 'a blind eye ... to some practices' (17.28), the management of the department is described as 'inward looking' and showing 'little sense of direction and little evidence of professional aspirations' (17.21).

As with most inquiry reports, little time is devoted to looking for explanations or to attributing blame beyond the immediate circumstances of the local event. It is interesting to note that at no point does the Inquiry seek to locate pindown in the context of previous residential child care scandals such as the relatively recent Leeways inquiry (Lawson, 1985) or the Kincora scandal (Hughes, 1985).

Recommendations

The Report makes some 39 detailed and specific recommendations in total, covering such matters as 'measures of control', the role of the statutory visitor, the education of children in residential care, staffing, training, line management arrangements, supervision and complaints procedures. Most of these recommendations are of an 'operational' nature, although they do also address matters of local policy. Whilst they might well have wider implications and be applicable elsewhere, they are, as per the original terms of reference of the Inquiry, designed to 'draw out the strengths and weaknesses and legality' of local practices.

The Report does give some consideration to the 'national implications' of its findings. Whereas the formal recommendations are considered in some detail in the context in which they derive, the national implications do not give rise to specific recommendations. Rather they are expressed more in terms of hopes and broad exhortations: residential care for children 'should be resourced, staffed, supported and managed' in order to meet the needs of children (21.3); the education of children in care 'should be given ... a much sharper focus nationally' (21.4); the health of looked-after children 'is an aspect which should receive more attention nationally' (21.5); 'the needs of children who are

16 or over have ... been inadequately met in the past and there is ample evidence that this is a problem on a wide scale' (21.8).

It is not the purpose of this chapter to establish quite how pindown came to be practiced in the way that it was, at this time and in these precise circumstances (but see Westcott, 1991; Wardhaugh and Wilding, 1993; Butler, 2002 for more detailed accounts of the process of institutional abuse). Our interest is in how such practices came to be understood as scandals.

The uses of scandal

The process whereby routine child care practice in Staffordshire became a scandal has to some extent followed a recognisable pattern and the Inquiry and its Report shown to have adopted familiar techniques to fix the narrative in a very particular framework for understanding such events. But this does not explain the wider paradigm shift that must have taken place between the revelations of Leeways, Kincora, Crookham Court or even the Short Report, such that this Inquiry achieved the emblematic status that it did and which still attaches to it. This, we would suggest, was largely a matter of timing.

Central to the scandal of pindown is the question of children's emerging status as rights-holders. This was a scandal precipitated by a lawyer and pursued through the courts. It was 'sponsored' by organisations such as NAYPIC and engaged with by groups with an interest in civil liberties. At the centre of the abuses of pindown was the restriction of children's liberty, their isolation, their exclusion from education and normal social intercourse and the degradation and humiliation at being denied even their own clothes. It is their civil rights that were at issue rather than the more obvious cruelties or abuses that formed the substance of previous scandals in residential care. In this way, Pindown echoed and amplified the concerns of the Short Report that had demonstrated a 'growing conviction that children should have enforceable rights as individuals' (para. 18). It confirmed the conclusions of the Cleveland Inquiry that a child was a person and not simply an object of concern and it did so before a government in the process of redefining the welfare state in such a way that a premium was attached to notions of individual rights and personal freedoms.

This is not to suggest that this was a government willing to pursue a children's rights agenda as such. As Parton (1991) convincingly argued at the time, government interest in rights has to be understood in terms of the 'new politics of welfare' (McCarthy, 1989; see also Deakin,

1994; Gamble, 1994) which it was trying to establish. This speaks a language of 'consumer choice' more than political or civil rights. Building on a coincidence of critiques of the postwar welfare state, the Thatcherite interest, certainly after the 1987 election (see Le Grand, 1990), was in reducing public expenditure through the marketisation of welfare. This implied weakening the administrative discretion of welfare professionals and reducing the role of the local state in the provision of services thus enabling such 'consumer choice' to flourish. One should recall that Tony Newton, the Health Minister, was approvingly cited in the Short Report directly conflating the ideas of children's rights and the consumer interest (Short Report, para. 18). Pindown was another timely reminder both of the dangers of local authorities' incompetent excesses but also of the need to protect fundamental freedoms, at least in so far as this might further the commodification of welfare. In this respect, Pindown is closer to Cleveland than the substance of both sets of events might initially suggest. Thus, as with other scandals, events in Staffordshire provided a case in point for an argument that was already in progress, evidence for a series of policy propositions that were already being advanced.

The immediate response by government to Pindown was to commission a 'special review of residential care in England' undertaken by William Utting and published as *Children in the Public Care*. As well as establishing residential care as a 'necessary service for children' (105), Utting made several recommendations aimed at improving the status of residential care 'as an occupation fulfilling an important purpose for important people' (105), mainly through better training of staff. He recommended also a greater degree of participation by children and young people in decisions made affecting their lives. But the greater part of his recommendations were aimed at improving the management of residential services through improved planning (107.2; 109.2) better inspection and monitoring (107.3; 109.3; 109.4), stronger guidance from the centre and through the operation of the law (107.5; 109.1; 109.5). As well as confirming Parton's contention that the child care scandals of the early 1990s secured the place of 'legalism' in the political economy of child care (see chapter 4), Utting's Report is also evidence of the growing strength and confidence of the managerialism that was implicit in the Pindown Report.

Many of Utting's concerns were to be rediscovered and re-asserted in the ten years following Pindown. By 1996, Berridge and Brodie (1996: 188) were able to list no less than 15 'initiatives' to address problems in institutional care for children undertaken either by central or local government or national voluntary organisations between 1991 and 1994.

Their list includes the reports of several inquiries into child abuse in children's homes but not the 18 Circulars that the DOH and Welsh Office issued between 1992 and 1996 nor the four Circulars published by the DFEE (DOH, 1997). To this growing list should be added at least four other central government initiatives, one Act of Parliament and another White Paper. By any measure, the care of children looked after away from home has been a very active concern of policy-makers over the last decade. Indeed, as we have noted elsewhere (Butler, 2002), the sheer volume and complexity of the available regulations and guidance is increasingly being recognised as a problem in itself. In his later Report (DOH, 1997), Utting noted that far from being a 'tool for practitioners', guidance and regulation is more a 'subject for their research' (p. 172) and overall Utting's final view (DOH, 1997) is a not necessarily wholly unambiguous one. He notes (our emphasis) that (p. 17): 'Regulations, statutory guidance and other forms of advice provide a full and detailed *web* of safeguards.' The 'need for procedure, procedure and more procedure' (Corby et al., 1998: 74) seems to have been the defining characteristic of the 'politics of enforcement' (Parton, 1999: 17) that have determined professional practice throughout the personal social services and elsewhere in the last decade. How far such a politics has furthered the case for children's rights, which we have argued, was central to the general experience of residential care and the particular construction of pindown as a scandal, is another matter.

After Pindown

Of the four major residential child care inquiries in the ten years following Pindown, the Report into Practices in Ty Mawr (Williams and McCreadie, 1992), a community home with education in South East Wales, is closest in spirit as well as chronologically. It too presents a picture of untrained, unsupported and ill-equipped staff working with too little direction and in a climate of low morale, distant management and budgetary constraint. However, the signal inquiries of the last decade have been those into events at Castle Hill School (Brannan et al., 1993), the Frank Beck Inquiry (Kirkwood, 1993) and the North Wales Inquiry (Waterhouse, 2000). It is beyond the scope of this chapter to examine in detail the findings of these inquiries, but an important common factor to note is that each exposed not so much the routine or particular failures of institutional care but the predatory practices of 'career paedophiles' (Stanley, 1999: 21). This is not to suggest that these reports do not also describe familiar deficiencies. Corby (1998: 70) finds in the abdication by management in Leicestershire of any responsibility for residential services a situation that 'Dame Myra Curtis would have recognised' as having the potential for abuse and Waterhouse found that the management structure of at least one local authority in North Wales was 'confused and defective without adequate expertise' (Waterhouse, 2000: 207). But in the activities of Ralph Morris at Castle Hill, an independent boarding school in Shropshire, Frank Beck, a manager of various children's homes in Leicestershire between 1973 and 1986 and Peter Howarth, Stephen Norris, John Allen and many others in North Wales, a completely different policy agenda has begun to form around the practice of residential care.

The tone in which this agenda is set is exactly captured by the 1997 review of those measures put in place since 1991 to protect children living away from home, the *Safeguards Review* (Utting, 1997) which notes (p. 5):

> This Review was precipitated by the past activities of sexually and phys- ically abusive terrorists in children's homes. Such persistent abusers may be a small proportion of those who harm children, but they create havoc with their lives. A single perpetrator is likely in a lifetime's career to abuse hundreds of children, who suffer pain, humiliation and tor- ment, and incur permanent emotional damage … They are very dan- gerous people.

The hue and cry for paedophiles that was launched by the *News of the World* in the summer of 2000 is clearly foreshadowed in the text of the *Safeguards Review*. Whatever the merits of public 'naming and shaming' campaigns, it remains to be seen whether the acute concern with the activities of a few will do very much to protect the interests of the many. We would suggest that the effect of the latest inquiries into the residen- tial care of children has been in part to reintegrate the dialogue of chil- dren's rights into the far less emancipatory paradigm of child protection once again and that the progress of children towards a much less condi- tional civil status has been somewhat obscured. We do not trace this to any particular systematic reaction nor to the progress of the political emancipation of children and young people or to a growing confidence amongst welfare professionals and a renewed determination to regain lost territory (indeed, see Butler and Drakeford, 2001b). It may be no more than a measure of the relative weakness of the underlying political will to secure children's rights.

The balance is now very finely poised. In Wales, the National Assembly has appointed the UK's first Children's Commissioner whose duties explicitly revolve around the implementation of the UN Convention on the Rights of the Child. In England, there are to be local 'children's rights directors'. How far either will succeed in securing a more equitable civil status for children waits to be seen.

Conclusion

The residential scandals of the last ten years, or indeed of the last 150, have provided windows onto the relatively closed world of the child in public care. Sometimes, no doubt, on their own merit but often it would seem as part of other agendas, already in train. Such scandals, and the policy initiatives which have followed them, have ensured considerable progress in protecting children from the casual cruelties of institutional life and the particular wickedness of some individuals. But taken one by one, they serve, even in aggregate, to reinforce the idea that the problems of institutional care are sporadic, acute and somehow peculiar to the institutional world. This separation of the institutional abuse of children from the wider societal context in which it appears mirrors the separation of specific institutions and their residents from their wider communities. But, as we have noted already, it is in the relative powerlessness of *all* children that the particular abuse of *some* children must be located. In this sense, the scandals of residential care are no more than specific instances of the more general scandal that places children on the margins of public policy and which permits them only partial citizenship.

10
Scandal, Welfare and Public Policy

Introduction

At the start of this book it was suggested that the most important issues which arise out of the dynamic relationship between scandal, Committees of Inquiry and welfare policy would best emerge in the account which we would attempt to offer of actual events and real inquiries. Now, at the end of our investigations, it is time to draw together the different threads and answer some of the questions with which this book began. Chapter 1 set out three broad areas of inquiry through which the particular scandals recounted here were to be interrogated.

Firstly, we have been concerned with the anatomy of welfare scandal itself – how and why some events emerge from the routine particularity of everyday misdeeds to become emblematic of a far more general and significant sense of wrongdoing. In attempting to gain some understanding of scandalous events in this way, we have focused upon three factors: the possibility that inherent characteristics of particular events assist in placing them apart from the mundane; the activities of different 'claims-makers' – individuals or organisations who have a part to play in the transformation of particular events into symbols of more general significance; and the impact of the wider policy and political context within which individual instances of scandal occur.

Secondly, we have been interested in the Committee of Inquiry itself as a response to scandal, both because of the way in which it, too, becomes part of the ongoing construction of social reality and because of the way in which, through the production of official 'truth', such inquiries illuminate the means which sources of power and influence in our society employ to shape that truth.

Thirdly, we have been concerned to investigate the impact which Inquiries might make upon future social policy. Are they merely, as Blom-Cooper (1996: 57) suggests, 'an instrument of dampening and dissembling public disquiet about a scandal', or do inquiries have a more positive after-life in which their findings and recommendations make a difference to social policy and social welfare practice?

Anatomising scandal

Characteristics of events themselves

We have suggested that potentially emblematic events possess particular characteristics, such as an inherent dramatic content. Whilst this might be said of scandals occurring in other fields such as politics or other forms of showbusiness, scandals in the field of welfare practice and policy can be distinguished from other such instances in a number of ways. In other fields, very often scandal follows notoriety. In our field, this has not been the case. The scandals with which we have been concerned involved ordinary people who become involved in events that are viewed by others as extraordinary. They were generally neither eminent in their own fields, nor even much noticed by their neighbours. They were also, for the most part, only peripherally concerned with the twin pillars of sex and money around which the daily diet of media scandals revolve – although, in the case of institutional scandals in particular, they were almost always concerned with questions of power or misuse of office, of which sex and money are particular outcrops, and with the denial of responsibility.

The general business of social welfare can also be distinguished from other forms of public scandal in being messy and mundane, rather than glamorous or spectacular. Its methods of organisation and reporting are bureaucratic rather than dramatic. In the case of some scandals, the essential narrative (viewed in a particular way) can acquire all the urgency and excitement of the popular novel. Although the tragic ending is already known, most readers of the 1979 Report into the death of Darryn Clarke will follow the increasingly frantic efforts made to find him in the last few days of his life with the irrational hope that these efforts might still meet with some success. The fate of Isabel Schwartz seems inevitable yet somehow escapable, right up to the point where she sat working late in her office, alone. While events need to be capable of 'successful use in story-telling' (Nichols, 1997: 325), for emblematic scandals, we argue, a particular sort of story has to be told, that of the morality tale, where there are 'revelations and allegations, denials followed by explanations' (Cavender et al., 1993: 152) and where individual acts are reducible to the symbolic struggle between good and evil and actors are capable of being divided into heroes and villains. In the case of Maria Colwell or Jasmine Beckford, for instance, innocence is confounded by brutality. The death of a child at the hands of its parents; the petty thefts and minor acts of violence which are often involved in institutional scandals can be lifted from the routine or the insignificant into the scandalous by the fact that they occur in settings which are conspicuously dedicated to the care and well-being of others. It is, as Katz (1987: 55) suggests, the status of place and persons involved, rather than the structure of the events themselves, which accounts for the attention devoted to them. While such characteristics may be a necessary component of scandal, however, they are not a sufficient condition.

Our conclusion is that those who seek an understanding of social welfare scandal, make their best start by exploring the process of its construction, the practicalities through which, as Nichols (1997) suggests, mundane deviance is transformed into high moral drama. While, however, like Chesler (1972) we might agree that scandals are 'like all atrocities – only everyday events, writ large', this is not to suggest that the experiences that lie behind the 'atrocities' are not real or meaningful in themselves. Rather, it is to emphasise the way in which additional meanings are created and sustained in particular social, professional and political contexts. For, even though the raw material of scandals is very often quotidian, they are carried to public prominence in a way that converts their everyday nature into something altogether extraordinary. From those that have been examined in this book, we believe that we can discern key elements in the process of scandal construction.

At its most basic, scandal involves unanticipated exposure, followed by disapproval. Those involved in welfare scandals are almost always, in our assessment, taken unawares by the drama which engulfs their lives. Within institutions, as we have seen, the practices which become the focus of inquiry are usually of long-standing. Even afterwards, in many cases, such as at Farleigh Hospital, a significant body of internal opinion remained unconvinced that anything untoward, let alone scandalous, had ever taken place. It is only when institutional actors step outside the confines of internal routines that scandal becomes a conscious possibility. Nurses at Normansfield were alert to the scandalous possibilities of strike action. The authorities in Staffordshire were conscious that questions might be asked of Tony Latham's Fundwell activities. As to fieldwork scandals, the unanticipated element here refers to the events themselves. While Committees of Inquiry argue that the passage of affairs, in general, could have been altered by different decisions earlier in the chain of circumstances, few attempt to apply this rather banal conclusion to the particular event which form the focus of their investigation. The inherent unpredictability of acute mental illness and the stresses and volatility of circumstances in which child deaths occur are not amenable to anticipation. Scandal in social welfare, therefore, does not usually involve the sort of conscious risk-taking which is an integral part of scandals in other domains such as those involving politicians or big business (viz. Jeffrey Archer or Nick Leeson).[1] Rather, it involves processes whereby the private actions of individuals or the routine practices of institutions attract public censure in ways entirely unforeseen by those directly involved.

This lack of anticipation helps explain one of the paradoxes of social welfare scandal, which is the way in which, generally, Committees of Inquiry spend so little time in dealing with those individuals most directly responsible for what had taken place. The sense that staff within institutions and clients in the field were not consciously involved in deliberate wrongdoing (at least by the lights of their peers and the context within which they operated) means that culpability has to be sought in the wider, rather than the individual, sphere. The recent Inquiry into events at Bristol Royal Infirmary (Kennedy, 2001: 4), involving both an institution and the death of children, captures this feeling most directly in its claim that the Report provides:

> an account of people who cared greatly about human suffering, and were dedicated and well-motivated. Sadly, some lacked insight and their behaviour was flawed. Many failed to communicate with each other, and to work together effectively for the interests of their patients. There was a lack of leadership, and of teamwork.

Lack of anticipation is thus a crucial feature of social welfare scandals. It colours the nature of events, the reaction of those caught up in them and also the response of those appointed to inquire into them.

The second test identified earlier was that of exposure. Put simply, events and actions which remain undiscovered or unnoticed do not result in scandal. As earlier chapters have made clear, institutional scandals are particularly characterised by the exposure of practices which

1. The possible exception to this is the Waterhouse Inquiry and the criminal activities of the paedophiles who preyed on children in their care. It should be noted that even here, there is some suggestion that abusers were able to persuade a great many others that their practices were not harmful or in any way exceptional.

have been long embedded in the day-to-day culture of organisations. Nor, in these circumstances, is discovery usually an easy or unproblematic business. Institutions are especially capable of absorbing and minimising scandal. The Nolan Commission, reporting on that most venerable institution, the House of Commons, noted the 'culture of slackness' and 'the tolerance of corruption' which can characterise institutional responses to the behaviour of insiders. Even when the violations which lead to scandal concern the most basic human rights to life and liberty, institutions set up to provide care and promote welfare have proved remarkably resistant to investigation. In either case, however, scandals occur when a set of constituent elements engenders a particular response which transforms them into something beyond themselves. That response, as discussed more fully below, is provided in scandal by energetic individuals, determined to bring attention to their discoveries. Sometimes this response is immediate in its transformative power, as in the case of the Ely Hospital Inquiry. At other times, such as in the case of Pindown, the process was long-drawn-out and was achieved only through considerable effort. Even fieldwork scandals, where the events themselves are more directly dramatic, can struggle for the sort of official exposure which Committees of Inquiry provide. The four-year gap between the death of Isabel Schwartz and the inquiry into her death has already been highlighted in chapter 7. Even Jayne Zito, involved in the most high-profile way in one of the landmark scandals of recent times, described the events which followed the murder of her husband in this way. 'We screamed from the rooftops' she told *Psychiatry in Practice* in 1996, 'to open the doors for the Ritchie Inquiry to take place publicly.' Moreover, the importance of exposure in social welfare scandals does not relate simply to the specific events themselves. Rather, as the series of Inquiries which followed Colwell and which continue to dominate newspaper headlines, discovery in one place, or one instance, produces further revelation in the same field. And in doing so, a further paradox emerges. Exposure, which is fundamental to scandal generation, becomes on repetition a barrier to that same generation. Scandal demands the unexpected, if not the unanticipated. Repeated uncovering of the same conditions means that this essential element is eroded to the point where its impact has ceased and scandal no longer arises.

Finally, in the three basic tests set out in our simple definition, comes the issue of disapproval. As noted earlier, Committees of Inquiry are often not centrally concerned with the most conspicuous targets of disapproval – those individuals at whose hands scandalous events have taken place. Rather, they focus primarily upon professional 'sin', and on the extent to which the particular events in question can be seen as characteristic or typical of such practices in general. In this way, scandal implies a ready audience of competing interests, within and beyond the organisations and individuals concerned, which makes the explication of the underlying actions and practices a matter of dispute and a struggle over meaning. Disapproval forms a crucial site of this struggle. Indeed, the transformation of particular occurrences into the raw material of scandal only takes place when it is possible to place a construction upon the underlying events which emphasises the extent to which they have departed from officially sanctioned, socially shared or emergent codes of conduct. The process of construction is often contentious and contested. The practices in Pindown, for example, were considered, by those held responsible, as simply administrative indiscretions, in which failure resided in violation of presentational rather than substantial rules. In the case of Normansfield, a direct struggle took place over public disapproval, with Dr Lawlor attempting to secure that disapproval for the nursing staff and the nursing staff attempting to secure it for him. All were involved in the disputed nature of events themselves. Where should disapproval rest in the Normansfield circumstances? Upon the strike action? Upon the reduced circumstances at the hospital? Upon the culpable neglect of those who had allowed this deterioration to take place? Even where the events at issue quite clearly represent an essential violation of shared moral norms – as in cases of murder – a struggle will take place to define the significance of contributory factors and to allocate responsibility between the individuals and organisations involved. Disapproval is thus a necessary condition for scandal, but the allocation of that disapproval is formed out of competing interpretations and the interests they represent.

Claims-making and counter-claims-making

Beyond the inherent characteristics of the raw material of scandal, a second element is required for their generation, that which social constructionists call claims-makers, individuals or interest groups which carry out Nichols' (1997) transformation of the raw material of routine events into landmark instances. For some writers, such as Fine (1997: 297), this element is the most important of all – 'a scandal suddenly appears, from the either – a chance occurrence that moral entrepreneurs seize for their own ends'. Best (1990) has suggested a classification of primary, secondary and tertiary claims-makers, in which the primary group are social problem activists – those who strive, for example, to bring the conditions of discharged mental health patients or young people in care to the attention of the public. In this book we have been concerned to highlight the wide range of claims-makers who play a part in social welfare, spanning the spectrum from the relatively well-connected and organised efforts of Barbara Robb and AEGIS to the isolated but determined actions of Mr Pantelides or the 'mothers of Maresfield Road'. Primary claims-makers in social welfare, however, share one key characteristic. They are almost always outsiders, either in the sense of bringing a fresh eye to circumstances where general sensibilities have been blunted or in the sense of being part of a group who do not have a place on the dominant policy agenda.

The secondary group in Best's (1990) analysis are the representatives of the mass media who take up and publicise particular events or causes, conveying them to a wider public. The *Times* letter which led to the *Sans Everything* reports is an example at the simplest end of this process. Of course, as will have become clear from any of the individual scandals explored in this text, this 'conveyance' is a complex matter which involves direct and indirect interpretations of events, far more than any simple telling of the 'truth'. As Cavender et al. (1993: 153) make clear, 'the media do not simply report facts; instead, they convert events into news stories through frames of coverage – selection principles that determine what is reported as news, and how it is reported.' Katz (1987: 51–2) provides a useful insight into the frame most often adopted in the case of scandal when he suggests that virtually all such events 'deemed newsworthy are depicted as endangering one or another foundation of collective identity... Such stories have an unspoken melodramatic quality: they implicitly tap the folk ideas about vulnerability of collective identity'. The 'Cinderella' motif in press coverage of the Maria Colwell Inquiry is an excellent example of the direct connection between folk stories and scandal. More generally, the degree of force with which the danger to collective identity might be felt increases with the extent to which events occur in places which are themselves symbolic of such collectivism. Many of the social welfare scandals explored in this book have gained some of their momentum from the violation which thefts or neglect of duty represent in places ostensibly dedicated to the protection of the vulnerable and the provision of care. When patients can be killed by nurses in a hospital – as in the Whittingham scandal of the 1970s or the Allitt scandal of the 1990s – then a very direct assault has taken place also upon the collective sense of security. Secondary claims-makers develop this theme in social welfare to the point where they themselves become actors in the nexus between scandal and social policy. Chapter 7, for example, explored in some detail the role played by the media in the changing of official approaches to the care of the discharged mental health patient.

What is it about social welfare which makes it so attractive to the news media? Clearly not all institutions are equally available for investigation or, more significantly in our context, representation as a source of scandal. Our suggestion would be that the organisations most vulnerable to such representation are those which already occupy an ambivalent or distrusted position within the public domain. Thus, politicians are always open to scandal because the involvement of any individual in moral or financial corruption strikes a chord with the public's view of politicians as a whole. So, too, with social welfare. Social workers, notoriously, have suffered a bad press at the hands of the powerful right-wing elements within the British media. 'Welfare' institutions, suspiciously regarded, provide a receptive context within which secondary claims-makers can operate relatively freely, knowing that individual mistakes or misdemeanours are unlikely to be sheltered within the protective shadow of a benignly-regarded institution or beneath the powerful legal policing of private corporations. Scandals, in this sense, occur when it is possible to present the unexpected and the exceptional as confirmation of a more hidden or submerged expectation. Thus, acts of cruelty in an institution, or the killing of someone by a discharged mental health patient are exceptional events – and newsworthy as such – but only become scandals, requiring a formal response at the level of a Committee of Inquiry, by tapping into a belief that they are emblematic of something far less unexpected. The folk-fear of the dangerous madman or the folk-memory of the workhouse lurk behind the social welfare scandals presented in this text. News values depend upon an initial appeal to novelty and moral distaste but rest, thereafter, on feeding rather than disrupting the prejudices, beliefs and mind sets of their audiences.

In the Best (1990) analysis, the audience for social welfare scandal represents the tertiary group of claims-makers, to whom the efforts of the first two groups are directed. In this sense, the unfolding story of scandal emerges as significant. A number of the events with which this book has been concerned took place over a substantial period of time with the sense of scandal accruing to them as events followed one upon another. The ongoing dispute at Normansfield as to the nature of any Inquiry to be conducted became part of the struggle to fix public disapproval discussed earlier. Public engagement is fundamental to the particular response to scandal with which this book has been concerned. As Blom-Cooper (1996: 57) puts it, 'the most compelling reason' behind the decision to set up an independent Inquiry in social welfare, lies in 'the assuaging of public revulsion or repugnance that will not be satisfied by the traditional methods of remedial action'. Without a reaction of that sort from the public, the claim to scandal, particularly of any emblematic of symbolic significance, will have been lost, as events at St David's Hospital, Carmarthen, set out in chapter 9, amply demonstrated.

Lastly, in this section it is important to discuss the crucial role played by counter-claims-makers in scandal generation, for as well as individuals and organisations who have an interest in attempting to mark out the general significance of a particular scandal, there are powerful players and institutional interests who will attempt the opposite: to suggest that the events under consideration, and their own part within them, have to be understood in quite different ways. As Fine (1997: 313–14) suggests:

> the mobilisation of response to scandal by moral entrepreneurs typically does not go unanswered. Institutions mount energetic campaigns to blunt collective action. Where critics themselves cannot be attacked then individual deviants within organisations are scapegoated, claims are made for the self-regulation of organisations concerned in the hope that threats can be limited. Where the defence that the complained-of behaviour amounts only to business-as-usual cannot be sustained, organisations also attempt to defend themselves by claiming that their behaviour differs little from that in other professions.

A number of such techniques have emerged in the accounts provided here, as well as those which are identified by Cavender et al. (1993: 153) as 'denials, mystification, and countercharges against those who demand accounts'.

Thus, in the case of Pindown, denial involved the strenuous efforts by local and national players to avoid the establishment of an Inquiry at all. Within particular Inquiries, denial of responsibility is routine: some individuals refuse to attend at all, other witnesses appear expressly in order to defend their own part in events. Organisations mobilise denial in a number of characteristic ways, suggesting, for example, that the events under consideration represent ordinary practice or minor violations of a low-level nature which have been misunderstood or misconstrued by others. Thus, in the case of the *Sans Everything* Inquiries, it was suggested that the witnesses were either well-motivated but simple-minded (as in the case of Nurse Craybourne) or deliberately determined to misrepresent normal and acceptable nursing practice as something extraordinary and unacceptable (as in the case of Mrs Robb). In this latter case, for example, the Committee dismissed complaints that patients were understimulated with the explanation that, 'many of these older patients desire nothing more than just to sit or loaf around owing to their mental condition. They may appear bored and dejected: in fact they are often incapable of animation.' Even the Ely Inquiry rejected one of the complaints of Mr Pantelides – that patients had deliberately and callously been kept outside in cold and distressing conditions – on the grounds that this was ordinary practice which he had misinterpreted because he 'is not used to the cold'.

Even where complete denial cannot be sustained, then counter-claims-making can attempt to mobilise denial by suggesting that code violations were either minor or understandable in the particular circumstances under investigation. Where complaints cannot be dismissed as simple misinterpretation of ordinary events, then organisations require other forms of denial. One which has been evident in a series of Inquiries investigated here is the 'bad-apple' denial. Sometimes this appears as a form of whole-class denial, usually when more powerful interest groups attempt to shift the blame for anything untoward down the chain of command, in a diffusion of responsibility which is characteristic of hierarchically-organised institutions. Cavender et al. (1993: 158), in their investigation of the Iran-Contra scandal suggest, 'superiors in hierarchical organisations blame inferiors while subordinates protect superiors from incriminating information.' This reverse form of deniability is evident in the Ely Inquiry, for example, where the Medical Superintendent – a man liked and respected by all – was protected from incriminating knowledge when a suspicious death at the hospital was processed without ever being brought to his attention. The progressive 'weeding-out' of adverse information as reports of events at Staffordshire children's homes were passed up the social services ladder provides a similar instance.

Where whole classes of individuals could not be found wanting, then the 'bad-apple' denial often has recourse to a particular individual, or group of individuals. The 'bad-apple' approach reaches its height in the Normansfield Inquiry, where a whole barrelful are rounded on in the final sequence of the 800-page Report and expunged from the hospital and, in some cases, from the Health Service. Most importantly, however, the barrel itself is left intact. As Cavender et al. (1993: 163) suggest, 'the purging of problematic individuals confirms the system's legitimacy'.

In addition to denial, some counter-claims-makers can also follow a strategy of mystification. This occurs when individuals or organisations admit that something has gone wrong, but attempt to deny either the seriousness of such events, or their emblematic nature, by appealing to factors which either cannot be revealed, or which lie beyond the comprehension of outsiders or which, for reasons which cannot be fully explained, cannot be fully explained. The medical profession, as a series of scandals have suggested, is especially skilled – and successful – at mystification as a response to those who suggest that particular events should be credited with more general significance. When, in *Sans Everything*, Mrs Robb complained that Miss Webb had been inappropriately treated by electro-convulsive therapy, the Friern Committee of Inquiry (1968: 34) were in no doubt. The Report records a set of statistics, included in order to establish both the complexities of these matters and the defence of local practice. It concludes, however, by making it clear that none of these elaborations really mattered. Whatever Mrs Robb might have thought, 'the doctors and nurses were the best judges of the appropriate treatment'.

To denial and mystification can be added the counter-claims-making technique of counter-charging. Counter-charges in scandal exist, essentially, as means of attempting to discredit those claims-makers who attempt to offer a view of particular events which emphasises their emblematic nature, or which seeks to locate responsibility with more powerful actors within a policy context. Councillors who argued for public inquiries in the cases of Maria Colwell and Pindown were dismissed as trouble-makers, seeking personal or party advantage. Individual workers in these and other Inquiries routinely argue that they were simply carrying out the policies of their employing organisations, or that their conduct was modelled upon, and endorsed by, their superiors.

The point we seek to make is that scandal is not simply the product of those who seek to draw attention to its existence. It can also be formidably opposed by others, often in positions of relative power. The conditions in which scandal is generated involve disagreements not only about the explanations which lie behind events which all agree to be in need of explanation. More fundamental, first-principle disputes can occur as to whether scandal has ever taken place.

Just as this book has been concerned to trace the conditions in which scandal in social welfare takes place, so we have also had to consider the conditions in which scandals fail to make an impact, either upon the public, or upon policy-making, or both. Two different, but linked components have been traced, in relation to the impact which scandals make in public consciousness.

Inflation

Scandal generation relies upon novelty as well as intensity. In order to make an impact, media claims-makers have to be able to show not only that events are inherently disturbing, but that they represent some new departure in depravity or depredation. Scandals in both institutional and fieldwork settings have shown how both primary and secondary claims-makers have responded to this thirst for originality by stoking up the temperature of the stories they unfold, unveiling ever more bizarre or aberrant behaviours. Eventually, our account suggests, the bubble of scandal inflation bursts and the capacity for scandal generation by this means subsides.

Fatigue

Alongside scandal inflation, we suggested the phenomenon of scandal fatigue. There are only so many times when it is possible to draw attention to apparently similar events and suggest that each represents an episode which stands out from the surrounding landscape in a way which demands and commands attention. Moreover, landmark scandals require landmark solutions, in the sense that each is paraded before the public on the premise that this is a story worth telling, in order to ensure that it will not be repeated in the future. When events proliferate, as in the mental health inquiries following homicide of the 1990s or the child care inquiries of the 1980s, then that basic claim to public attention recedes and fatigue at the repetition of events and the failure of solutions leads to dissipation of effect. Even amongst those most closely connected, this sense of exhaustion is apparent. Inskip and Edwards (1979), reporting on their own experience of chairing Inquiries during the 1970s, concluded, 'Major hospital inquiries burn up money that is desperately needed to improve the health service, disrupt the work of the hospital and often have a devastating affect on individual and group morale, leaving in their wake a legacy of corrosive bitterness. They should be avoided wherever possible.'

Saturation

In addition to inflation and fatigue, we have tried to identify the phenomenon of saturation as a further factor in the anatomy of social welfare scandal. Put simply, this suggests that, just as a sponge can hold only so much water, so there is only so much public space available for scandal. If that space is occupied by one form of scandal, there may be little room left for alternative examples. This may act so as to limit the attention for social welfare scandal at all, or – and, as it seems to us, more often – it limits the range of scandal within the social welfare sphere itself. The final years of the Major government of 1992–97 were punctuated by an accelerating series of public relations disasters, in which Tory ministers, members of the parliamentary party and senior Conservative apparatchiks became engaged in scandal inflation which ran from David Mellor's mistress to 'cash-for-questions' and beyond. At the end of the period, the tide of social welfare scandal had receded sharply from its Clunis highpoint. Fatigue at repeated inquiries following homicide was part of the explanation for this diminution in effect and public attention, but competition for space in an increasingly crowded scandal field was also a factor. Within social welfare, too, we suggest, a period in which public space has been captured by one particular form of scandal can have the effect of crowding out others. The decade from 1983 to 1993 was largely (although not wholly) free of mental health scandals. This was partly because of the policy hegemony established by care in the community, but it was also influenced by the extent to which child welfare issues – Jasmine Beckford, Kimberley Carlile, Orkney, Cleveland, Pindown – had come to be the focus of press and public interest.

Context

Finally, in this discussion of why certain scandals rise above others, attracting a sense of defining a particular period or a particular policy, the account in which we have been engaged has highlighted those contextual factors – the policy background, the political climate, the resources available to individuals and institutions – which have an impact both upon the shaping of particular events and their explication. Scandals arise in specific circumstances and that specificity has been shaped by the policy and practice measures prevailing at the time. The sense which is then made of the events – the struggle to construct a meaning from them, and especially a meaning which suggests a significance beyond the immediate events themselves – also takes place within that general context.

Committees of Inquiry

The second major focus of this book has been upon the Committee of Inquiry as a particular response, by the State, to scandal in the practice of social welfare. Most scandals have no formal resolution. A leading politician or soap opera star might be caught *in flagrante* but neither he nor she would be likely to appear before any conventional tribunal. Those examples which do find themselves resolved by formal processes are, almost always, confined to the internal mechanisms of particular organisations. For example, the England cricket captain relaxes before a Test Match with a barmaid, and finds himself in the arms of the England and Wales Cricket Board; a children's television programme presenter uses cocaine and is sacked by his employers. Where scandals cannot be confined to internal proceedings, then the Law Courts are the usual stage upon which the final act is concluded, from Fatty Arbuckle in the 1920s (see Fine, 1997) to Jonathan Aitken eighty years later. In only a tiny minority of instances are the bounds of scandal broken beyond these mechanisms in the form of a particular state-sponsored tribunal of investigation. The Committee of Inquiry is thus both one of the most important bonds which links the different scandals discussed in this book and a proper object of investigation in its own right.

By the time an Inquiry comes to be set up, the task of defining a particular set of events as out-of-the-ordinary has already been accomplished. The establishment of an Inquiry ipso facto demonstrates that claims-makers have been successful in transforming a set of particular events into something of wider significance. In many ways, the fact of an Inquiry lends additional weight to the connection which has been drawn between particular scandals and emerging social problems. As Fine (1997: 297) suggests, this is a process in which scandals, by capturing public attention, 'may influence (magnifying, concretising, transforming or minimising) the development of the social problem they are said to represent. The depiction of the scandal comes to symbolise the problem for the public and, thus the response to scandal shapes the response to the social problem.'

In fact, the position in social welfare scandals is somewhat more complex. Committees of Inquiry are far from uniformly set up in order to investigate scandal. Rather, they are often set to perform a more preliminary role, being charged with establishing whether or not an alleged scandal did in fact take place in the way described and interpreted by primary claims-makers. Many of the early mental hospital scandals of 1968–83, and some later ones, were framed in this way. The Inquiries discharged their function not by taking scandal as an established fact, but by seeking, in the first instance, to establish if the complained-of events had ever taken place. Even where the actual occurrence of a particular event was not in dispute – as in all the social welfare scandals which involve the death of an individual – Committees of Inquiry almost always have, as part of their remit, the reconstruction of the circumstances leading up to the event and the event itself. This role is often and disingenuously described in the Reports of Inquiries as one of 'establishing the facts'. In that single phrase, the central assumption of Inquiries is made clear: that there is an objective reality that can be discovered and represented in language where meanings will be shared and unambiguous. This is precisely the opposite of the socially constructed nature of scandal that we have emphasised in this book. In carrying out their task of discovery and communication, Inquiries operate in a way described by Bogen and Lynch (1989: 197) as establishing a 'master-narrative', in which 'all partial and contingent narratives [are subsumed] in the greater whole'. The result is a report which lays claim to objectivity and neutrality, which provides linear chronologies of events pieced together from often-conflicting sources but without the 'disclaimers, qualifications and partial recollections' (Bogen and Lynch, 1989: 199) which will have been characteristic of the original testimony. Indeed, if – as we argue – social welfare scandals exist in the space where morality play and soap opera meet, then in dealing with its cast of heroes and villains, Inquiry Reports aspire to represent Everyman, in their attempts to weld together the competing particular accounts of individuals into a general narrative which can be 'true' for anybody.

The purpose of this book, in its account of the mechanism of the Inquiry, is to consider the construction of such a narrative, which, for all its claims to objectivity and veracity, is only one partisan version of many possible accounts. As Bogen and Lynch (1989: 200) suggest, Inquiries represent the point at which 'history is up for grabs'. The relationship between the Inquiry and the scandal under investigation is dialectical. The Inquiry, in its attempt to define and judge, becomes a player in the contested terrain, contributing its own voice to the construction of the original events. The contested nature of the 'truth' which emerges is perhaps most vividly illustrated in those cases where a minority report provides an alternative version of events, as in the Maria Colwell Inquiry which formed the subject of chapter 5. The application of the Committee of Inquiry to scandal is significant, then, because it allows a moment of insight into what Schlesinger et al. (1991: 398) term 'the conflictual processes that lie behind the moment of definition'. The master-narratives of dominant institutional and political interests are framed, as are Inquiry Reports themselves, in an habitual discourse of common-sense objectivity – as though the account that they offer is the only possible version of events. We have suggested that they are not, sharing instead Peay's (1996a: 2) contention that Inquiries 'take on a life of their own. They are not an event, but a social process.'

Moreover, in this sense, of course, the social process involves a large measure of interpretation of what has taken place. Events may have occurred, but Committees of Inquiry are charged with developing an understanding of what has taken place in order to support or deny the contention that these were scandalous affairs, traceable to culpable moral or professional failures and/or the denial or evasion of responsibility. In this sense, Inquiries are themselves forms of secondary claims-making, being the media through which the original contentions of primary claims-makers are assessed and published to a wider audience. They are, however, highly privileged secondary claims-makers whose apparent independence gives rise to self-assertions of disinterestedness and objectivity. The accounts offered here both of the majority and minority Reports in the case of Colwell, and in the 'behind-the-scenes' negotiations which Public Record Office documents reveal in the case of Ely, cast these claims into the constructionist perspective which, in our account, provides the most fruitful lens through which social welfare scandals can be understood. Inquiries, as much as any other medium of communication, devise and develop accounts and interpretations of events which aim to persuade others of their particular understandings.

As well as reconstructing accounts of the past, Committees of Inquiry are most often charged with making proposals for the future. Indeed, the single most frequently cited rationale for shining attention upon the events reported in this book is 'to make sure that this sort of thing will never happen again'. Such claims are more widespread than social welfare scandals. The Inquest report of the jury into the death which led to the 1920s Hollywood scandal involving Fatty Arbuckle recorded their wish that 'the district attorney of the city and county of San Francisco take steps to prevent a reoccurrence of the affairs similar to the one in which this young woman lost her life.' Indeed, as the case of the hospital scandals of 1968–83 or the child death inquiries of the 1970s, 1980s and 1990s, demonstrated, the diminishing credence which could be attached to such claims – as scandals of similar sorts repeated themselves, despite earlier Inquiries – produced a diminution in scandal itself.

We have identified too that the actual mechanics of the inquiry process can help shape the truths such inquiries tell. The formality of the courtroom in the case of Colwell, the determination of the Chair in the case of Ely, the narrative style of the reports that such Committees of Inquiry produce all contribute to the truth of the events that they leave in the reader's mind. Amongst the earliest decisions which have to be made about Inquiries, or which Inquiries have to make for themselves, concerns the method by which investigations should be conducted. A basic choice has to be made between adversarial and inquisitorial approaches, the former involving relatively formal, court-derived methods, conducted in public, the latter deploying a deliberately more relaxed atmosphere and conducted in private. Cecil Clothier (1996: 52–3), for example, who chaired the Committee of Inquiry into the deaths caused by nurse Beverley Allitt, and a partisan advocate of inquisitorial methods, describes the choice between the two approaches in this way:

> I believe that inquiries in public seldom, if ever, arrive at the innermost truth underlying the apparent miscarriage of some public affair...
>
> On the other hand in the quiet atmosphere of a small and private room, with no more persons present than are necessary to conduct the inquiry and record the proceedings, the truth in my experience has a way of eventually coming to the surface, sometimes in a remarkable outburst of candour such as could never have been uttered at a public inquiry.

Other Inquiries have concluded that the balance of advantage lies more with adversarial and public methods. Such advocates point to the protections which witnesses are able to obtain when questioning has to be carried out within agreed conventions and where individuals whose conduct is under investigation have the benefit of representation by lay or legal counsel. The interests of the public are also, it is claimed, more directly answered in public proceedings, where the cathartic effects of hearing traumatic events interrogated and explained can be obtained, and where any suspicion of 'cover-up' or concealment can be avoided.

For the purposes of this book, the importance of this debate, and of others related to the mechanics of inquiry hearing, lies not in suggesting the superiority of one approach over another, but in showing that such choices have an impact upon the findings which emerge. We have already suggested that the forensic search for 'the truth' is an apparently simple strategy which, in reality, conceals a complex set of competing versions of the same events. The conclusion we reach here is not only that there is no simple 'truth', as many Inquiries claim, but that 'truth' is influenced by the institutional framework within which the seeking-after it is conducted.

Policy impact

If scandals are constructed, then, they are manufactured with a purpose.

Crepaz-Keay (1996), for example, has provided a detailed demonstration of the way in which media coverage of the *Boyd Confidential Inquiry into Homicides and Suicides by Mentally Ill People* portrayed the problem it identified in a way which implicitly advocated particular remedies. The Report provided what Crepaz-Keay (1996: 43) describes as 'simple reliable information' which undermined the usual stereotyping of 'dangerous' mental health patients. Instead, newspapers and the broadcast media, from the most tabloid to the most serious-minded, 'ignored the truth, for the sake of a story' (Crepaz-Keay 1996: 44) and reported the Inquiry in terms of 'Scandal of loonies freed to kill' (*Daily Star* 18 August) and 'One murder a fortnight by mentally ill' (*Daily Telegraph* 17 August). The final major question upon which we have concentrated is exactly this policy impact of scandal – the particular remedies which emerge from their construction, investigation and resolution. Inquiries provide a highly instructive opportunity to investigate this policy-making process. While, for the most part, official policy-making proceeds along apparently smooth paths, scandal disrupts this carefully contrived exterior, breaking through the surface and illuminating the normally hidden actions of powerful individuals and organisations which lie below.

In taking advantage of the opportunity which is thus presented we have argued that, from time to time, social welfare scandals have been influential in the development of policy which has followed after the particular events have taken place. That influence, we have suggested, is limited in a number of ways. To have an impact an individual scandal needs to take place at a time of policy strain and, with the fluidity which this produces, to be capable of catching a tide which is already beginning to run in a fresh policy direction. Such tides might involve the flight from institutions or organisations which have become the focus of public disenchantment. Policy strain is significant because, as chapters 4 and 5 have demonstrated, events which would have been constructed as scandals in one era can go neglected in another. Ely Hospital produced a scandal partially, at least, because it occurred at a time when the policy of looking after mentally ill people within institutions was being overturned in favour of community care. St David's Hospital in Carmarthen failed to make any substantial impression upon the public partially, at least, because the policy issues which it illuminated were no longer a matter of contention and community care had established its brief period of policy hegemony. Nor are such findings confined to the field of social welfare. Tumber (1993: 351), for example, explores the case of the Gerald Ratner scandal which emerged when the owner of the eponymous jewellery chain was pilloried in the mass media for describing his firm's products as 'crap'. It emerges in Tumber's exploration that Ratner's 'comments about his products were not new lines. According to press reports, he had used them several times before to financial jour-nalists and City advisers.' What had changed, however, was the climate in which the remarks were made. When the company was expanding and prosperous, disparaging remarks about its products by their owner did not appear to matter. With the advent of economic recession and declining sales, however, the views took on a new significance. The con-textual tide had changed, and what had previously been a non-event was now the raw material of scandal. At other times, scandals mark the intrusion of new currents into the ebb and flow of policy formation such as the advent of consumerism and the rhetoric of rights in the New Right's attempt to re-shape the politics of welfare.

Beyond the policies and practices of social welfare systems and work-ers there are a range of wider implications in the resolution of scandal through the mechanism of the Committee of Inquiry which need to be drawn together in this concluding chapter. Inquiries juggle the who, the what and the why of the events with which they deal. We have already suggested that Committees of Inquiry seldom concentrate upon the direct actors engaged, for example, in the death of a child or the act of homicide by someone who is mentally ill. This is not to say, however, that they do not focus upon those social welfare actors who, within institutions or fieldwork practice, were responsible for the provision of services. In the case of asylums, Normansfield and Ely stand at opposite ends of the 'blaming-and-shaming' spectrum, but both parade a series of individuals against whom judgement is made. The culpability of Diana Lees and Tony Latham remains one of the clearest impressions which the reader takes away from the Colwell and the Pindown Inquiries. Cavender et al. (1993: 159) suggest that the morality play framework within which scandals are cast by Inquiries and the media is directly in the interests of powerful players, allowing the focus to be directed to the question, 'who did it?' and thus diverting attention from organisations onto individuals. Peay (1996b: 11) develops a different critique when she suggests that Inquiries offer a faulty basis for iterating between individ-ual cases and the generalisability of policy-making. Looking at the way in which Inquiries tend to focus upon individual culpability, she asks: 'subject to this level of analysis, which of us would be likely to be found completely without fault?' This criticism has been widely echoed in the professional press, where Inquiries have sometimes been portrayed as in the business of personal assassination, rather than independent and rounded evaluation of evidence. Yet, while scandals arise in very specific circumstances, the emblematic Inquiries which we have considered in this book are most often precisely those which have proved capable of convincing others that the events they describe lead to a more general set of conclusions.

A concentration upon the 'who' of scandal is often, in the Inquiries we have considered, bound in with a focus on 'what' has taken place. Peay (1996: 4) is critical of Inquiries because of what she regards as their willingness to be too often content to explore 'what' occurred, rather than 'why' these events took place, suggesting that 'it is not clear whether we wish to learn from Inquiries or to learn about the events they explore.' Our own reading suggests that this dichotomy is not a wholly real one. Inquiries, in the construction of the 'what' took place, are almost always selecting from a set of competing accounts. The selection of material contributes to the emerging answer to the 'why' of scandal which Inquiry teams are advancing. When the 'what' issues revolve around the actions of particular individuals – the 'who' of scandal – then, as Peay (1996: 7) puts it, avoidance of the 'why' usually entails an avoidance of the 'more inaccessible issues of resources and management strategies'. Instead, explanations focus on the motivation of individuals, shifting attention away from organisations and onto what Cavender et al. (1993: 159) describe as 'accounting for the scapegoats' motivations'.

The conclusion of this analysis is to suggest that, beyond the detail of social welfare itself, the Inquiry is a process by which the immediate consequences of scandal can be managed, while leaving intact the wider institutional order. This finding is consistent with our earlier contention that, while scandal can accelerate a rising policy tide, it cannot, of itself, originate a change in policy direction, or alter the course of a policy which is already well established. The standard outcome of Inquiries is the identification of individual culpability or micro-systems failure. Larger questions of historical or structural significance are avoided, even where Inquiries deal with some of the most fundamental and contentious issues of contemporary society – the nature of parenting, children's rights, the treatment of mental illness, the operation of the criminal law and so on. In this way, as Cavender et al. (1993: 162) suggest, Inquiries contribute to a discourse in which scandals are treated as flaws in an essentially sound system, crises which will pass and where order and authority will be restored. Individual wrongdoing and minor policy adjustments attract the attention which might otherwise have been directed towards structural causes and thus minimise the need for extensive social change. Even when the corruption of care is as manifest as in some of the institutions which have appeared in the pages of this book, the weakness and cynicism which is characteristic of those organisations which are inherently incapable of making the image and the reality of care match each other only rarely emerges with any force from the pages of an Inquiry.

Conclusion

There is no end to the generation of scandal in social welfare. During the period in which this book has been in preparation, a persistent trickle of stories of abuse in the rapidly growing residential care sector for older people has found their way into the public domain. Many of the themes familiar from the institutional scandals discussed in this text are to be found in such accounts. At the same time, the headlines as we write are dominated by the start of the Committee of Inquiry into the death of a child killed at the hands of her great-aunt. Claims that the Committee's report will produce profound change in the organisation and delivery of social work services, and that these changes will prevent such tragedies in future are prominent in the discourse of those most closely involved. The task of understanding the relationship between scandal, Committees of Inquiry and policy generation is such a necessary one, precisely because the relationship is so enduring, and one which seems set to continue well into the future. This book has set out to provide a contribution to that understanding, a process which, just as scandal itself, will need to continue well into the future.

Bibliography

Books and Articles

Aries, P. (1960) *L'Enfant et la vie familiale sous l'ancien regime*, Paris: Libraire Plon, translated by R. Baldick as *Centuries of Childhood* (1962), London: Jonathan Cape.

Armstrong, D. (1983) *The Political Anatomy of the Body: Medical Knowledge in Britain in the Twentieth Century*, London: Warburg Institute.

Arnot, M. (1994) 'Infant death, child care and the state: the baby farming scandal' and the first infant life protection legislation of 1872', *Continuity and Change*, 9:2, 271–311.

Atkinson, J.M. (1996) 'The community of strangers: supervision and the new right', *Health and Social Care in the Community*, 4:2, 122–5.

Bacon, R. and Eltis, W. (1975) *Britain's Economic Problem: Too Few Producers*, London: Macmillan.

Baker, E. (1997) 'The introduction of supervision registers in England and Wales: a risk communications analysis', *The Journal of Forensic Psychiatry*, 8:1, 15–35.

Ballance, G. (1973) 'Fostering' in J. Stroud (ed.), *Services for Children and their Families: Aspects of Child Care for Social Workers*, Oxford: Pergamon Press.

Barclay, P. (1982) 'The Report and its Implications' in T. Philpot (ed.), *A New Direction for Social Work? The Barclay Report and its Implications*, Sutton, Surrey: IPC Business Press.

Barker, P. (1975) 'Social work as reflected in press coverage of the Aukland inquiry', *Social Work Today*, 6:18.

Barnardo, S.L. and Marchant, J. (1907) *Memoirs of the Late Dr. Barnardo*, London: Hodder & Stoughton.

Barth, R.P., Courtney, M., Berrick, J.D. and Albert, V. (1994) *From Child Abuse to Permanency Planning*, New York: Aldine de Gruyter.

Barton, R. (1959) *Institutional Neurosis*, Bristol: John Wright.

Bayley, M. (1973) *Mental Handicap and Community Care*, London, Routledge & Kegan Paul.

Behlmer, G. (1982) *Child Abuse and Moral Reform in England 1870–1908*, Stanford, CA: Stanford University Press.

Berridge, D. and Brodie, I. (1996) 'Residential child care in England and Wales: the Inquiries and after' in M. Hill and J. Aldgate (eds), *Child Welfare Services: Developments in Law, Policy, Practice and Research*, London: Jessica Kingsley.

Best, J. (1990) *Threatened Children: Rhetoric and Concern about Child-Victims*, Chicago: University of Chicago Press.

Bhugra, D. (ed.) (1996) *Homelessness and Mental Health*, London: Routledge.

Black and in Care (1984) *Black and in Care: Conference Report*, Black Rose Press.

Blom-Cooper, L. (1996) 'Some reflections on Public Inquiries' in J. Peay (ed.), *Inquiries After Homicide*, London: Duckworth.

Blom-Cooper, L. (1997) 'Colwell to North Wales' in *Cleveland Ten Years On: Child Protection What Really Matters*, Bristol: National Council for Family Proceedings, University of Bristol.

Bogen, D. and Lynch, M. (1989) 'Taking account of the hostile native: plausible deniability and the production of conventional history in the Iran-Contra Hearings', *Social Problems*, 36:3, 197–221.

Bornea, J., Pereira, C., Pilgrim, D. and Williams, F. (1977) (eds), second edition, *Community Care: a Reader*, Milton Keynes: Open University Press.

Borsay, A. (1998) 'Returning patients to the community: disability, medicine and economic rationality before the industrial revolution', *Disability and Society*, 13:5, 645–63.

Bowlby, J. (1953) *Child Care and the Growth of Love*, London: Penguin.

Box, S. (1980) 'Where have all the naughty children gone?' in National Deviancy Conference (eds), *Permissiveness and Control: the Fate of the Sixties Legislation*, London: Macmillan.

Bullock, R. (1999) 'The Children Act 1948: Residential Care' in O. Stevenson (ed.), *Child Welfare in the UK*, Oxford: Blackwell Science.

Busfield, J. (1986) *Managing Madness: Changing Ideas and Practice*, London: Hutchinson.

Busfield, J. (1993) 'Managing Madness: changing ideas and practice' in Busfield, J. (1996) *Men, Women and Madness: Understanding Gender and Mental Disorder*, London: Macmillan.

Buckrill, J.C. (1880) *The Care of the Insane and Their Legal Control*, London: Macmillan.

Butler, I. (1996) 'Children and the sociology of childhood' in I. Butler and I. Shaw (eds), *A Case of Neglect? Children's Experiences and the Sociology of Childhood*, Aldershot: Avebury.

Butler, I. (2002) 'Institutional abuse' in K. Wilson and A. James (eds) *The Child Protection Handbook*, London: Bailliere Tindall.

Butler, I. and Drakeford, M. (2001a), 'Tough enough? Youth justice under New Labour', *Probation Journal* 48:2, 119–24.

Butler, I. and Drakeford, M. (2001b) 'Which Blair Project?', *Journal of Social Work*, 1:1, 1–14.

Butler, I. and Owens, D. (1993) 'Canaries among sparrows: ideas of the family and the practice of foster care', *Community Alternatives: International Journal of Family Care*, 5:1, 25–42.

Campbell, A.C. (1968) 'Comparison of family and community contacts of mentally subnormal adults in hospital and local authority hostels', *British Journal of Preventative Social Medicine*, 22:3.

Carlebach, J. (1970) *Caring for Children in Trouble*, London: Routledge & Kegan Paul.

Carpenter, M. (1851) *Reformatory Schools for the Children of the Perishing and Dangerous Classes and for Juvenile Offenders*, London: Woburn Press 1968 (Reprint of the London 1851 Edition)

Carpenter, M. (1853) *Juvenile Delinquents – their Conditions and Treatment*

Castle, B. (1983) *Diaries*, London: Weidenfeld and Nicholson. London: W. & F.G. Cash.

Cavender, G., Jurik, N.C. and Cohen, A.K. (1993) 'The baffling case of the smoking gun: the social ecology of political accounts in the Iran-Contra Affair', *Social Problems*, 40:2, 152–64.

Chesler, P. (1972) *Women and Madness*, New York, Avon, reprinted in J. Heller, J. Reynolds, R. Gomn, R. Muston and S. Pattinson (eds), *Mental Health Matters*, Buckingham: Open University Press.

Chibnall, S. (1977) *Law and Order News: an Analysis of Crime Reporting in the British Press*, London: Tavistock.

Clarke, J. (1980) 'Social democratic delinquents and Fabian families' in National Deviancy Conference (eds), *Permissiveness and Control: the Fate of the Sixties Legislation*, London: Macmillan.

Clarke, J. and Newman, J. (1997) *The Managerial State*, London: Sage.

Clothier, C. (1996) 'Rumination on Inquiries' in J. Peay (ed.), *Inquiries after Homicide*, London: Duckworth.

Cohen, S. (1973) *Folk Devils and Moral Panics*, London: Paladin.

Corby, B. (2000) *Child Abuse: Towards a Knowledge Base*, 2nd edition, Buckingham: Open University Press.

Corby, B., Doig, A. and Roberts, V. (1998) *Residential Child Care and Child Abuse Inquiries: Research Report 1*, Liverpool: Liverpool Business School, John Moores University and Department of Sociology and Social Work, University of Liverpool.

Crepaz-Keay, D. (1996) 'A sense of perspective: the media and the Boyd Inquiry' in G. Philo (ed.), *Media and Mental Illness*, London: Longman.

Crompton, F. (1997) *Workhouse Children*, Stroud Sutton Publishing.

Crossman, R. (1977) *The Crossman Diaries*, London: Magnum.

Cunningham, H. (1995) *Children and Childhood in Western Society Since 1500*, London: Longman.

Daniel, P. and Ivatts, J. (1998) *Children and Social Policy*, Basingstoke and London: Macmillan – now Palgrave Macmillan.

Davies, M. and Woolgrove, M. (1998) 'Mental health social work and the use of supervision registers for patients at risk', *Health and Social Care in the Community*, 6:1, 25–34.

Davies, T.G. (1996) 'Mental mischief: aspects of nineteenth-century psychiatric practice in parts of Wales', in H. Freeman and G.E. Berrios (eds), *150 Years of British Psychiatry Volume II: the Aftermath*, London: Athlone.

Deakin, N. (1994) *The Politics of Welfare: Continuities and Change*, Hemel Hempstead: Harvester Wheatsheaf.

Department of Health (1991) *Child Abuse: a Study of Inquiry Reports 1980–1989*, London: HMSO.

Department of Health (1994a) *Guidance on the Discharge of Mentally Disordered People and their Continuing Care in the Community*, HSG (94)27, London: Department of Health.

Department of Health (1994b) *Introduction of Supervision Registers for Mentally Ill People*, Circular HSG (94)5, London: Department of Health.

Department of Health (1995) *Building Bridges: a Guide to Arrangements for Inter-Agency Working for the Care and Protection of Severely Mentally Ill People*, London: Department of Health.

Department of Health (1996) *Attitudes to Mental Illness: Summary Report*, London: Department of Health.

Department of Health (1997) 'Plans for psychiatric hospital closures to be vetted by new group', press release, 97/222.

Department of Health (1998) 'Frank Dobson outlines third way For mental health', press release, 98/311.

Department of Health/Social Services Inspectorate (1991) *Children in the Public Care: a Review of Residential Care* ('The Utting Report'), London: HMSO.

Department of Health and Social Security (1982) *Child Abuse: a Study of Inquiry Reports 1973–1981*, London: HMSO.

Department of Health and Social Security (1985) *Social Work Decisions in Child Care: Recent Research Findings and their Implications*, London: HMSO.

Dingwall, R., Eekelar, J.M. and Murray, T. (1983) *The Protection of Children: State Intervention and Family Life*, Oxford: Blackwell.

Dingwall, R., Eekelar, J.M. and Murray, T. (1984) 'Childhood as a social problem: a survey of the history of legal regulation', *Journal of Law and Society*, 11:2.

Doig, A. (1988) 'The dynamics of scandals in British politics', *Corruption and Reform*, 3:3, 323–30.

Donnison, D.V. (1954) *The Neglected Child and the Social Services*, Manchester: Manchester University Press.

Drewry, G. (1988) 'The Parliamentary response to child abuse' in *After Beckford: Essays on Themes Related to Child Abuse*, London: Department of Social Policy, Royal Holloway and Bedford New College.

Eastman, N. (1995) 'Anti-therapeutic community mental health law', *British Medical Journal*, 310, 1081–2.

Elias, N. (1939) *Über den Prozes der Zivilisation (The Civilising Process)*, Basel: Falken.

Elliot, F.R. (1986) *The Family – Change or Continuity?*, London: Allen & Unwin.

Ferguson, H. (1990) 'Rethinking child protection practices: a case for history' in Violence Against Children Study Group, *Taking Child Abuse Seriously*, London: Unwin Hyman.

Fine, G.A. (1997) 'Scandal, social conditions and the creation of public attention: Fatty Arbuckle and the "problem of Hollywood"', *Social Problems* 44:3, 297–323.

Fisher, N. (1994) 'The discharge of mentally disordered people and their continuing care in the community', *Psychiatric Bulletin*, 18, 435–6.

Fotterell, D. (1990) 'Asylum for psychiatric patients in the 1990s', *The Lancet*, 335:468.

Fox Harding, L. (1991) *Perspectives in Child Care Policy*, London: Longman.

Fox Harding, L. (1996) *Family, State and Social Policy*, London: Macmillan.

Frankenburg, S. (1934) *Common Sense in the Nursery*, London: Cape.

Freeman, H. (1998) 'Mental health policy and practice in the NHS: 1948–79', *Journal of Mental Health*, 7:3, 225–39.

Froude, J.A. (1849) *The Nemesis of Faith or the History of Markham*, London: Routledge (reprinted 1903).

Fulcher, J. and Scott, J. (1999) *Sociology*, Oxford: Oxford University Press.

Galtung, J. and Rouge, M. (1965) 'The Structure of Foreign News', *Journal of International Peace Research*, 1:1.

Gamble, A. (1994) *The Free Economy and the Strong State: the Politics of Thatcherism*, 2nd edn, Basingstoke: Macmillan – now Palgrave Macmillan.

Giller, H. and Morris, A. (1981) *Care and Discretion: Social Workers' Decisions with Delinquents*, London: Burnett Books.

Gittins, D. (1998) *Madness in its Place: Narratives of Severalls Hospital 1913–1997*, London: Routledge.

Glennerster, H., Korman, N. and Marsden-Wilson, F. (1983) *Planning for Priority Groups*, Oxford: Blackwell.

Goffman, E. (1961) *Asylums: Essays on the Social Situation of Mental Patients and Other Inmates*, Garden City, NY: Doubleday.

Golding, P. and Middleton, S. (1982) *Images of Welfare: Press and Public attitudes to Poverty*, Oxford: Robinson.

Goodwin, S. (1989) 'Community care for the mentally ill in England and Wales: myths, assumptions and reality', *Journal of Social Policy*, 18:1, 27–52.

Gorst, J. (1906) *The Children of the Nation*, London: Methuen and Co.

Greenland, C. (1986) 'Inquiries into child abuse and neglect (CAN) deaths in the United Kingdom', *British Journal of Criminology*, 26:2, 164–72.

Haines, K. and Drakeford, M. (1998) *Young People and Youth Justice*, London: Macmillan.

Hallett, C. (1989) 'Child abuse inquiries and public policy' in O. Stevenson (ed.), *Child Abuse: Professional Practice and Public Policy*, London: Harvester Wheatsheaf.

Harding, L.F. (1991) *Perspectives in Child Care Policy*, London: Longman.

Harris, R. and Webb, D. (1987) *Welfare, Power and Juvenile Justice*, London: Tavistock Publications.

Hatfield, B. and Mohamad, H. (1996) 'Case management in mental health services: the role of community mental health support teams', *Health and Social Care in the Community*, 4:4, 215–25.

Hayden, C., Goddard, J., Gorin, S. and Van Der Spek, N. (1999) *State Child Care: Looking After Children*, London: Jessica Kingsley.

Hazel, N. (1981) *A Bridge to Independence*, Oxford: Blackwell.

Hendrick, H. (1994) *Child Welfare: England 1872–1989*, London: Routledge.

Hernshaw, L.S. (1964) *A Short History of British Psychology: 1840–1940*, London: Methuen.

Hervey, N. (1985) 'A slavish bowing down: the Lunacy Commission and the psychiatric profession, 1845–60', in W.F. Bynum, R. Porter and M. Shepherd, *The Anatomy of Madness: Essays in the History of Psychiatry*, Vol. 2, London: Tavistock.

Heywood, J.S. (1959) *Children in Care*, London: Routledge & Kegan Paul.

Heywood, J.S. (1973) 'Services for children and their families' in J. Stroud (ed.), *Services for Children and their Families: Aspects of Child Care for Social Workers*, London: Pergamon Press.

Heywood, J.S. (1978) *Children in Care: the Development of the Service for the Deprived Child* London: Routledge & Kegan Paul.

Higgins, R., Oldman, C., and Hunter, D.J. (1994) 'Working together: lessons for collaboration between health and social services', *Health and Social Care*, 2: 269–77.

Holman, R. (1975) 'The place of fostering in social work', *British Journal of Social Work*, 5:1, 3–29.

Holman, R. (1988) *Putting Families First*, Basingstoke: Macmillan – now Palgrave Macmillan.

Holman, R. (1998) 'From Children's Departments to Family Departments' *Child and Family Social Work*, 3, 205–11.

Home Office (1951) *Sixth Report on the Work of the Children's Department*, London: HMSO.

Home Office (1955) *Seventh Report on the Work of the Children's Department*, London: HMSO.

Home Office (1960) *Report of the Committee on Children and Young Persons* ('The Ingleby Report'), Cmnd 1191.

Home Office (1961) *Eighth Report on the Work of the Children's Department*, London: HMSO.

Home Office (1972) *Report of the Departmental Committee on the Adoption of Children* ('The Houghton Report'), Cmnd 5107, London: HMSO.

Hopton, J. and Glenister, D. (1996) '*Working Partnership*: vision or pipe dream?', *Critical Social Policy*, 16:2, 111–19.

Houghton, E. (1957) *The Victorian Frame of Mind 1830–1870* (1985 edition), New Haven and London: Yale University Press.

Howard Association (1896) *Annual Report 1896*, London: Howard Association.

Howells, J.G. (1974) *Remember Maria*, London: Butterworths.

Hughes, R. (1998) 'Children Act 1948 and 1989: similarities, differences, continuities', *Child and Family Social Work*, 3, 149–51.

Humphries, S. and Gordon, P. (1993) *Labour of Love: the Experience of Parenthood in Britain 1900–1950*, London: Sidgwick & Jackson.

Hutchison, R. (1986) 'The Effect of Inquiries into Cases of Child Abuse upon the Social Work Profession', *British Journal of Criminology*, 26:2, 178–81.

Ignatieff, M. (1978) *A Just Measure of Pain: the Penitentiary in the Industrial Revolution, 1750–1850*, London: Macmillan.

Ingelby, D. (1985) 'Professionals as socialisers: the "Psy Complex"' in A. Scull and S. Spitzer (eds), *Research in Law, Deviance and Social Control*, New York: JAI Press.

Inskip, J.H. and Edwards, J.G. (1979) 'Mental hospital inquiries', *Lancet*, 24 March, 658–60.

James, A. and Prout, A. (eds) (1990) *Constructing and Reconstructing Childhood: Contemporary Issues in the Sociological Study of Childhood*, London: The Falmer Press.

James, A.N. (1998) 'Supporting families of origin: an exploration of the influence of the Children Act 1948' *Child and Family Social Work*, 3, 173–81.

Jones, K. (1967) *The Development of Institutional Care*, London: Association of Social Workers.

Jones, K. (1972) *A History of the Mental Health Service*, London: Routledge & Kegan Paul.

Jones, K. (1983) 'Community care' in K. Jones (ed.), *Issues In Social Policy*, London: Routledge & Kegan Paul.

Jones, K. and Fowles, A.J. (1984) *Ideas on Institutions: Analysing the Literature on Long Term Care and Custody*, London: Routledge & Kegan Paul.

Jones, L. (1996) 'George III and changing views of madness' in J. Heller, J. Reynolds, R. Gomn, R. Muston and S. Pattinson (eds), *Mental Health Matters*, Buckingham: Open University Press.

Jones, R. and Kerslake, A. (1979) *Intermediate Treatment and Social Work*, London: Heinemann.

Jordan, B. (1981) 'Prevention', *Adoption and Fostering*, 5:3, 20–2.

Kahan, B. (1993) 'Children living away from home' in G. Pugh (ed.), *Thirty Years of Change for Children*, London: National Children's Bureau.

Kates, V. (1985) 'Success, strain and surprise', *Issues in Science and Technology*, 2, 46–58.

Katz, J. (1987) 'What makes crime "news"?', *Media, Culture and Society*, 9, 47–75.

Kempe, C.H (1968) 'Some problems encountered by welfare departments in the management of the Battered Child Syndrome' in R.E. Helfer and C.H. Kempe (eds), *The Battered Child*, Chicago: The University of Chicago Press.

Kennedy, I. (2001) *Inquiry into the management and case of children receiving complex heart surgery at the Bristol Royal Infirmary*, Norwich: The Stationery Office.

Key, E. (1900) *Barnets Århundrade* (English edition: *The Century of the Child*, 1909, New York and London).

Kirkpatrick, A. and Feldman, P. (1983) 'Is anyone out there listening?', *Hospital and Health Services Review*, January, 17–21.

Klein, R. (1995) *The New Politics of the National Health Service*, 3rd edition, London: Longman.

Korman, N. and Glennerster, H. (1990) *Hospital Closure: a Political and Economic Study*, Milton Keynes: Open University Press.

La Fontaine, J.S. (1979) *Sex and Age as Principles of Social Differentiation*, London: Academic Press.

Le Grand, J. (1990) 'The state of welfare' in J. Hills (ed.), *The State of Welfare: the Welfare State in Britain since 1974*, London: Oxford University Press.

Liddiard, M. (1928) *Mothercraft Manual*, London: 6th Edition. London: J and A Churchill.

MacFarlane, A. (1986) *Marriage and Love in England: Modes of Reproduction*, Oxford: Blackwell.

Maluccio, A.N., Fein, E. and Olmstead, K.A. (1986) *Permanency Planning for Children: Concepts and Methods*, New York: Tavistock.

Martin, B. (1988) 'Moral messages and the press: newspaper responses to a child in trust' in *After Beckford: Essays on Themes Related to Child Abuse*, London: Department of Social Policy, Royal Holloway and Bedford New College.

Martin, J.P. (1984) *Hospitals in Trouble*, Oxford: Basil Blackwell.

de Mause, L. (ed.) (1976) *The History of Childhood*, London: Souvenir Press.

Mayer, J.A. (1983) 'Notes towards a working definition of social control in Historical Analysis' in S. Cohen and A.T. Scull (eds), *Social Control and the State*, Oxford: Basil Blackwell.

McCandless, P. (1981) 'Liberty and lunacy: The Victorians and wrongful confinement' in A. Scull (ed.), *Madhouses, Mad-Doctors, and Madmen*, London: Athlone.

McCarthy, M. (1989) 'Personal social services' in M. McCarthy (ed.), *The New Politics of Welfare: an Agenda for the 1990s?*, London: Macmillan.

Merrick, D. (1996) *Social Work and Child Abuse*, London: Routledge.

Millham, S., Bullock, R., Hosie, K. and Haak, M. (1986) *Lost in Care*, Aldershot: Gower.

Molotch, H. and Lester, M. (1974) 'News as purposive behavior: on the strategic use of routine events, accidents and scandals', *American Sociological Review*, 39, 101–12.

Morris, A., Giller, H., Szwed, E. and Geach, H. (1980) *Justice for Children*, London: Macmillan.

Muijen, M. (1995) 'Scare in the Community: Britain in moral panic', *Community Care*, 7–13, September.

Muncie, J. (1984) *The Trouble with Kids Today*, London: Hutchinson.

Nichols, L.T. (1997) 'Social problems as landmark narratives: Bank of Boston, mass media and "Money Laundering"', *Social Problems*, 44, 324–41.

NISW (National Institute for Social Work) (1982) *Social Workers: Their Role and Tasks* ('The Barclay Report'), London: Bedford Square Press.

Parker, R.A. (1988) 'An Historical Background' in I. Sinclair (ed.), *Residential Care: the Research Reviewed*, London: National Institute for Social Work.

Parker, R.A. (1990) *Away from Home: a Short History of Provision for Separated Children*, Barkingside: Barnardos.

Parry-Jones, W. Ll. (1981), 'The model of the Geel Lunatic Colony and its influence on the nineteenth-century asylum system in Britain' in A. Scull (ed.), *Madhouses, Mad-Doctors, and Madmen*, London: Athlone.

Parton, N. (1985) *The Politics of Child Abuse*, Basingstoke: Macmillan – now Palgrave Macmillan.

Parton, N. (1991) *Governing the Family: Child Care, Child Protection and the State*, Basingstoke: Macmillan – now Palgrave Macmillan.

Parton, N. (1999) 'Ideology, Politics and Policy' in O. Stevenson (ed.), *Child Welfare in the UK*, Oxford: Blackwell Science.

Payne, S. (1996) 'Psychiatric care in the community: does it fail young men?', *Policy and Politics*, 24:2, 193–205.

Payne, S. (1999) 'Dangerous and different: reconstructions of madness in the 1990s and the role of mental health policy' in S. Watson and L. Doyle (eds), *Engendering Social Policy*, Buckingham: Open University Press.

Peay, J. (ed.) (1996a) *Inquiries After Homicide*, London: Duckworth.

Peay, J. (1996b) 'Themes and questions: the inquiry in context' in J. Peay (ed.), *Inquiries after Homicide*, London: Duckworth.

Pinchbeck, I. and Hewitt, M. (1973) *Children in English Society*, London: Routledge & Kegan Paul.

Pollock, L.H. (1983) *Forgotten Children: Parent–Child Relations from 1500 to 1900*, Cambridge: Cambridge University Press.

Porter, R. (1996) 'Two cheers for psychiatry! The social history of mental disorder in twentieth century Britain' in H. Freeman and G.E. Berrios (eds), *150 Years of British Psychiatry Volume II: the Aftermath*, London: Athlone.

Powell, R.B., Hollander, D. and Tobiansky, R.I. (1995) 'Crisis in Admission Beds: a Four-year Survey of the Bed State of Greater London's Acute Psychiatric Units', *British Journal of Psychiatry*, 167, 765–9.

Powell, E. (1961) Address to the National Association for Mental Health. Published in *Report of the Annual Conference of Mental Health*, London: National Association for Mental Health.

Prior, L. (1996), 'The appeal to madness in Ireland', in D. Tomlinson and J. Carrier (eds), *Asylum in the Community*, London: Routledge.

Quartrup, J. (1994) 'Recent developments in research and thinking on childhood', Paper the XXXI International Sociological Association Committee on Family Research, London, 28–30 April.

Reder, P., Duncan, S. and Gray, M. (1993) *Beyond Blame: Child Abuse Tragedies Revisited*, London: Routledge.

Reith, M. (1998) *Community Care Tragedies: a Practice Guide to Mental Health Inquiries*, Birmingham: Venture Press.

Repper, J. and Brooker, C. (1996) 'Public attitudes towards mental health facilities in the community', *Health and Social Care in the Community*, 4:5, 290–9.

Ridley, F.F. (1988) 'Scandal, morals and politics', *Corruption and Reform*, 3:3, 293–306.

Rogers, A. and Pilgrim, D. (1996) *Mental Health Policy in Britain: a Critical Introduction*, London: Macmillan.

Rogers, R. (1980) *From Crowther to Warnock: How Fourteen Reports Tried to Change Children's Lives*, London: Heinemann.

Rose, D. (1997) 'Trial by television', *Community Care*, 4–10 December, 30–1.

Rose, N. (1985) *The Psychological Complex: Psychology, Politics and Society in England 1869–1939*, London: Routledge & Kegan Paul.

Rowe, J. and Lambert, L. (1973) *Children Who Wait: a Study of Children Needing Substitute Families*, London: British Agencies for Adoption and Fostering.

Ruskin, J. (1886) 'Of Queen's Gardens' in Ruskin, *Works* edited by A.D.O Wedderburn and E.T. Cook, London, 1903.

Schlesinger, P., Tumber, H. and Murdock, G. (1991) 'The media politics of crime and criminal justice', *British Journal of Criminology*, 42:3, 397–420.

Scull, A.T. (1979) *Museums of Madness: the Social Organisation of Insanity in Nineteenth Century England*, London: Allen Lane.

Scull, A.T. (1981) *Madhouses, Mad-Doctors, and Madmen: the Social History of Psychiatry in the Victorian Era*, London: Athlone Press.

Scull, A.T. (1985) *Social Control and the State: Historical and Comparative Essays*, Oxford: Blackwell.

Scull, A.T. (1996) 'Asylums, utopias and realities' in D. Tomlinson and J. Carrier (eds), *Asylum in the Community*, London: Routledge.

Scull, A.T., MacKenzie, C. and Hervey, P. (1996) *Masters of Bedlam: the Transformation of the Mad-Doctoring Trade*, Chichester and Princeton, NJ: Princeton University Press.

Sedgwick, P. (1982) *Psycho Politics*, London: Pluto Press.

Shearer, A. (1979) 'The legacy of Maria Colwell', *Social Work Today*, 10:19.

Shorter, E. (1976) *The Making of the Modern Family*, London: Collins.

Showalter, E. (1981) 'Victorian women and insanity' in A. Scull (ed.), *Madhouses, Mad-Doctors, and Madmen*, London: Athlone.

Sinclair, I. (1988a) 'Common issues' in I. Sinclair (ed.), *Residential Care: the Research Reviewed*, London: National Institute for Social Work.

Sinclair, I. (1988) 'The client reviews: children' in I. Sinclair (ed.), *Residential Care: the Research Reviewed*, London: National Institute for Social Work.

Small, J. (1985) 'Transracial placements: conflicts and contradictions' in S. Ahmed, J. Cheetham and J. Small (eds), *Social Work with Black Children and their Families*, London: Batsford.

Spicker, P., Anderson, I., Freeman, R. and McGilp, R. (1995) 'Discharged Into the Community: the Experience of Psychiatric Patients', *Social Services Research*, 1, 27–31.

St Aubyn, G. (1935) *Family Book*, London: Arthur Baker.

Stanley, N. (1999) 'The abuse of children: an overview of policy and practice' in N. Stanley, J. Manthorpe and B. Penhale (eds), *Institutional abuse: Perspectives Across the Life Course*, London: Routledge.

Stevenson, O. (1979) 'Tragedies Revisited', *Social Work Today*, 10:21, 23 January.

Stevenson, O. (1998) 'It was more difficult than we thought: a reflection on 50 years of child welfare practice', *Child and Family Social Work*, 3, 153–61.

Stone, L. (1977) *The Family, Sex and Marriage in England 1500–1800*, London: Weidenfeld & Nicolson.

Stroud, J. (1973) 'Residential Care' in J. Stroud (ed.), *Services for Children and their Families: Aspects of Child Care for Social Workers*, Oxford: Pergamon Press.

Sullivan, P. (1998) 'Progress or neglect? Reviewing the impact of care in the community for the severely mentally ill', *Critical Social Policy*, 18:2, 193–213.

Taylor, R. (1995) 'Alienation and integration in mental health policy', *Critical Social Policy*, 42, 81–90.

Taylor, W.C. (1874) 'What influence has the Employment of Mothers on Infant Mortality?', *Transactions of the National Association for the Promotion of Social Science* cited in I. Pinchbeck and M. Hewitt (1973) *Children in English Society*, London: Routledge & Kegan Paul.

Thoburn, J. (1999) 'Trends in foster care and adoption' in O. Stevenson (ed.), *Child Welfare in the UK*, Oxford: Blackwell Science.

Tidmarsh, D, (1995) 'Homicide and care in the community', *The Journal of Forensic Psychiatry*, 6:1, 1–5.

Tidmarsh, D. (1997) 'Psychiatric risk, safety cultures and homicide inquiries', *Journal of Forensic Psychiatry*, 8:1, 138–51.

Timmins, N. (1996) 'Major in mental health rethink', *The Independent*, 16 July.

Titmuss, R. (1963) 'Community care – fact or fiction?' in H. Freeman (ed.), *Trends in the Mental Health Services*, London: Pergamon Press.

Tumber, H. (1993) '"Selling scandal": business and the media', *Media, Culture and Society*, 15, 345–61.

Utting, W. (1997) *People Like Us – The Report of the Review of the Safeguards for Children Living Away from Home*, London: DOH/WO.

Van Every, J. (1992) 'Who is the family? The assumptions of British social policy', *Critical Social Policy*, 33, 62–75.

Walton, J. (1981) 'The treatment of pauper lunatics in Victorian England: the case of Lancaster Asylum, 1816–1870' in A. Scull (ed.), *Madhouses, Mad-Doctors, and Madmen*, London: Athlone.

Walton, J. (1985) 'Casting, out and bringing back in Victorian England: pauper lunatics 1840–70 in W.F. Bynum, R. Porter and M. Shepherd (eds), *The Anatomy of Madness: Essays in the History of Psychiatry Vol. II Institutions and Society*, London: Tavistock.

Walton, R. and Elliot, D. (1980) 'Criticisms and Positive Aspects of Residential Care' in R. Walton and D. Elliot (eds), *Residential Care: a Reader in Current Theory and Practice*, Oxford: Pergamon Press.

War Office (1922) *Report of the War Office Committee on Enquiry into Shell-Shock*, Cmnd 1734, London: War Office.

Wardhaugh, J. and Wilding, P. (1993) 'Towards an explanation of the corruption of care', *Critical Social Policy*, 63, 4–31.

Webster, C. (1998) *The National Health Service: A Political History*, Oxford: Oxford University Press.

Wells, J.S.G. (1997) 'Priorities, "street level bureaucracy" and the community mental health team', *Health and Social Care in the Community*, 5, 333–42.

Westcott, H.L. (1991) *Institutional Abuse of Children – From Research to Policy. A Review*, London: NSPCC.

White, M. (1998) 'Staff back Dobson on mental health reforms', *Community Care*, 10–16 December, 1.

Wintersberger, H. (ed.) (1996) *Children on the Way from Marginality to Citizenship: Childhood Policies. Conceptual and Practical Issues*, Vienna: European Centre for Social Welfare Policy and Research.

Wroe, A. (1988) *Social Work, Child Abuse and the Press*, Norwich: University of East Anglia Social Work Monographs.

Young, A.F. and Ashton, E.T. (1956) *British Social Work in the Nineteenth Century*, London: Routledge & Kegan Paul.

Parliamentary Papers and Non-departmental Government Reports

First Annual Report, Parliamentary Papers, 1835, xxxv, Poor Law Commission.

Fourth Annual Report, Parliamentary Papers, 1838, xxxviii, Poor Law Commission.

Health Committee of the House of Commons (1994) *Better Off In the Community? The Care of People who are Seriously Mentally Ill*, London: HMSO.

'Ingleby Committee' (1960) *Report of the Committee on Children and Young Persons*, Cmnd 5107, London: HMSO.

Mental Health Commission (1993) *Fifth Biennial Report of the Mental Health Commission*, London: HMSO.

Report from the Commissioners on the Administration and Practical Operation of the Poor Laws, Parliamentary Papers, 1834, xxxvi, Poor Law Commission.

Report of the Departmental Committee on Reformatories and Industrial Schools, Parliamentary Papers, 1913, xxxix.

Report of the Select Committee on Protection of Infant Life; Together with Proceedings of the Committee, Minutes of Evidence, Appendices and Index Parliamentary Papers, 1871, vii.

Report on Quarantine, Parliamentary Papers, 1849, xxiv, General Board of Health.

'Seebohm Report' (1968) *Report of the Committee on Local Authority and Allied Personal Social Services*, Cmnd 3703, London: HMSO.

'Short Report' (1984) *Second Report from the Social Services Committee: Children in Care*, vol. 1, London: HMSO.

Inquiry Reports

'Cleveland Report' (1988) *Report of the Inquiry into Child Abuse in Cleveland, 1987.* Presented to the Secretary of State for Social Services by Rt. Hon. Lord Justice Butler-Sloss, Cmnd 412, London: HMSO.

'Colwell Report' (1974) *Report of the Committee of Inquiry into the Care and Supervision Provided in Relation to Maria Colwell*, London: HMSO.

Curtis Committee (1946) *Report of the Care of Children Committee: presented by the Secretary of State for the Home Department by the Minister of Health and the Minister of Education by the command of his Majesty*, London: HMSO.

'Darryn Clarke Report' (1979) *Report of the Committee of Inquiry into the Actions of the Authorities and Agencies relating to Darryn James Clarke.* Presented to the Secretary of State for Social Services, Cmnd 7730, London: HMSO.

'Waterhouse Report' (2000) *Lost in Care – Report of the Tribunal of Inquiry into the Abuse of Children in Care in the Former County Council Areas of Gwynedd and Clwyd since 1974*, London: Stationery Office.

Report of the Committee of Inquiry into Allegations of Ill-Treatment of Patients and Other Irregularities at Ely Hospital, Cardiff (1969), Cmnd 3975, London: HMSO.

Report of the Farleigh Hospital Committee of Inquiry (1971), Cmnd 4557, London: HMSO.

Report of the Committee of Inquiry into Whittingham Hospital (1972), Cmnd 4861, London: HMSO.

Report of the Committee of Inquiry into Normansfield Hospital (1978), Cmnd 7397, London: HMSO.

Brannan, C., Jones, J.R. and Murch, J.D. (1993) *Castle Hill Report: Practice Guide*, Chester: Shropshire County Council.

Clyde, J.J. (1992) *Report of the Inquiry into the Removal of Children from Orkney in February 1991*, Edinburgh: HMSO.

DHSS (1975) *Report of the Committee of Inquiry into the Provision and Co-ordination of Services to the Family of John George Aukland*, London: HMSO.

Hughes, W.H. (1985) *Report of the Committee of Inquiry into Children's Homes and Hostels (Kincora)*, Belfast: Northern Ireland Office.

Kirkwood, A. (1993) *The Leicestershire Inquiry 1992*, Leicester: Leicestershire County Council.

Lawson, E. (1985) *The Leeways Inquiry Report*, London: London Borough of Lewisham.

Leicestershire County Council and Leicestershire Area Health Authority (Teaching) (1980) *Carly Taylor: Report of an Independent Inquiry*, Leicester: Leicestershire County Council.

London Borough of Brent (1985) *A Child in Trust: the Report of the Panel of Inquiry into the Circumstances Surrounding the Death of Jasmine Beckford*, London: London Borough of Brent.

London Borough of Greenwich and Greenwich Health Authority (1987) *A Child in Mind: Protection of Children in a Responsible Society. The Report of a Commission of Inquiry into the Circumstances Surrounding the Death of Kimberley Carlile*, London: London Borough of Greenwich.

London Borough of Hillingdon Area Review Committee (1986) *Report of the Review Panel of the London Borough of Hillingdon Area Review Committee on Child Abuse into the Death of Heidi Koseda*, London: London Borough of Hillingdon.

London Borough of Lambeth (1987) *Whose Child? The Report of the Public Inquiry into the Death of Tyra Henry*, London: London Borough of Lambeth.

Ritchie, J. (1994) *The Report of the Inquiry into the Care and Treatment of Christopher Clunis*, London: HMSO.

Shropshire County Council (1973) *Report of the Inquiry into the Circumstances Surrounding the Death of Graham Bagnall*, Shrewsbury: Shropshire County Council.

Staffordshire County Council (1991) *The Pindown Experience and the Protection of Children* (Allan Levy and Barbara Kahan), Stafford: Staffordshire County Council.

Stokes, J. (1988) *Report of the Committee of Inquiry into the Care and After-Care of Sharon Campbell*, London: HMSO.

Williams, G. and McCreadie, J. (1992) *Ty Mawr Community Home Inquiry*, Cwmbran: Gwent County Council.

Author Index

Subject Index